GW00577979

CONTENTS

The
KINGS & QUEENS
of WALES

The KINGS & QUEENS *of* WALES

TIMOTHY VENNING

AMBERLEY

Front cover: Caswallon fab Beli from *History of the Kings* (Peniarth MS 23C).
(Supplied by Llyfrgell Genedlaethol Cymru / The National Library of Wales)

First published 2012

Amberley Publishing
The Hill, Stroud
Gloucestershire, GL5 4EP

www.amberley-books.com

Copyright © Timothy Venning 2012

The right of Timothy Venning to be identified as the Author
of this work has been asserted in accordance with the
Copyrights, Designs and Patents Act 1988.

All rights reserved. No part of this book may be reprinted
or reproduced or utilised in any form or by any electronic,
mechanical or other means, now known or hereafter invented,
including photocopying and recording, or in any information
storage or retrieval system, without the permission in writing
from the Publishers.

British Library Cataloguing in Publication Data.
A catalogue record for this book is available from the British Library.

ISBN 978 1 4456 0905 8

Typeset in 11pt on 13pt Minion Pro.
Typesetting and Origination by Amberley Publishing.
Printed in the UK.

1

PRE-ROMAN TRIBAL SOVEREIGNS: LEADERSHIP IN IRON AGE SOCIETY

'Celtic' British Kingdoms?

The Roman invasion of southern Britain by Julius Caesar in 55 BC – undertaken after alleged local support to his enemies in Gaul – provides us with our first written evidence of rulers in Britain. According to his own (carefully 'spun') memoirs he found tribal polities similar to those in northern Gaul, dominated by the extensive kingdom of the Catuvellauni led by King Cassivelaunus. This expanding state, based north of the Thames in Hertfordshire, had some sort of – partially resented – overlordship over the smaller tribes of south-eastern Britain, including Kent where Caesar landed, and one of his objectives was to reduce its power as a potential source of aid to Gallic rebels. The southern British 'Belgae' were explicitly stated by him as an 'invading' branch of the Gallic confederation of that name, and the British war was thus an extension of his current Gallic wars – though this may have been played up in case his enemies in Rome accused him of going beyond the remit of his command in Gaul. His expedition to Kent in 55 BC was barely more than a reconnaissance. But interestingly, his larger-scale invasion in 54 BC was fought to a virtual standstill by the Britons and his need to return to Gaul before the autumn gales meant that he had to leave Cassivelaunus' state unconquered, though diminished in size. It was therefore both substantially resourced and well led to stand up to his veteran legions, and he admits to hard fighting and some reverses. The names he gives of the British leaders he encountered and the impression he received of their polities shows cultural affinities with the world of the north Gallic tribal polities he was already fighting, implying some cross-Channel connections. How old and how close these were – and whether any southern British elites had physically crossed from Gaul – is another matter. The literary record is silent, and the valuable recent studies into British DNA cannot define whether any genetic similarities between this and north Gallic/Belgian DNA dates to the pre-Roman or post-Roman period. The similarities imply some migration to Britain from Gaul – but was this in the first century BC or the fifth century AD?

It is not clear due to the absence of a literary tradition how far back the existence of the tribal kingdoms found by the Romans can be traced. Nor is it clear whether their geographical extent had fluctuated much in preceding centuries, or had been relatively stable. It is probable that there had been some growth and decline of kingdoms depending on the personal power exercised by strong leaders over a warrior aristocracy, and that unrecorded kingdoms had previously achieved the sort of domination over their neighbours that Caesar recorded the Catuvellauni as establishing over the lower Thames basin when he arrived. The competitive nature of and continuous aggression by similar chiefly states, plus the high status given to warriors in such a society, suggests that a degree of strife and predation was normal. What is uncertain is how long the Catuvellauni's dominance of their neighbours had lasted by 55 BC.

The usual assumption by historians from the rise of 'nationalist' history in the nineteenth century until recently was that the pre-Roman states were a creation of the 'Iron Age' – so called from the use of iron as the predominant metal tool (as for weapons). The tendency of historians was to group areas of similar socio-economic development and artefacts (as found by archaeology) into 'cultures', each neatly dominated by a 'people' (i.e. a homogeneous ethnic group). The lead in this was taken by pioneering nineteenth-century German historians in searching for evidence of an ancient 'German' people; all the independent tribes who Roman records list as their regional enemies clearly had similar cultures and political structures from the Rhine to the Vistula, as seen by archaeology. In Britain a similar process by historians led to pre-Roman British cultures being assumed to be the creation of one 'British' people (the original name for the inhabitants of the island noted by the ancient Greeks apparently being 'Pretani', i.e. Britons). The use of this one term for (and presumably by) the inhabitants implies a sense of unity among the tribes on the island, as one 'people' or culture – but the political element of this is less certain. The first known Greek contact with the island was by the explorer Pytheas of Massilia around 300 BC – but his account only survives in second-hand references from Imperial Roman authors and does not mention the societies and rulers he encountered. Guesswork is thus necessary, supplemented by the contemporary Roman sources' details of which tribe occupied what territory when they invaded plus the second-century AD details of tribal regions in the Romano-Egyptian scientist Ptolemy's *Geographia*.

The nineteenth- and early twentieth-century historians' usual assumption was to extend Caesar's account of a Belgic 'invasion' in the first century BC to other tribes and whole cultures, and to reckon that the arrival of the use of iron from the Continent in southern Britain around 500 BC marked the physical arrival of a new 'people', as well as a new culture, and that the two were necessarily connected. Use of iron gave militarily aggressive 'newcomers' the means to dominate and/or suppress earlier cultures – as in the Greek parallel the literary evidence referred to the conquest of most of Greece by invading 'tribes' at the end of the Mycenean age around 1100 BC. The concept of successive 'ages' indeed came from Greek culture, where the eighth-century BC poet Hesiod had written of the successively degenerating 'Ages' – the prosperous Golden Age, the poorer Silver Age, the Bronze Age when the heroes of Greek myth had held sway, and the present Iron Age. The lack of the same size or wealth of possessions as in southern Britain among settlements in northern Scotland during the final centuries BC could be traced to a different and culturally 'inferior' society – who it was assumed had been pushed out of the richer south and east of Britain by 'Iron Age' warriors.

Similarly, the emergence of defensible 'hill-forts' across the most geographically suitable culturally advanced area of Britain could be linked to inter-tribal warfare aided by iron weapons. The archaeological evidence of the concentration of the population across a wide area of (hilly) south-central England in large hill-situated fortresses, marked by (defensive?) banks and moats, was linked to this Iron Age 'people'. There had been no such concentrated settlements under the dominant culture before around 500 BC, which used bronze rather than iron; indeed it had only small farming settlements rather than concentrations of people in larger sites (or evidence of defensive banks and ditches). The change in culture was taken to imply a change to a more warlike state of affairs, and probably also a leadership able to command sufficient manpower resources for the work. Was the lack of 'defensive' earth-banked forts in the lowlands of eastern Britain due to a lack of useful, easily defensive hilltop positions or due to a different, less aggressive 'leadership class' (or less centralisation to enable the concentrated use of labour?). Hence the 'Iron Age' was linked to the arrival of a new, more warlike people and their presumed violent dispossession of their predecessors. Cultural change and political change could be linked and assumed to be the results of aggression by outsiders, presumably from the 'homeland' of the working of iron in Central Europe, principally Switzerland (called the 'La Tene' culture from a major excavated site). The 'La Tene' 'Celts' were assumed to have displaced the previous Central European 'Hallstadt' culture – so called from its principal archaeological site. This certainly accounted for the evidence of why hill-forts first appeared in southern Britain around 600–500 BC and then became larger in the 'Late Iron Age' around 200 BC – the new, warlike polities had both more material goods to safeguard and a predatory class of competitive warriors attacking neighbouring tribes. As proto-'states' competed, the fortifications of the 'winners' became ever more elaborate. This convenient nineteenth-century theory was still in vogue at the time of the major post-Second World War research into southern British hill-forts carried out by archaeologists such as Barry Cunliffe, and forts such as Danebury in northern Hampshire were shown as becoming larger and more elaborately defended as generations proceeded. The largest forts, such as Mai Dun (Maiden Castle) near Dorchester, which Sir Mortimer Wheeler excavated in the 1930s, were logically tribal 'capitals' and their elaborate defensive systems of ramparts and dykes implied a military need for such work.

This explanation for the evolution of pre-Roman British settlements has now been substantially discredited, starting with the observations of Roy Hobson in the early 1960s that pottery found at settlements could show that the 'hostile' and 'non-contemporaneous' 'Bronze Age' and 'Iron Age' cultures cohabited simultaneously. This would imply a gradual change to new forms of living, not military expulsion of one culture by another. But had new methods of living, e.g. use of iron and more advanced crop-farming, been introduced by new arrivals whether or not they had expelled the earlier residents? As a compromise, it was suggested by Colin Renfrew that new ideas in farming etc. had spread out in 'waves' from where they were first used, with 'Iron Age' practices coming to Britain from northern Gaul which in turn had received new ideas from the south. It is more generally accepted now that cultural changes such as the use of iron could evolve peacefully, usually by trade, and need not imply physical conquest. Indeed, the crucial British DNA evidence shows that the majority of the present British population can trace descent in the female line from the pre-Iron Age Neolithic Era. There was thus no 'ethnic cleansing' by 'Iron Age' conquerors from the Continent – or, for that matter, by Angles, Saxons, and Jutes after AD 400, of which more later. There were however genetic inheritances from more than one remote Continental ancestor, implying some post-1000 BC settlement from abroad. But what does this new theory mean for the evolution of kingdoms if there were no dynasties of aggressive 'Iron Age' conquerors ruling as warlords?

The absence of a written tradition means that the history of these kingdoms has been lost, while we rely to a large extent on the Greco-Roman literary assessment of their hostile 'Celtic' neighbours for an insight into society. Indeed, the central concept of this society across Europe – from Britain to the northern fringes of Greece – as 'Celtic' derives from its identification as one distinct culture by the Greeks and Romans. The term 'Celts' as a collective description for all the European peoples involved in this culture was revived in the modern era by the French archaeologist Joseph Dechelette in 1914, though it is now less certain that this is 'racially' or linguistically accurate. Even Caesar, our first literary source for the state of affairs in 'Celtic' Gaul in the 50s BC, uses the term 'Celt' for the inhabitants of central Gaul rather than all the region, let alone their culturally similar German and British neighbours.

Caesar recorded the culture that he found in 'Celtic' Gaul when he overran it and its similarities with what he found when he landed in Britain in 55 and 54 BC, indeed regarding the two peoples as parts of the same society. Technically, he only gave the actual name 'Celts' to the inhabitants of part of Gaul, and called the tribes nearer the Channel 'Belgae' as with the predominant tribe in Hampshire; the use of the name 'Celt' for all Gauls was done by nineteenth-century writers. The Britons apparently gave aid and refuge to tribesmen resisting Caesar in the early 50s such as the Veneti of Brittany, on which grounds he justified his invasion.

The southern British forts – similar to those on the Continent, particularly in Gaul whose tribal warrior-society was detailed by its conqueror Caesar – could be portrayed as the 'capitals' of warrior-chieftains, the British equivalent of the leaders who fought Caesar in Gaul. The larger hill-forts were seen as bases for an entire region's warlords, e.g. Mai Dun (Maiden Castle) outside Dorchester for the Durotriges tribe of Dorset. They could also be compared to 'hill-fort'-type fortresses found in parts of Ireland, most notably at Navan (Emain Macha), where society had evolved without Roman influence into the early Christian era and the – unique – surviving

'Celtic' post-Roman literature of the society portrayed a 'heroic' world of provincial kingdoms ruled by dynamic war-leaders with their war bands and Druid advisers. The Iron Age society of Roman-era Ireland, especially the forts and the warrior elite known to the 'Ulster Cycle' legends, could be portrayed as the same society which the Romans had disrupted in Britain. Thus the 'Cycle's great Ulster king Conor Mac Nessa, whose war band featured heroes such as Cu Chulainn, would have had his British equivalents – and the formidable Queen of Connact, Maedb (Maeve), was an Irish equivalent of Britain's Boudicca. For that matter, comparisons could be made between the obsessions of Irish Iron Age heroes with honour and personal combat and the way that the 'Heroic Age' warlords of Greece were portrayed in the *Iliad*. Crucially, all of them fought – or at least journeyed to battle – with chariots, as recorded separately for the Homeric heroes, the warriors who fought Caesar in Kent, and the legendary Cu Chulainn in Ulster. Recently expensive 'high-status' Iron Age chariots have been found in Britain, as at Wetwang.

The evolution of the southern British hill-forts from smaller to larger sizes between the fifth century and the first century BC could be seen as showing the expansion of the lands controlled by warrior-kings analogous to the men featured in Greco-Roman histories and Irish heroic poetry – the creation of embryonic tribal 'kingdoms'. The names given for tribal leaders in Greek and Roman accounts are akin to those of ancient Britain, suggesting linguistic affinities over a wide area, while the tribal structure of the Celtic polity set up in conquered 'Galatia' in the 270s was similar to that of Celtic Gaul. Even though there was no recorded history for these British 'kingdoms', comparison of British 'hill-fort area' archaeology with that of Gaul and Ireland and use of the literary information available on those two countries could suggest how society and culture had evolved in the centuries leading up to the Roman invasions. The only 'Celtic' tribal states that preserved any degree of dynastic history were those of the Irish, whose heroic legends dealt both with the origins of the Irish people and with the early kings and warriors of the kingdoms that existed in historic times (particularly the conflict of Ulster and Connacht). Our extant written records only date from the Christianised era post-AD 450, but the archaic 'pagan' society pictured therein was clearly preserved for centuries before that. As Caesar recorded, the early historical traditions were supposedly memorised by the 'class' of bards in epic poetry and recited at feasts rather than written down. Even with the wealth of material available in Ireland it is unclear how accurate its memories were of events hundreds of years in the past – the 'heroic' High Kingship of all Ireland, centred at Tara, and its third-century AD militia of 'Fianna' warriors under Fionn mac Cumhaill are unlikely to be historic. Nor are the lengthy genealogies that were eventually written down in the Christian era, dating back to the invading 'Sons of Mil' around 1000 BC – though oral tradition might well have been able to preserve the basic 'king-lists' of past centuries there. It has emerged, however, that the DNA of much of Ireland and western Britain does have more affinities with Spain than with the residents of northern France or Belgium, suggesting that the legend of the 'sons of Mil' – and perhaps the British traditions of 'Brutus the Trojan' from the Mediterranean, of which more later – have some link to ancient folk-memory.

The heroic 'origin myths' of peoples as a distinct, incoming society that conquered or expelled their predecessors have more to say about their need for a sense of a distinct identity than about accurate memories of precise historical events, and are often expressed in anachronistic contemporary terminology. A parallel can be seen in the question of the 'Dorian invasions' in Greece, where the Classical Era peoples of much of the Peloponnese chose to identify themselves as ethnically distinct from the Ionians (including the Athenians) and as having invaded the country from the north at the end of the heroic Iron Age to supersede the 'Mycenaean' states. In all these cases, however, some memories of a genuine movement of peoples – or at least of a smaller invasion by a new 'leadership elite' – cannot be ruled out. There were genuine linguistic differences between the post-1100 BC Greeks of 'Ionian' and 'Dorian' regions, even if these were 'rationalised' by later myths as having an ethnic origin. Was the same true of different regions in Britain and Ireland and their varied cultural traditions?

We have not any similar 'record' for the early history of the kingdoms of pre-Roman Britain, although some garbled early Welsh traditions may have been used in the elaborate constructions by Geoffrey of Monmouth in the 1130s. The 'book of early history' which he claimed to have been given and to have used as a source may only be a literary device, and his version of pre-Roman events is clearly seriously flawed. Crucially, where we do have other written evidence – for Roman Britain – Geoffrey's version is contradicted, and it seems to be patriotic myth. The medieval idea of a 'Kingdom of Britain' from around 1000 BC is clearly anachronistic, and was placed by Geoffrey in the setting of a twelfth-century-style chivalric society rather than anything with plausible 'Celtic' contexts. He was suspiciously fond of referring to places that were politically important in the twelfth century to his readers, such as the Normans' homeland and other regions of France, rather than to obscure places – mentions of which would have been more free from suspicion of contemporary relevance. The Greek master-poet Homer, by contrast, referred in his 'ancient history' poems to places such as Mycenae and Troy that were defunct by his own times, around 400 to 500 years after the events. Above all, the notion of Britain as called after the heroic ancestor of its kings – 'Brutus the Trojan' – was clearly an invention, though not of Geoffrey's as it had been mentioned by the Welsh writer 'Nennius' around AD 830. The 'Trojan' link of the ruling dynasty of Britain in Geoffrey's work, where Brutus was a member of the exile Trojan dynasty in Italy, was clearly an attempt to fit British history into that of the Greek *Iliad* and *Odyssey*, the Latin *Aeneid*, and the contemporary French myths of their people's 'Trojan' origin. As a descendant of Aeneas, the royal Trojan hero of the *Aeneid* and cousin of King Priam, 'Brutus' had a suitably 'high-status' origin. The *History of the Kings of Britain* was written in twelfth-century terminology, for twelfth-century political purposes of creating a suitably ancient mythology for the Norman-led 'British' political order centred on the Kingdom of England, with no concept of what real-life pre-Roman society was like. Geoffrey's leaders held contemporary titles, e.g. 'dukes' of Cornwall and kings of Wales and Scotland, not archaic ones. The term 'duke', from the Latin 'dux' ('leader'), only originated as a Late Roman military office around AD 300.

There is no archaeological evidence of a centralised royal-led society in pre-Roman Britain, or of any of the early towns that Geoffrey presents. But it is possible that the archaeological record of increasingly large hill-forts during the 'Late Iron Age' in Britain indicates that there was a degree of insecurity lacking in earlier eras, arising from increased wealth and increased competition to possess it. It is logical to presume that this increased competition in society implies the existence of an acquisitive warrior aristocracy led by dynasties of chieftains in the last few centuries BC – a British variant on the 'heroic' society idealised by the Irish legends, bearing some similarities with the competitive, ritualised world of warriors in the works of Homer in Greece. But this cannot be taken for granted, as there is no definitive agreement among modern archaeologists about the purpose of hill-forts – particularly the larger ones that were too extensive to contain a settled population. Places such as Maiden Castle or Danebury were too large to be 'proto-townships' for the contemporary population of first-century BC Britain, their populace living safely behind defensive ramparts in the manner of Greek or Roman cities. But the fact that there was substantial building at Danebury in the second and first centuries BC would imply that it was used partly for permanent settlement, not just as a trading centre or a place of refuge in wartime. It is risky to assume that the Greco-Roman concept of a walled (or not) residential urban site was in existence in Britain at that time; the few 'proto-urban' concentrated settlements of the decades before Roman conquest, such as Silchester or St Albans/Verulamium, known as 'oppida' (a Mediterranean not local term), seem to contain both 'urban' settlement, based on trade and crafts, and farms with fields. They were more like sprawling suburbs, or modern Third World 'shanty-towns', than planned urban 'show-pieces' as in the Greco-Roman tradition. These 'oppida' had ramparts or ditches, but this may have been primarily as boundaries and defensibility been a lesser purpose.

The hill-forts rarely contain many identifiable residential structures, although logically they would have served as temporary refuges for people and livestock in time of war. Danebury is thus unusual. But we cannot say that being a wartime refuge was their primary purpose or that their evolution represents a new and violent society with a contest over resources –this theory may be 'back-dating' assumptions based on later, Dark Ages society into a different world. The concentration of resources at these sites may have been for trade and/or distribution rather than for safety, with the leadership of society using them as administrative centres. Refuge in wartime may have been a minor or later use for them, with the conflict of contending tribal kingdoms recorded for southern Britain in the later first century BC and early first century AD by Roman historians being a new development of that era.

The Belgae, who were rulers of much of south-central England by Claudius' time, were apparently relative newcomers to their position of power, as stated by Caesar. Were they resented as such by their neighbours the 'Atrebates' of eastern and northern Hampshire, whose lands they had usurped? The main 'oppida' – not exactly translatable as 'towns' in the Roman sense, due to the presence of rural settlement and fields within the defensive circuit of earthworks – were at Calleva (Silchester) in northern Hampshire and the Belgae's 'Venta Belgarum' (Winchester) a little to the south. The Belgae, coming from Gaul, are thus likely to have seized the coastal districts of the Atrebates. The existence of an identical tribe of 'Belgae' in northern Gaul makes it probable that the tradition is accurate which portrays them as part of the same 'people' as the British Belgae. Many of them fled Gaul after Caesar's victory over Vercingetorix in 52 BC to join their kinsmen in Britain. Caesar, incidentally, reckoned the northern third of what is commonly called 'Gaul' to be Belgic by tribal identity; technically he placed the 'Gauls' to their south, in Aquitaine.

It is probable that Commius of the Atrebates, a former Gallic chieftain in Caesar's service who joined the rebellion, was not the only prominent figure in Britain who arrived in the late 50s as a refugee from Caesar and seized lands or a kingdom for himself. Other unrecorded migrations of individuals or tribes from the Continent may well have occurred earlier, though Britain lacks the complex mythology of a series of invasions that survived in Irish literature. The extension of the 'empire' of the Catuvellauni in the Thames valley and southern East Anglia by dynamic rulers such as Cassivelaunus in the first century BC indicates another probable area of turbulence. The emergence of the use of coinage by the main tribal rulers of South East England in the first century BC gives us the first definite evidence of royal leadership, with increased trade with the Continent leading to emulation of Roman civilisation and the usage of Roman luxury goods. The last half-century or so before the invasion of 55 BC is accordingly now known by archaeologists as the 'Contact' era. But it is not known if it was only now, with a wealthier society and fiercer competition to control resources, that the kingdoms which the Romans found evolved and warfare broke out among them.

The 'empire' that the Catuvellauni of the Hertfordshire area built up, overrunning their eastern neighbours the Trinovantes, and the Belgae's aggression against the Atrebates may have been a new phenomenon, with dynamic leaders seizing resources to build up war bands and plundering their neighbours. The use of coinage, a visible source of advertisement and prestige for successful rulers, was certainly new though we cannot say if it was only in the first century BC that British rulers came into contact with the use of coinage due to the growing prosperity and Roman trade of neighbouring Gaul. Our only literary reference to Britain before the era of 'Contact' is the uncertainly dated exploration of the British coasts by Pytheas of Massilia, probably in the later fourth century or early third century BC. (This is only preserved in later, Roman-era histories.) For what it is worth, our sketchy details of Pytheas' mission make no reference to the rulers in Britain or to any distinct kingdoms, suggesting that either there were no such polities or that he was only concerned with the geography not the political situation.

It used to be a general scholarly opinion that the Celts, as the peoples who Caesar found in possession of southern Britain in 55 BC were all categorised, had arrived as a tribal migration from the Continent a few centuries earlier. They had brought the use of iron with them, thus creating a sharp divergence of their 'Iron Age' from the previous 'Bronze Age' when weapons had been made of bronze. It could be assumed that the superiority of iron implements over bronze ones meant that more 'advanced' Celtic warriors using iron had subdued their bronze-using predecessors. Other instances of Celtic migrations could be used as evidence of what 'must' have happened in Britain, such as the Celtic descent on northern Italy around 400 BC recalled by Livy and the Celtic invasions of Greece in 279 and Asia Minor thereafter. A Celtic 'Iron Age' around 500 thus succeeded an earlier Bronze Age, whose poorly armed and less organised polities collapsed in the face of 'Celtic' aggression. The use of hill-forts by the Iron Age Celts showed that they had a more warlike society, with people and goods needing to be defended from attackers, and the increasing size of hill-forts from around 400 to 50 BC showed that the Celtic polities had become larger and better organised. The Bronze Age societies – with smaller, less well-defended settlements – had in turn replaced the Neolithic age where there had been only scattered farming settlements, with each advance in technology brought by more 'advanced' peoples who had used their new weaponry to subdue or drive out their predecessors. Even in the Neolithic Age, a series of more 'primitive' societies – as identified by their household goods, discovered in the long and round barrows of southern England – had each been superseded by a more 'advanced' culture, presumably by conquest. Early archaeologists even chose to name whole eras of the Neolithic after the specific material goods of the age found in British sites, such as the supposed 'Beaker Folk' whose distinctive pottery flourished from around 2700 to 1700 BC.

The 'Celtic' influx, presumably from Gaul and involving warriors of the type depicted in the surviving Iron Age literature of Ireland, was supposed to have brought Britain into a Europe-wide tribal culture that stretched as far as the tribes threatening the Romans and Greeks in the fourth and third centuries BC. The Celtic 'homeland' was located in the area of the most distinctive archaeological sites of their culture, in Switzerland and Austria where the Hallstadt site sometimes gave its name to the early Celtic culture until around 600 and the La Tene site to the subsequent era. The Celts spread out from this area of Central Europe in a series of migrations, and were supposed to have expanded east and west by trade and/or conquest. Some sort of disruption of an earlier order certainly seems to have occurred in northern Italy, where one possible 'wave' of invaders around 600 and then the one recalled by Livy around 400 brought new material cultures to the Po valley and pushed the earlier Ligurians and Veneti back to the areas now named after them on the west and east coasts. The resulting tribal groups of the central Po plain who the Romans found there in the third century – the Insubres, Cenomani, and Boii – bore cultural traits akin to those of the Celts in Gaul, making the Romans see them as parts of one people, and the Boii bore a name suggesting an origin in Bohemia.

Historians now believe that there was no mass 'Celtic' influx as such into Britain, and that the 'Iron Age' culture they represented emerged gradually during the period from around 700 to 450 BC. There was no radical 'break' such as that of 1066, with one mass-migration of conquerors, or even an influx over a few generations; the new material goods seem to have come into use over several centuries. Logically, this would represent a change of 'fashion' among settled inhabitants rather than invasion. Indeed, the whole notion of a 'Celtic' people with a distinctive 'Iron Age' culture, stretching from the Atlantic to the tribes bordering Greece and centred on the main discovered archaeological sites in Austria, is now disputed. The tribes over this area may have shared the same 'hallmarks' of culture and had inter-connected languages, also sharing a common pantheon of gods, but this does not mean that they all shared a common origin and dispersed outwards from their original 'centre'. The 'Celtic' tribes who invaded Macedonia and sacked Delphi in 279 BC under a ruler called 'Brennus' (Celtic for 'King'), one branch of them then settling in the significantly named 'Galatia' in western Asia Minor, undoubtedly had linguistic and cultural affinities with the tribes of ancient Gaul, which were recognised by their Roman conquerors. The personal names of their senior chieftains were strikingly similar. There were also affinities with the 'Gaulish' tribes which terrified the Romans in northern Italy in the third century BC and whose wars are recounted by Livy.

The Romans may have been correct in assuming that the tribes they encountered in northern Italy were the same people as the warriors who had invaded Etruria and sacked Rome itself at a date variously reckoned as 390 or 387/6 BC – and the legendary name of the invaders' commander, 'Brennus' as with the Celtic leader in Greece, is similar to the later Welsh word for 'king' ('Brenin'). But this does not make them – or the Late Iron Age Britons – one ethnic 'people'. Culture could be spread by trade and fashion as much as by migration, and elites adopt new names and cultural terms without these being imposed by conquerors. A change in the form of material culture in Britain, e.g. from using bronze to using iron, need not imply that a new 'people' arrived to impose new customs and technology on those that they conquered or drove out – rather that 'fashions' changed among an existing populace. Nor is it necessary to assume that the use of iron enabled a 'people' that had adopted it to drive out or subdue those societies that used bronze, rather than the new metal being gradually adopted over centuries as a result of trade with only occasional use in warfare.

The latest researches in British DNA certainly suggest that there was less movement of peoples or arrival of new tribes from the Continent in the first millennium BC than used to be thought, with many modern Britons having a genetic connection to the Neolithic inhabitants. If written tradition was taken as accurate, the successive 'waves' of Iron Age Celts, Romans, Anglo-Saxons, and Normans should have diluted the original DNA to a far greater extent than this. The arrival of new material goods need not imply that they were brought by a distinctive people, rather that society developed – though it is certainly possible that some ambitious new 'leaders' of a more militarised Iron Age culture did come from the Continent or adopted ideas that they had found there through trading. Ambitious men, some of foreign origin or training, then used military and political power to impose new ideas on a far larger but less militarised population (as did the Normans). The influx of Belgae from Gaul by Caesar – or the flight of Commius to take over the British tribe of the Atrebates – may have been part of a pattern over centuries. Thus, as in the Saxon and Norman worlds, a ruling 'class' of aristocratic warriors could emerge and engage in the sort of ritualised, 'chivalric' warfare seen in the stories of Late Iron Age Ireland. It should also be said that historians are now less certain about using linguistic evidence of affinities between the languages spoken in the 'Celtic fringes' of the British Isles to 'prove' the existence of one 'Celtic people' – or two 'groups', speaking the 'P'- and 'Q'-Celtic dialects. This theory dates back to speculation by James VI and I's tutor George Buchanan in the late sixteenth century, built on by Edward Lluyd (pioneering linguist and Keeper of the Ashmolean Museum, Oxford) a century later.

The archaeological evidence of the Iron Age hill-forts suggests that some sort of central tribal authority directed their building in the last four or five centuries BC and that the later, bigger hill-forts were accordingly built by stronger – larger? – authorities than the early ones. The hill-forts were concentrated in the central part of southern England, with a few in the central West Midlands, rather than being dispersed across all of England – or over all of the hilly areas. Settlement was elsewhere in smaller, sometimes (not often in the east) fortified farms. Accordingly it could be suggested that there were significant cultural 'sub-divisions' within the larger picture of Iron Age culture. Central 'government', in the sense of an authority directing the building of hill-forts to concentrate resources, was thus stronger in the area with larger hill-forts though the leadership may still have built the forts primarily for trade at regular agricultural markets or to collect supplies of tribute, not for defence. The most experienced of current archaeologists dealing with the period, Barry Cunliffe, in his *Iron Age Communities of Britain* (1971, 3rd ed. 1991), proposed five major divisions. The hill-forts were concentrated in a 'south-central' zone of Britain; other divisions consisted of the 'east' (with mainly unfortified farming settlements), the 'south-west' (where evidence suggested an emerging aristocracy living off the produce of subordinate farms), and the 'north-east' (from Humber and Mersey to Forth) and 'north-west'. It is debatable whether hill-forts' main purpose was as 'towns', i.e. residential and/or trading centres, given that the amount of settlement in them was limited. It is now regarded as probable that they were centres for trade and/or meetings, where people and their invaluable domestic livestock could be secured in times of conflict. The very fact that forts were erected then but not in Neolithic times would suggest an aggregation of wealth (portable goods or livestock) that was worth stealing and/or an increase in insecurity and warfare, allied to new chiefdoms that directed the building.

Warfare and Kingship

The unique literary evidence which Homeric-style oral poems preserved of conditions in neighbouring Late Iron Age Ireland suggests a culture where inter-tribal raids for cattle and other loot and fights between prestige-seeking champions and/or larger forces of warriors occurred from time to time. The Irish culture, with fortresses such as Navan (Emain Macha) and kings carrying out annual sacred rituals, certainly looks similar to conditions on the mainland at the time that Caesar invaded. A powerful 'over-king' with a large and predatory war band, such as that of the kingdom of Ulster in the Irish legends, could be seen in the position of Cassivellaunus of the Catuvellauni in 55 BC or Cunobelinus a few decades later. There was also an interesting parallel with the 'Heroic Age' of Greece, as immortalised in Homer's epics, and its kings (e.g. of Mycenae). It seemed that in all these cases there was (at least in retrospective memory) a predatory 'culture' of aggressive warlords, dominating their neighbours and surrounded by war bands of expert swordsmen keen to prove their prowess in combat. Was there a British equivalent of Cu Chulainn or Achilles?

The large hill-forts were presumably useful for the collection of civilians and livestock in time of war to evade raiding tribal warriors rather than withstanding long sieges. These kingdoms must have had rulers and probably ruling dynasties among whose ablest menfolk the kingship descended, or even the occasional woman ruler like the British Boudicca and Cartimandua and the mythical Irish Maeve/Medb of Connacht. There have been dubious arguments about 'matriarchal' rule existing in some kingdoms or cultures, based on a mixture of the power exercised by queens like Boudicca (or Medb in legend) and the theories of Robert Graves (see below). One argument about the uncertain means of hereditary descent in the 'Pictish' kingdom of Scotland has led to a theory that they practised matriarchal succession (see later), and linked this to their retention of ancient practice.

Unlike in Ireland even the most renowned men's names of the British Iron Age do not seem to have survived into later myth unless one or two were present in Dark Age Welsh and Breton tradition and were picked up by Geoffrey of Monmouth. Survivals of ancient names and traditions may also appear in the collection of eleventh- and twelfth-century Welsh stories known since Lady Charlotte Guest's 1840s translation as the *Mabinogion* – particularly those concerning the ancient giant-size King Bran 'the Blessed' and the South Wales king Pwyll and his wife Rhiannon (a 'Celtic' goddess). There has also been intense debate about the precise nature of kingship, in particular its sacral context. The kings that ruled over Iron Age society may well have had a priestly role, not least as the symbols of their people and intercessors with the gods on whose goodwill agriculture depended. The Irish – and to a lesser extent Welsh legends of ancient rulers have some of them 'marrying' figures representing the lands they ruled over. This may reflect a rite carried out on accession. The concept of a sacrificial king being killed at the end of a fixed term of rule or in a crisis to appease the gods is more contentious, and is now to some degree discredited. As shown by the discoveries in peat-bogs, the 'Celts' did practice human sacrifice (often by ritual drowning) – and were reviled for it by the Romans. But it is unclear if this ritual had a connection with a role established for kingship, such as symbolising the annual cycle of the crops with a new king every spring, or if it did how widespread this was.

Robert Graves has traced this practice and its accompanying mythology in parallel Greek legends, as well as proposing the theory that the earliest rulers were from matriarchal dynasties reflecting the role of an all-powerful 'Mother Goddess' in early mythology. The Asian Astarte/Cybele, with her junior consort Adonis, was regarded as a survival of the original order of theology across Europe, with her equivalent in the Celtic Matrona. The all-powerful female goddesses and their earthly equivalents were thus superseded at some time in the last millennium BC by 'patriarchy' – as in Greek culture the 'original' version of the leading male god Zeus, junior to the Mother Goddess in Cretan culture, became the supreme sky-god. The 'White Goddess' theory, with a powerful female ruler representing the supreme goddess and a succession of temporary consorts who may have been ritually sacrificed like Adonis, is still highly contentious and the evidence is not strong enough to make it certain.

The main ancient British myth that may reflect pre-Roman history is that concerning Stonehenge which found its way into the later Arthurian legends. The main stone circle, the 'Giants' Dance', was supposed to have been erected during the reign of an overlord of all Britain – in this case Ambrosius Aurelianus – as a monument to the massacred councillors of his predecessor Vortigern. The construction was allegedly carried out by his magician Merlin, who moved the stones from Killara in Ireland after Ambrosius had defeated the local king. It has been suggested that although the date given of around AD 460 is totally inaccurate (and the association with Merlin arose from Dark Age bards seeking an explanation for the 'magic' of the massive construction work at the site) there was a genuine folk-memory of the site's erection by a genuinely powerful 'over-king' in the Neolithic era. The Irish connection was given credence as a dim folk-memory when it was found that the central 'bluestones' of the circle came from the Presceli Mountains in Pembrokeshire, formerly an area of Irish settlement in the fifth century. Thus the story of the man who ordered the circle's construction was allegedly assimilated with that of Ambrosius, a similar 'national' re-builder of society after a period of strife from many hundreds of years later. In similar vein, it was claimed that the legend preserved in Geoffrey's works of his successor 'Arthur' ruling over vassal-kingdoms on the Continent is a dim memory of the triumphs of later rulers of this dynasty in the Neolithic period.

Admittedly the authorities responsible for the work on Stonehenge would have needed to call on large-scale resources over a substantial period to undertake such a project, and must have been figures of some prestige and ability to coerce assistance. But archaeologists have no idea as to whether a monarchy controlling a number of sub-kingdoms (including one in the Presceli Mountains where the 'bluestones' originated?) or a widely venerated priesthood controlling a 'national' sacred centre were responsible. Given the dispersed, small-scale, and agricultural nature of Neolithic settlements and the absence of signs of a ruling warrior-class that kings could lead in battle, it is more likely that there was no centralised secular leadership for society in this period. Kingship may rather have evolved in the 'heroic' era of hill-forts in the later Iron Age, where the more sharply stratified society and the apparent need for some form of defences for men and their wealth would suggest a greater need for warrior-leaders.

The Pre-Roman and Roman Conquest-Era Tribal Leadership

Evidence: partly literary (Roman sources and some Dark Age legends, plus the source of the later work of Geoffrey of Monmouth). The Roman accounts of the 55–54 BC invasions by their leader, Caesar, and of the post-AD 43 invasions by Tacitus and Suetonius are the main sources. The names and locations of each tribal territory in Britain are given by Ptolemy (around AD 120) in his *Geographia*. Some is archaeological, e.g. tribal leadership's coinage for the final decades before the Roman conquest.

Catuvellauni (based on Hertfordshire, expanding to cover much of Britain around the lower Thames basin)

The Real and the Legendary Lines of Kings
Geoffrey of Monmouth in the 1140s claimed to be citing earlier books in giving a list of rulers before Cassivellaunus, the ruler who fought Caesar in 55–54 BC. The 'kingdom of Britain' which he referred to did not exist, showing his lack of basic historical information that can be corroborated from other sources. His kings included the 'Lud' who supposedly founded London and built Ludgate, and other assorted eponymous rulers whose names more likely derived from medieval legends explaining local place-names. King Leir ('Lear'), later used by Shakespeare, was connected to Leicester. Geoffrey's enterprising genealogy listed kings of Britain back to the legendary Brutus the Trojan of around 1000 BC, all of it anachronistic and most of it evidently fabricated – though there seems to have been a Dark Ages origin for some of it which appears in the ninth-century *Historia Brittonum*, e.g. the 'Brutus' story. We cannot say when the 'Brutus' story was invented, though the name was presumably an imaginative 'back-formation' from the name of Britain; a guess would be that the idea came from the Frankish literary 'Trojan origin' story written by Fredegar in the seventh century.

The list and approximate dating of the rulers given by Geoffrey is as follows, given that the date of the 'Trojan War' was most commonly calculated at around 1185 BC in the Classical period:

Name	Length of reign (years)	Date
Brutus	23	Twelfth century BC
Locrinus (first King of 'Logres': Wales to Camber, Scotland to Albanactus)	10	
Gwendolen	15	
Maddan	40	
Mempricius	19	
Ebraucus	40	Eleventh century BC (contemporary of Saul)
Brutus (Greenshield)	12	
Leil	20	Tenth century BC (contemporary of Solomon)
Hudibras	39	
Bladud	20	Ninth century BC (contemporary of Elijah)
Leir	60	
Maglaurus (Albany) & Henwinus (Cornwall)	*c.* 4?	
Leir (ii)	3	
Cordelia	5	
Marganus & Cunedagius	2	
Cunedagius	33	
Riwallo	?	
Gurgustius	?	
Sisillius	?	
Jago	?	
Kimmarcus	?	

Gorbuduc	?	
Ferrex & Porrex	?	

The civil war between Ferrex – who was killed – and Porrex, and the latter's murder by their mother, then ended the dynasty of Brutus. Civil strife followed for an indefinite time. The date of the next king in Geoffrey's list could however be worked out by 'back-dating' from the known date of the sack of Rome, 390/87 BC.

Dunvallo Molmutius	40	440s–400s BC
Belinus & Brennius (i)	5	400s BC
Belinus	2?	
Belinus & Brennius (ii)	2?	

Brennius then settled in Italy, having led the Celtic army that sacked Rome.

Belinus (ii)	>30?	Early 380s BC–?
Gurguit Barbtruc	?	Mid- to late fourth century BC?
Guithelin	?	
Sisillius	?	Early third century BC?
Kinarius	?	
Danius	?	
Morvidus	?	
Gorbonianus	?	Late third century to early second century BC?
Archgallo (i)	?	
Elidurus (i)	5	
Archgallo (ii)	10	
Peredurus & Ingenius	7	
Peredurus	?	
Elidurus (ii)	?	
Anon. (son of Gorbonianus)	?	

Marganus	?	Mid-second century BC?
Ennianus	?	
Idvallo	?	

Succession of minor kings, mostly of unknown connections. Geoffrey puts them as ruling in succession, but unless they had very short reigns the time-scale between Brennius and Lud does not allow for this.

Heli	40	*c.* 120–80 BC?
Lud	?	*c.* 80–60s BC?

The Trojan link clearly derived from an attempt to give the British monarchy as respectable a pedigree as the ancient Roman 'Trojan' link, literarily celebrated in the *Aeneid*, and more recently the Frankish legends linking the origins of the Britons' arch-rivals across the Channel to another supposed Trojan migration. Thus 'Brutus', whose names could be connected to 'Britain', was linked to the lineage of Aeneas established in Italy after the Trojan War, making the British royal house junior relatives to the line of the Caesars in Rome that claimed descent from Aeneas and his son Ascanius/Iulus. It was posited that he had arrived at Totnes around 1000 BC to rid Britain of its earlier race of giants (an established part of Dark Age folklore probably invented to explain the gigantic scale of the megalithic stone-works found across the country). He was given three sons with names linked to the constituent parts of the main British island in Geoffrey's time – Locrinus of 'Logres' (England), Kamber of 'Cymry' (Wales), and Albanactus of Alba (Scotland). The name 'Cymry' presumably comes from the Latin for 'companions', 'Comites', evolving into 'fellow countrymen' some time after AD 450; the use of 'Alba' for Scotland only appears around AD 900.

Other invented figures established a shaky royal line descending to the time of Julius Caesar. Some names that Geoffrey used were genuine ones from later northern genealogies, e.g. 'Gorbonianus' from the 'Germanianus' in the line of Coel 'Hen'. It is possible that there were some vaguely remembered local figures who had ruled areas of Britain, were recalled in Welsh or Breton legend, and could be inserted into Geoffrey's story – e.g. Bladud, the legendary leper prince turned swineherd who discovered the medicinal springs at Bath but in the expanded version of his story was now made a King of Britain who tried to fly and crashed off the roof of a temple in his capital. A probably genuine British king of uncertain geographical context in the fifth or sixth century AD, Dyfnwal Molmud, was taken back in time to around 400 BC and made the wise national ruler who originated the 'Molmutine Laws', no doubt an attempt to give the British their own version of the Roman 'Twelve Tables'. Brennus, the ruler of the Celtic Gauls in northern Italy who sacked Rome around 387 BC, was patriotically made a Briton (as Dyfnwal's son) and given a co-ruling brother Belinus, whose name was derived from a Celtic god. King 'Leir' may have been the traditional mythological founder of 'Leircester', i.e. Leicester, and the story of the king abdicating and being ill-used by his ungrateful daughters had been an extant twelfth-century romance that Geoffrey picked up. As with the mythical rivalry of Kings Ferrex and Porrex, the story was to become a favourite of later romancers and be embellished by Tudor drama. The latter, like Geoffrey's work, was not over-concerned with the 'historical' truth as opposed to a good story – Shakespeare embellished and altered Geoffrey's version of the Lear story and in *Cymbeline* had the Romans land at Milford Haven like Henry Tudor in 1485.

But Geoffrey did not include one of the most well known of the current Celtic legends concerning a King of Britain, namely that of Bran 'the Blessed' who invaded Ireland after the mistreatment of his sister Branwen, wife to its ruler Matholwch, and was mortally wounded after which his magical severed head ended up buried at the 'White Mount' in London (Tower Hill) as a national talisman. It has been suggested that the claim in the legend that the sea between Wales and Ireland was much narrower at the era of Bran's crossing is a dim folk-memory of a time when this was actually the case and that the prototype for Bran was therefore a genuine wide-ruling British ruler who attacked Ireland several thousand years before the start of the Christian era. But there is no indication from archaeology that the limited population of Britain at this stage could sustain a chieftainship of more than local powers. Nor is it probable that this story of heroic warfare could have survived, uniquely, through the Iron Age and Roman era to be picked up by Dark Age Celtic writers over a thousand years later – at least in Ireland a whole body of mythology surrounding ancient Ulster kings survived, for a more believable four or five centuries according to the accepted chronology. There is equally no evidence for other mythological 'ancestral hero' rulers of the pre-Roman era who appear in Welsh legend but did not make it into Geoffrey's story, such as Pwyll ('Wisdom'), Prince of Dyfed, and his son Pryderi. Their mythical origins have been investigated at length by Roger Loomis and other scholars.

The line created – or expanded from earlier Welsh or Breton books – by Geoffrey emerges into history as the royal house of the Catuvellauni in the first century BC, though even here he is grossly anachronistic in his portrayal of their urban 'capital' at London and his work is conspicuously inaccurate when it can be placed in comparison with other written sources (most notably Caesar and Cassius Dio) or archaeology. London may have derived its name from a local ruler, but the existence of a much earlier 'Trinovantium' on the site was clearly an attempt by the patriotic Geoffrey to give the city a pedigree to rival that of Rome (as he did other twelfth-century towns and cities). It has been claimed that for London to grow to the size it reached by the time of Boudicca's sack in AD 60 – seventeen years after the earliest date for a Roman foundation – there must have been a settlement there earlier, but this remains speculative unless any archaeological evidence is found. It is however true that there were 'towns' in pre-Roman Britain, albeit in the sense of large, sprawling settlements which included farms and small crafts workshops within their perimeters. These 'oppida' included the Catuvellauni's 'capital', Colchester, and the core of the later Roman Verulamium (St Albans) which possessed a large sprawling residential area in the first century BC.

Once Geoffrey's story reaches the time of the Roman Empire he produces all sorts of patriotic stories about British kings ruling the island autonomously that are not supported by any Roman literary sources and seem designed to assert as much British independence for the period as he could get away with. Arviragus, younger son of Cymbeline (Cunobelinus), is presented as King of Britain rather than of the local south-eastern kingdom of the Catuvellauni, fights the Roman invasion of AD 43 on equal terms, and ends up as the son-in-law of and governor for Emperor Claudius. The whole story in Geoffrey's history of Claudius' campaigns against Arviragus has no basis in the Roman sources, and there is no mention of Claudius' supposed daughter 'Genvissa' or the two rulers' joint foundation of Gloucester; at best it must have come from contemporary romance or vague Welsh legends connected to Gloucester. Kings such as Arviragus' 'son' Marius and his second-century AD son Lucius, inviter of the first Papal Christian mission to Britain in the second century, are made to seem independent, and no mention is made of Roman governors. Patriotically, one Emperor who campaigned in Britain, Septimius Severus, is given British family connections that no Roman literary source mentions – as is the Britain-based rebel Carausius who seems in reality to have come from 'Menapia', either modern Belgium or Ireland. There is also confusion over the various 'walls' erected in northern Britain, with one of them falsely connected to Severus rather than Antoninus Pius and placed from north to south rather than from east to west. A recent study by Steve Blake and Scott Lloyd (*The Keys to Avalon*, 2000) has claimed that the confusion over the wall may have arisen from Severus commissioning the 'original' ditch separating the civilian from military zones in Wales that was taken over and extended by Offa in the eighth century, as this does run from north to south. But this cannot be proved unless adequate Roman evidence is found at the site.

It is unknown if the sixty or so differing post-twelfth-century Welsh versions of the Geoffrey of Monmouth legendary history, the *Brut y Brenhinedd*, derive entirely from Geoffrey. The earliest of these versions, known as 'Llanstephan Mss. 1' in the British Library, dates to the early thirteenth century (as mainstream scholars agree); most are later thirteenth- to fourteenth-century, divided into six main versions including the *Brut Dingestow* (from Dingestow Court in Monmouthshire) and the *Brut Tyssilio* (originally attributed to a seventh-century Welsh prince, Tyssilio). Some hopeful writers have alleged that at least some of them, e.g. the *Brut Tyssilio*, derive from pre-Geoffrey originals and the differences between them and Geoffrey's version show which details he altered or made up; could one of them (or its lost 'original') even be Geoffrey's original source? This theory would suggest that some of the data about 'mythical' pre-Roman or Roman-era kings came from early sources and is thus based on actual names and events. But most scholars would deny this; and the stories in Geoffrey and the *Bruts* are at variance with our Roman sources, as in the detail of the alleged war of Claudius with Arviragus. Similar doubt persists over the 'Roman era' names in the tenth-century Welsh royal genealogies of Hywel Dda's ancestors, preserved in BL Harleian Mss. 3589 – which include alleged British kings such as 'Afallach' and 'Beli' and their relationship to the family of the Virgin Mary.

Kings of the Catuvellauni

Name	Accession	Years ruled	Death
Beli?	100s BC?	*c.* 40 (Geoffrey)	60s BC?
Cassivellaunus	60s BC?	20–30?	40s BC?
Tasciovanus	40s BC?	25–30?	*c.* AD 10?

Andoco	*c.* AD 10?	A few years?	*c.* AD 10/15
Cunobelinus (prev. ruled Trinovantes)	*c.* AD 15?	Over 25	AD 41?
Togudumnus (Northern lands)	AD 41?	2?	AD 43
Caratacus (Southern lands)	AD 41?	2?	AD 43

Trinovantes (based on Essex)

Geoffey of Monmouth posited the original town of London as the tribal capital, 'Trinovantium'. It is not known if he had any genuine evidence for this; it was pure literary invention for him to claim that the name came from 'Troia Nova', 'New Troy'. A weaker southern neighbour of the powerful Catuvellauni, its initial conquest by the latter was reversed by Julius Caesar as a means of weakening his main enemies with an exiled prince being restored as the new king. Either he or a successor was removed by the Catuvellauni some time around the birth of Christ, once it was safe to do so due to the weakening of Rome's immediate military threat.

Cunobelinus' name means 'Hound of (the god) Belinus'. Geoffrey turned this god, presumably especially revered by the Trinovantes, into a king. Cunobelinus forcibly united the two kingdoms; it is unclear if Trinovantian resentment at this aided the Romans in obtaining local cooperation during and after their invasion in 43.

Name	Accession	Years ruled	Death
Imanuentius	?	?	55 BC

Conquest by Cassivelaunus of the Catuvellauni.

Mandubracius (restored by Julius Caesar)	54 BC	?	?
Cunobelinus (prince of the Catuvellauni)	*c.* AD 1	Around 40?	AD 41

Atrebates (based on northern Hampshire)/Belgae (southern Hampshire)
The name means 'the inhabitants', 'Ad-treb-a-tes' in proto-Brittonic.
Precise boundaries unclear, except that Winchester (Venta Belgarum) was
the principal 'oppidum' of the Belgae and Silchester (Calleva Atrebatum)
of the Atrebates; the latter may also have had Noviomagus (Chichester) as
their southern 'oppidum' and the 'Regni' thus had been a branch of their
people. The existence of a kingdom of the Belgae in northern Gaul – which
has given its name to Belgium – may imply a 'migration' of Belgic warrior-
aristocrats to rule Hampshire some time in the first century BC, possibly
exacerbated by flight from Julius Caesar's invaders after 58 BC, or just a
cultural link. Caesar states that some Gallic Belgae had moved to southern
Britain and seized territory before his time, and the fact that the Atrebates'
'capital' of Calleva/Silchester was further inland than the Belgic 'capital 'of
Winchester would imply that the Belgae drove the Atrebates northwards.
The southern British aid to anti-Caesar rebels in Gaul which the Roman
general mentions suggests that the locals still had kin and/or trading
interests in Gaul as of 55 BC. Culturally the Atrebates, Belgae, and Regni
(see below) were akin, e.g. in adopting Roman-style coinage; personal links
among their nobility are probable. There was also an 'Atrebates' tribe in
northern Gaul, centred around Arras; it is not known if they, like the Gallic
'Belgae', were kin of (in the original home of?) the Hampshire Atrebates.

The earliest known Atrebatic ruler, Commius, was a north Gallic prince
who had served in Caesar's army in Gaul in the 50s BC before defecting
to the rebel Vercingetorix in the revolt of 52. Forced to flee to Britain at
Caesar's victory, he probably brought Roman cultural influences with him.
The kingdom was evidently a regular conduit for Roman imports before the
conquest, and was probably a political ally too – Augustus is known to have
maintained friendly relations with southern British kings and there have been
recent archaeological findings indicating even a temporary Roman military
camp dating to before 43 on the kingdom's Solent coast. The substantial size
of pre-Roman Calleva, recently excavated, is suggestive about the kingdom's
power – and possibly about proto-urbanisation (with or without Roman
influence in this concept and in the building of large aristocratic residences).
Tincommius/Tincomarus, who is mainly known from his coinage and from
its location seems to have been the ruler at Calleva in the first decade AD,
was probably the fugitive ruler of the Atrebates who sought sanctuary in
Rome towards the end of the Emperor Augustus' reign and was recorded as
his client-king on the 'Res Gestae', a monumental summary of the Emperor's
achievements at Ancyra (Ankara, Turkey).

There is no information as to whether Rome assisted his restoration to power and this then brought greater Roman influence to his kingdom, but the high level of trade and the semi-'Romanised' nature of pre-conquest Calleva might support this theory. It has been suggested that the style of his coinage resembles that of another contemporary Roman client-king, Juba II of Mauretania (son-in-law of Cleopatra), and he may have acquired this model while in exile. Verica's expulsion by the kingdom's aggressive northern neighbour, the Catuvellauni, around 40 and flight to Rome was one of the immediate causes for the invasion in 43. But whatever promises Rome may have made to restore him to secure the Atrebates' aid they annexed the kingdom as far as is known.

Recent archaeological discoveries at Calleva (Silchester), the main 'oppidum' of the Atrebates, have however indicated that a substantial 'aristocratic' mid-first-century building there may have belonged to a post-AD 43 British client-ruler, rather than a Roman landowner. If so, was this Verica or a relation who Rome installed as a client-king for the 40s and 50s? The date and mixture of Roman and British building styles used imply that the building, like the Fishbourne palace (see below), was an Imperial gift – probably by Nero – to a loyal ally. No coins or literary evidence of this ruler survive, but he was probably contemporary with and analogous to Boudicca's husband, Prasutagas of the Iceni (d. 60). Possibly he was the same man as the owner of Fishbourne, but the Atrebates' territory had not included the latter area before 43 so if he was owner of both 'palaces' Rome must have extended his kingdom. It is suggested that the famous 'legionary' model eagle found in the ruins of the post-60s basilica built at Calleva (as used literarily by Rosemary Sutcliff) belonged to a statue of the Roman god Jupiter not a legionary standard, and that the eagle was a totem of the Atrebates. It is now considered possible by one group of historians that a Roman invading force of 43 landed in the area of the Solent to make use of friendly locals loyal to Verica, rather than invading via Kent where Reculver remains the most accepted main Roman landing-site.

Name	Accession	Years ruled	Death/deposed
Commius (Gallic refugee from Caesar)	*c.* 50BC	*c.* 30?	*c.* 20 BC?
Tincommius/ Tincomarus (north?)	*c.* 20 BC?	*c.* 25?	*c.* AD 5? (dep.)

Epillus (south?)	*c.* 20 BC?	*c.* 2/?	*c.* AD 7? (dep.)
Epatticus (Catuvellauni prince)	*c.* AD 7?	*c.* 5?	*c.* AD 12? (dep.)
Verica	*c.* AD 12?	*c.* 28?	AD 40? (dep.)

Catuvellauni rule, probably by Caratacus.

Verica?	AD 43/4?	*c.* 20?	*c.* AD 65?

Regni (based on Sussex)

The name 'Regni' is probably more accurate than the alternative suggested, 'Regnenses'; this identity for the kingdom based on Noviomagus (Chichester) comes from a second-century AD Roman itinerary listing the roads and towns of the Empire. It may have been the southern half of the tribal territory of the 'Atrebates', as above; it certainly had separate rulers from their main territory based on Calleva.

The Regni were probably one of the most 'Romanised' of the tribes, given the archaeological proof of their trading-links with the Empire well before AD 43. This centres on the Solent and the Portsmouth–Chichester area, a relatively easy sea-journey from the Roman Gallic coast, and recent archaeological evidence includes a possible Roman trading-post indicating a limited Roman presence pre-43 (contrary to all literary sources). The Regni's ruler Cogidubnus, or Togidumnus, was maintained in power for decades after the conquest as a Roman ally and may well have assisted the invasion. He is assumed to have been the wealthy nobleman for whom the vast 'palace' villa at Fishbourne, near the tribal capital of Noviomagus (Chichester), was constructed around AD 60–70 – though the extension of the building to mirror the Flavian emperors' palace in Rome must have been after Domitian's accession (81) and seems late for this man still to be alive. Was it built for his son, a Flavian-era governor of Britain? The extensive Roman use of harbours in the Regni territory immediately after 43 would suggest that the tribe's pro-Roman links provided the legions campaigning in south-west Britain with a route to bring in supplies from the Continent.

There is also a possibility that Cogidubnus or Togidumnus ruled the Atrebates in Hampshire in the 40s–70s rather than the Regni. This depends on where precisely the frontier between the two kingdoms lay, and if Chichester was in Atrebatic or Regnian lands after the Roman conquest.

Name	Accession	Years ruled	Death/dep.
Epillus of the Atrebates	20 BC?	*c.* 27?	*c.* AD 7 (dep.?)
Cogidumnus/ Togidumnus (Roman client)	AD 44/5?	*c.* 30	*c.* AD 75

Iceni (based on Norfolk)

It is not certain if Prasutagus, the second known king, was a member of an existing royal dynasty of short or long duration when Rome backed him as their client to take over the throne a few years after the invasion in 43. (The extensive 'high-status' settlement recently excavated near Thetford was probably his royal headquarters.) His obscure predecessor, Antedios, had been killed or evicted in an anti-Roman revolt in 47/8 – presumably as a collaborator. On his death, leaving only daughters, he left the kingdom jointly to them and Emperor Nero, presumably intending the latter to act as guardian. However it was common – if sporadic – Roman practice to annex client-kingdoms if there was no clear, adult male heir, as seen with the Anatolian kingdoms of Pergamum (allegedly willed to Rome) in 133 BC and Cappadocia in AD 17. The Emperor's local officials, probably led by chief financial officer (procurator) Decius Catianus, who was alleged to be venal, attempted to annex the kingdom and a 'rush' of Roman settlers eager for land followed. Their scornful brutality and the influx of Roman settlers and tax-collectors sparked off a massive anti-Roman revolt that threatened the Empire's whole position in the island. The leader of the rebellion, Prasutagus' ferocious widow 'Boudicca', was in the tradition of strong 'Celtic' warrior-queens seen throughout their history and legend and exemplified by the semi-legendary Maedb (Maeve) of Connacht in Ireland. The name apparently means 'Victory', and was hence used by the Victorians to compare her to their Queen Victoria and put a commemorative statue of her on the Embankment in London in the 1890s as a national inspiration to the Empire. The version 'Boadicea', in fact 'Voadicea', was first used by Anglo-Italian historian Polydore Vergil around 1500. The late first-century AD Roman historian Tacitus, son-in-law of a highly successful Roman governor of Britain (Agricola) so probably using second-hand but reliable reports, gives a short but graphic account of the rebellion in his *Annals*, and more details were added around 220 by the later writer Cassius Dio. The latter also gave a physical description of Boudicca – a tall, loud-voiced, intelligent and indomitable woman with red hair down to her waist, wearing a grand gold 'torque' neck-ring and a flowing cloak.

Luckily for the rebels the governor, Suetonius Paullinus, was in North Wales conquering Mon/Anglesey with most of his troops as the revolt broke out in 60. The Iceni were able to march on the main, wall-less towns of the province without major resistance. Boudicca's epic leadership of a huge army of tribesmen to sack Colchester, London, and St Albans and the defeat of the first Roman troops to attempt to stop her – the Ninth Legion, sent in haste down Watling Street under legate Petilius Cerialis – made her revolt the most serious threat ever to Roman rule. In London in particular the scale of the destruction and the number of those killed was impressive, though the contemporary figures given by Tacitus should be taken with caution. The story of a massacre at Wallbrook in London, possibly of captive legionaries, survived to Geoffrey of Monmouth's time and has been confirmed by archaeology. Boudicca was finally confronted by Paullinus and his main army as she marched north-west up Watling Street to meet his returning army. The date is unclear due to the Tacitean narrative of the revolt covering one or two years; it may have been winter 60–1 or spring 61. Paullinus had the Second (Augustan) Legion, one of those which had been in Britain since AD 43, and most or all of the Twentieth (Gemina), plus auxiliaries and probably remnants of the Ninth – a force estimated at around 15,000 men and clearly outnumbered.

The Romans chose a battlefield where the lie of the land enabled them to hem in the vastly larger British forces with a forest to the side of the open area, meaning that the British chariots could not surround them. The Roman army, fighting on a narrow front where the superior British numbers could not envelop them, withstood the rebel attack and routed their challengers. The latter were forced back onto their line of wagons in the rear, where their womenfolk were apparently installed, and trapped there and massacred at will. Boudicca allegedly committed suicide. But it is not even certain where the battle was fought, except that logically it was somewhere near the Romans' line of march south-eastwards from Chester to London – Watling Street. Lewis Spence's theory that Boudicca was buried at King's Cross Station in London is likely to be wide of the mark. Much else about the queen remains unclear. It is uncertain if she derived her authority solely as Prasutagus' widow or as the heiress of an earlier ruling line of kings. Hopeful feminist proponents of matriarchal rule in 'Celtic' kingdoms have suggested the latter.

Name	Accession	Years ruled	Death/dep.
Antedios (Roman client)	<AD 43?	>4?	AD 47
Prasutagus (Roman client)	AD 47?	12?	AD 59
Boudicca	AD 59	2	AD 61

Brigantes (based on Yorkshire and Lancashire)

The name is linked to the proto-Brittonic word for 'bright', and to the goddess 'Brigantia'; their principal 'oppidum' before Roman conquest was apparently at Aldborough in Yorkshire (Isurium Brigantium) rather than at the later Roman city of York. Their territory was the largest in south-central Britain, probably stretching as far as the Tyne and the Solway Firth to the north.

It is unclear if Cartimandua was one of a series of ruling queens or the heiress of an unknown pre-Roman king. But her successive husbands derived their authority from her, suggesting that she was the rightful ruler. She was cautious enough to hand over the fugitive British war-leader Caratacus after he arrived in her lands as a refugee from defeat in central Wales in AD 51, and loyally kept to her alliance with Rome. This led to discontented warriors mounting a rebellion, which she survived with the aid of Roman troops from the Ninth Legion. However her continued pacific path led to her deposition in AD 69, possibly because a majority of her senior sub-chieftains were now convinced that the post-Boudicca revival in Roman power would soon lead to a Roman attack and absorption into the Empire so 'appeasement' was useless.

Name	Accession	Years ruled	Death/dep.
Cartimandua (Roman client)	<AD 43	Over 25	AD 69 (dep.)
Venutius (husband, sole ruler after he expelled his wife)	?	?	AD 72

The Brigantes evidently survived as a tribe resisting Roman occupation into a later period, as evidenced by the number of Roman forts of the later first and early second centuries in their territory. It has been suggested that they were involved in the disturbances at the time of the Emperor Trajan's death in 117 and that Hadrian's Wall was constructed partly to prevent them receiving assistance from tribes in what is now southern Scotland, but if so the names of their leaders are not recorded.

Silures (based on South Wales)

This list is heavily dependent on later Welsh tradition that in its written form dates from centuries later, being picked up by Geoffrey of Monmouth in the twelfth century and written into his history of the fictitious British 'kingdom'. It is supposed to have originated in medieval records at Raglan Castle transcribed in the sixteenth century by Llewelyn Sion of Llangewydd, Glamorgan. Some historians discount them entirely, but they may well remember names of genuine rulers under the later medieval fictionalising. It is not known if the version of the list incorporating the leader of the tribal resistance to the Romans in the later 40s, the refugee Catuvellaunian prince Caratacus, as a Silurian prince accurately remembers a genuine link he had with the Silurian royal family (perhaps through his mother or his wife). He was certainly able to rouse the tribe into fierce resistance against Rome from the mid-40s, and no indication is given in the brief Roman record by Tacitus of them having any other king. After his defeat at the unknown hill-fort of 'Caer Caradoc', possibly in western Shropshire, in 51, he fled to the dubious sanctuary of the Brigantes and was handed over to Rome by Queen Cartimandua. According to Tacitus his noble bearing as he was paraded in front of Emperor Claudius with his family won public sympathy, and he successfully argued that pardoning him would win the Emperor greater renown than executing him (the normal fate for captured enemy leaders, e.g. Vercingetorix the Gaul). But he was required to stay in Rome, and later British literary legend claimed that some of his family converted to Christianity and helped St Paul's mission. St Linus, second Bishop of Rome in the late 60s and 70s, was claimed to be a Briton. His status as a 'resistance hero' against Roman imperialism won him the status of subject for patriotic plays and musical pieces from Elizabeth I's reign onwards, and in the late Victorian era Elgar (living near one possible site for his 'last stand', the Herefordshire Beacon at Malvern) composed a jingoistic opera about him.

Roman sources do not record the names of his successors leading the tribal resistance, but it seems to have continued into the 70s and a whole Roman legion had to be stationed at Caerleon to keep the Silures under control on a long-term basis. Arviragus, named from Hardyng's *Chronicle* in the sixteenth century as the ruler who welcomed Joseph of Arimathea to Britain in the AD 60s and if so claiming authority over the Somerset area, is a historical British client-ruler. He is recorded by the poet Juvenal as terrifying the Romans with his chariot in the time of Nero. His existence therefore pre-dates his appearance in Geoffrey of Monmouth's book and the thirteenth-century Welsh *Brut Tyssilio*, though the location of his realm is unclear. The continued occupation of the Cadbury Castle hill-fort near Glastonbury after the Roman conquest of the area in the mid-40s may indicate that the local Celtic ruler came to terms with Rome and became a vassal, in which case he may have been Arviragus (as suggested by Geoffrey Ashe). Alternatively, he may have been the obscure leader of the Silurian resistance to Rome in the 50s. The issue is complicated by the later Welsh story that Joseph's settlement at 'Llanilid' was not Glastonbury at all but was near Pencoed in Glamorgan – within the Silurian kingdom and so available to be granted by the Silurian ruler. The extant version of this claim is unfortunately only found in the *Iolo Manuscripts* (published 1848) compiled by Edward Williams and edited by his son Taliesin, so it depends on the veracity of Williams, also known as 'Iolo Morgannwg'. The latter forged his literary mythology in creating a pseudo-antique Druidic order and rituals, so his accurate use of genuine historical manuscripts cannot be taken for granted; Raglan Castle was sacked by the Parliamentarians at the end of a Civil War siege and the original documents lost.

It is uncertain if Juvenal's reference means that Arviragus was fighting Roman soldiers or, less likely, visited Rome as a client-king and used to drive his chariot round the city. Geoffrey Ashe has suggested that Arviragus was the man given a high-status pagan burial at the sanctuary in Glastonbury, who was discovered and identified as 'King Arthur' by enterprising monks in 1184. The style of the burial in a hollowed-out tree-trunk, evidently pagan and unlikely for a fifth-century Christian king, seems more likely for an Iron Age ruler.

Ceri, supposedly Caratacus' nephew and founder of a fleet, was from his dating the presumed leader of the Silurian resistance to Rome in the 60s and 70s. He was traditionally the ruler buried at Porthkerry ('harbour of Ceri') in Glamorgan. The antiquity of the name is uncertain, but as no Ceri is recorded as a ruler in the Dark Age genealogies he may have been a Roman-era landowner of tribal descent who made use of the growing prosperity of pacified Roman South Wales to build a harbour.

Lucius is the ruler remembered in Celtic Christian tradition as inviting the first Roman Christian missionaries to his dominions in the AD 170s;

he may have been a client-king ruling tribal lands outside the 'Romanised' area in South Wales. The story – though not locating his kingdom within Britain – first appears in the sixth-century *Liber Pontificalis* in Rome, so is independently verified; in around 732 the Venerable Bede included it in his *Ecclesiastical History of the English People*. One of the missionaries involved, Fagan (Paganus?), is commemorated at a well-known site outside Cardiff, now the National Folk Museum of Wales, but it is not known how long the connection goes back. It is evident from the archaeological evidence that the Roman-era inhabitants of the hillier regions of Wales and the North (and Cornwall and Devon) continued to live in Iron-Age style farms and that towns were few; 'Romanised' villa-estates only existed in the south-east lowlands. The tribal social and political structure of the local peoples clearly survived through the Roman period, so the native aristocracy may have done so too and nobles of 'royal' descent held some prestige as landowners. Such a man who had visited Rome and met up with the Christian community there could easily have invited missionaries to settle on his lands, and legends grown up about them amid that small Christian community which existed in Britain by the time of the Diocletianic persecutions.

The genealogies of the Silures contained in the supposed copy of Llewelyn Sion's work by Edward Williams ('Iolo Morgannwg') made around 1800 continue for a long list covering the period to around 400. Unfortunately it is too long to contain a correct father-son descent, and has been frequently denounced as spurious on account of Williams' other fabrications of ancient Celtic history. As with Geoffrey of Monmouth's work, it may contain garbled names of genuine rulers who gave their names to local features, e.g. the 'Bran' of Cwmbran, the 'Gorrwg' of Glyncorrwg, and the 'Tegid' of Llyn Tegid. Just because they have symbolic personal names, 'Bran' meaning 'Raven', or had geographical features called after them does not mean that they never existed. It also includes the historical rebel Emperor of Britain from 287 to 293, Carausius, as 'Casnar Wledig'. In reality Carausius was a 'Menapian' by birth, coming either from the area of modern Belgium around the Scheldt estuary or from southern Ireland, and had no recorded genealogical links with Britain though it is not impossible that some son or other relative of his married into a local dynasty and this fact was remembered in Silurian tradition. (There is however no other evidence that Carausius' 'son', a second Casnar, existed or of a family link with Gloucester.) A similar connection is made between the Silurian dynasty under Roman overlordship and the shadowy figure of

Octavius, 'Eudaf Hen', the father of the wife of Emperor Magnus Maximus (r. 383–388). This may well be guesswork based on the medieval tradition that Eudaf's daughter's patrimony included South East Welsh lands.

Name	Accession	Years ruled	Death/dep.
Arch or Caid (ruler at time of Roman invasion)	<AD 43	?	
Caratacus of Catuvellauni	AD 43/44	3/4	AD 47
Arviragus	fl. AD 60–70?		
Ceri	fl. late first century?		
Marius?	fl. *c.* 100?		
Baram and Bran?	fl. mid-second century?		
Lucius?	fl. late second century?		
Gorrwg, Meirchion (Marcianus), Einydd	fl. third century?		

Other States

The kings or war-leaders of other states are not known, even in southern Britain at the time of the Roman conquest. The Roman literary sources and the number of local hill-forts make it apparent that Rome faced serious resistance from the main tribe in modern Dorset, the Durotriges – whose chief centre of resistance was probably the immense hill-fort of Maiden Castle ('Mai Dun') near Dorchester, the largest in southern Britain, though it is uncertain if the contemporary burials there are of victims of the Roman attack. (Mortimer Wheeler's confidence about this in the 1930s now seems misplaced.) It is presumed that the early Roman port facility at Hamworthy, on Poole Harbour, was set up by the advancing Roman legions under Vespasian as a supply depot and thence the Romans advanced west to reduce the hill-forts, the nearer ones such as Badbury Rings first. There were probably a number of major sieges of sites in Dorset, and fierce resistance is probable where missiles were discovered at sites such as Maiden Castle and Hod Hill. After the conquest, the Romans seem to have required the British to abandon their defensible positions; the new centres of population which emerged from the 50s and 60s were undefended 'Romanised' towns in the valleys such as the major urban centre of Durnovaria (Dorchester). The names of the commanders of the resistance are unknown, even though they faced a future Emperor in the legionary legate Vespasian.

Similar resistance led by unknown commanders is probable from their neighbours in Devon and Cornwall, the Dumnonii, who received a temporary Roman military base at Isca (Exeter) in the 40s–70s to control them. The territory of the Dumnonii was to see less adoption of Roman urban and rural life than further east, with Isca being the only major town. Existing Iron Age farming seems to have survived unchanged for centuries, particularly in the west in Cornwall where Chysauster is the main site to have been excavated. Significantly, the Dumnonii were the only known tribal kingdom in southern Britain to retain enough sense of 'nationhood' to re-emerge as a geographical and political entity after the Roman period, using their original name. This suggests that the comparative sparsity of Roman villas and continuance of pre-Roman-style farms in their area was coupled with the warrior aristocracy retaining a sense of tribal identity and an active memorialisation of their past history, as in the more 'upland' areas of the north and west of Britain. Possibly adopting Romanised lifestyles was actively resisted. The chief 'oppidum' of the Dumnonii was at 'Isca Dumnoniorum' ('Waters of the Dumnonii'), later Exeter and the post-conquest Roman base for the region.

Roman literary accounts and the lack of archaeological evidence of defended hill-forts make it probable that the Dobunni, in Somerset and Gloucestershire, came to terms quickly with the Romans and acted as their loyal allies. Their one major hill-fort currently in occupation, Cadbury Castle, was probably used into the 60s and as such would have belonged to a Roman ally. Indeed, the territory of the Dobunni was being raided by the anti-Roman Silures in the late 40s when the Romans launched their next advance into South Wales under Ostorius Scapula. It is possible that the enigmatic Arviragus (see Silures) was a ruler of the Dobunni, not the Silures, if the later traditions of him being the local king who gave Joseph of Arimathea land at 'Inis Witrin' in the early AD 60s refer to Glastonbury. If so, Rome trusted him enough to let him retain a fortified headquarters at Cadbury until the 60s.

The tribal chieftains or kings of the Ordovices (based on southern Gwynedd) and Deceangli (based around the Menai Straits) in North

Wales, first defeated by Governor Suetonius Paullinus in 59–60 and finally overrun by Agricola around 77/8, are also unknown. The same applies to the Demetae in Pembrokeshire. The latter's identity and name re-emerged after Roman rule in the fifth century; the former two tribes seem to have vanished during Roman rule (due to harsher repression for being untrustworthy?). Pre-Roman styles of rural living certainly survived under Roman rule, the excavated second- and third-century AD 'round-house' farming sites in these regions being similar to those before the conquest; this may have reflected a sense of cultural identity as well as minimal penetration by 'lowland' Roman culture.

The Cornovii in the West Midlands and the Coritani/Corieltavi in Lincolnshire seem to have survived as tribal identities under Roman governance, with their respective 'capitals' at Viroconium (the Wrekin) and Lindum (Lincoln). (The 'Corieltavi' name was only identified as the more accurate term for the Lincolnshire tribe in the 1980s, due to inscriptions being found.) The Cornovii, though a lowland tribe whose territory lay within the 'Romanised' zone of Britain, retained a tribal identity as late as the fifth century unlike the Durotriges, Belgae, and Atrebates possibly as a formal administrative division of the Roman province of Britain.

They gave their name to Cornwall when some of their personnel moved or were sent into western Dumnonia to evict the Irish settlers, probably after the Roman 'withdrawal' from Britain. The Corieltavi's tribal territory was probably retained as a Roman administrative unit, later becoming post-Roman 'Lindsey' whose rulers retained 'British' names even into 'Anglo-Saxon' times (e.g. seventh-century King Caedbad).

The Carvetii around Carlisle, the Selgovae in Galloway, the Damnonii in Carrick, and the Votadini in Lothian were overrun by Agricola in the late 70s and appear to have come under Roman control for most of the period until the withdrawal to the line of Hadrian's Wall around 120, though the number of Roman forts in the southern Uplands suggest a sporadic continuing unrest that had to be strictly policed. The lands north of the Wall were reconquered briefly when the Roman frontier was advanced again to the line of the Clyde and Forth by Lollius Urbicus around 140, and after around two centuries of independence were probably reduced to some degree of vassalage by Theodosius 'the Elder' around 369/70 after the major northern Celtic/Irish/Saxon attack on Roman Britain of 367.

The contemporary history of Ammianus Marcellinus and the genealogical traditions of the Votadini and their neighbours preserved into later Welsh history suggest that the Roman government of the 370s overran the area north of Hadrian's Wall and imposed or supported a loyal chieftain of the Votadini called Paternus 'of the Red Tunic', son of Tacitus (?). Theodosius also established other local rulers including Quintilius Clemens on the Clyde, Catellius Decianus around the Forth, and possibly Antonius Donatus (regarded later as a son of Emperor Magnus Maximus) somewhere around Galloway and/or on the Isle of Man.

2

THE END OF ROMAN RULE: POST-ROMAN GOVERNMENT

In 406 the overrunning of Gaul by a massive Germanic influx across the Rhine cut Britain off from Rome, and a revolt followed among the troops. A pair of ephemeral Emperors, Marcus and Gratian, were raised to the throne and deposed before the more successful usurpation of Constantine III, a private soldier, who attempted to save the rest of the western provinces from ravaging at the cost of taking many troops abroad. Most of the army stationed in Britain appears to have left Britain with Constantine III in 407 for the Gallic campaign and did not return; Constantine failed to restore order and faced his own rebels, including a general called Gerontius (possibly the British name 'Geraint', common in the Dumnonian royal pedigree). He was eventually captured at his south Gallic headquarters, Arles, by the army of the central government in 411. (His coins are only found in south-east Britain, unlike those of earlier rulers.)

In 410, according to the historian Zosimus, Emperor Honorius – now residing in the impregnable marsh-bound city of Ravenna while the Goths ravaged Italy – wrote to the British civic authorities in response to a request for military aid, telling them to look to their own defences. Presumably the 'council' of the British provinces, a body representing the main urban centres as with the council of Gaul, had decided to abandon the failing cause of Constantine III and return to the allegiance of the central government. (Some historians have argued that the letter was not to Britain but to 'Bruttia' in southern Italy.) The current raiding may be connected to the probable date of the death of the Irish 'High King' Niall 'of the Nine Hostages', remembered in legend as a formidable raider, in the English Channel around 405. The obscure Irish accounts even had him reaching the Alps, but this may be a mistake for a similar name – possibly somewhere else named 'Alpa/Alba', i.e. 'White', such as the Isle of Wight.

The presumed response to this letter of creating or augmenting a local British militia to defeat raiders is supported by the writer Gildas in the 540s. He records that the British 'took up arms' themselves and drove out a massive Saxon raid around 411. This is supported by Zosimus, while the *Gallic Chronicle* records a major Saxon raid on the Channel coasts in 411. The British civic force presumably had a commander, who probably took the official or unofficial rank of 'Count of Britain' following the terminology used for the senior commander in Britain in the *Notitia* and Ammianus. Later Welsh legend recalled that a son of the former Emperor Magnus Maximus called Eugenius (or Owain) was the military leader of Britain at this time, Geoffrey of Monmouth calling him 'Dux Gewissae' which in the current administrative context could mean 'military commander' of the area including 'Ewias' at the head of the Bristol Channel (based at Gloucester?). He was succeeded by his brother or half-brother, Constantine 'the Blessed', who returned from Armorica at the request of local civic authorities. It is not known if Geoffrey used a genuine early Welsh or Breton source for this, possibly preserving a garbled account of real military leaders in post-410 Britain, and adapted it to twelfth-century terminology – or made most of it up. Logically, the military settlements in Armorica would have been a useful source of aid for a group of British provincial governors stripped of Roman troops by Constantine III's Gallic expedition in 407.

It is possible that the Roman civic order which St Germanus' biographer records as existing in 429 included a formal senior military officer, or even that some form of Roman authority was recognised and some Roman officials came over from the Continent in the 420s. No positive proof or names of the men involved has been found. (See further, section on the 'High Kings'.) It is only speculation to think that the apparent supreme civil and military British leader of the later fifth century, Ambrosius Aurelianus –or the elusive 'King Arthur' – may also have used the rank of 'Count of Britain' to formalise their command of an army operating over large parts of Britain. R. G. Collingwood came to this conclusion in the 1930s, but though it is logical there is no direct proof.

The question of post-Roman administrative survival into the mid-fifth century remains contentious, with the literary evidence – British and Gallic – indicating a 'clean break' and Germanic conquest from the 440s onwards and the archaeological evidence less 'clear-cut'. The archaeological evidence is unclear, with the lapse in the use of coinage meaning that this means cannot be used to identify rulers. The amount of hoards of pre-410 coins discovered across the country, and of silverware such as the 'Mildenhall Treasure', implies a major amount of insecurity leading to wealthy people hiding their valuables around 370–410. The *Anglo-Saxon Chronicle* in the ninth century preserved a tradition that in 418 the leading Romans in Britain hid their treasures in the earth and fled to Gaul. This insecurity was logically linked to the sacking of towns and villas by invading Saxons, Picts, and Irish, as recounted by Gildas and Bede for the war of 410/11.

Similarly, any evidence of destruction by fire at a town or villa was put down to violence by raiders – whereas the amount of wood used in building meant that many fires could be more prosaic. The amount of resources needed to keep the larger villas in repair, and the dependence of their economic viability on having a market for their estates' agricultural products (e.g. the Roman army), argue that insecurity, reduced trade, and the ending of the military presence would have caused economic collapse. Indeed, the conversion of small-scale farms in places such as Cranborne Chase to huge pastoral estates producing wool, and the fourth-century prosperity of villa-centred estates in corn-growing East Anglia, indicates that a substantial part of the British rural economy was tied to the demands of the huge fourth-century western Imperial army and civil service. (There is literary evidence of large-scale agricultural requisitioning from Britain, namely Ammianus on Emperor Julian's demands for the Rhine army in the 350s.) Thus the 'villa economy' that had produced such wealthy estates as Lullingstone and Hinton Saint Mary in the fourth century was unsustainable in a poorer, locally based economic system once the army collapsed, the central government ended its demands, and trade across an invader-ravaged Empire collapsed. The basis of rural life would gradually revert to small farms producing for local needs, and the villas would fall into disuse. The end of a political/military link with the Western Empire in 410, and the massive disruption of life in Gaul as a result of the Germanic incursions from 406, would also have caused a sharp drop in trade with the remaining Roman world. It has been suggested that a corresponding growth in links across the North Sea with the German peoples would cause an influx of German trade-goods through the early fifth century and thus a change in 'acculturation' from the world of the Empire to that of the Germans. This could account for the discoveries of fifth-century Germanic goods across eastern Britain, instead of archaeologists being able to 'pinpoint' each site of Germanic discoveries as an 'alien' Anglo-Saxon village established by hostile invaders at war with the locals. If this is accurate, it would make a nonsense of the careful maps of 'advancing' Anglo-Saxon settlement through the fifth century drawn up by earlier twentieth-century archaeologists. Notably, the use of local Romano-British pottery outside its 'home' area drops off sharply around 400 – due to a collapse in demand or production, or to a rise in insecurity?

It is now apparent from archaeology that there was less physical destruction in the fifth century than was supposed earlier. The physical destruction in towns, with a mixture of signs of fire (e.g. at gates) and piles of bodies indicating violent attack, is most apparent at three towns in the south-east easy of access to fifth-century raiders – Colchester, Caistor-by-Norwich, and probably Lincoln. These cases can be safely regarded as due to violence, and their geographical location would suggest the responsibility of seaborne invaders. The signs of violent destruction at Roman forts is only apparent at the smaller, isolated Yorkshire coastal 'lookout-posts' that would have been vulnerable to seaborne Picts or Saxons, and is datable to around 390–400. Similarly, the earliest 'Germanic' cemeteries containing Continental goods appear in east coast areas which were likely sites for incoming settlers who either took land by force, penetrating from the coast, or were positioned there as mercenaries to defend local towns – the Thames valley, northern Kent, East Anglia, and Lincolnshire. The approximate dates that archaeologists agree saw the introduction of specific styles of brooches – first the 'cruciform' types, then the 'saucer' ones – enable English discoveries to be placed within a few decades. They make 'Early', 'Mid', and 'Late' fifth-century grave-goods distinguishable, but no greater precision is possible. Also, the continuity of fourth- to sixth-century use found at some 'Late Roman' East Anglian farming sites that later become 'Anglo-Saxon' – e.g. Mucking in Essex, excavated in the 1970s – suggests that if 'Germans' did arrive to settle there was less violence than a sweeping interpretation of Gildas' melodramatic account indicates.

The archaeological sites containing Germanic goods datable to the later fifth century expand into the coastal areas of Sussex (agreeing with the traditional timing and site of Aelle's landing) and across the East Midlands from the Thames to the Trent, with a concentration in East Anglia and Lincolnshire but none north of the Trent and only a few in the Humber estuary. There were isolated pockets of settlement around Luton and Dunstable in the south-east Midlands, presumably existing by agreement with the local British around Verulamium/St Albans. One notable early concentration of sites with Germanic goods from around 400–50 was in the upper Thames basin around Dorchester-on-Thames, the later sixth- and early seventh-century centre of West Saxon power, with a major village having being excavated at Sutton Courtenay. The extent of the Germanic settlement so far inland – to the 'rear' of British areas in the Chilterns – indicates either an agreement with the local Britons or their powerlessness to intervene. In this crucial area, there is absolutely no literary evidence to explain such a divergence from the traditional picture of a 'regulation' gradual Saxon 'land-grab' advancing from east to west. The locations of these early settlements would imply penetration by rivers, particularly the Thames and the systems based on the Wash, and the inland sites in East Anglia are mostly within reach of the Icknield Way which would also provide a land-route to the upper Thames basin. Indeed, the traditional interpretation of these sites with Germanic goods as all belonging to 'Germanic settlers' has been argued against in recent years; see in detail later.

Some form of civic authorities presumably held power in the declining towns of southern Britain, where the absence of evidence of new building (except occasionally in wood) indicates a paucity of resources or interest in maintaining the physical infrastructure. Building did however occur at one or two isolated sites in the west of the 'lowland zone' into the sixth century – most importantly new civic structures in wood at Viroconium, 'capital' of Powys. There were post-Roman buildings even in the south-east, as at Verulamium/St Albans (including a rural corn-drying oven) and Camulodunum/Colchester. In other places the occupied area seems to have shrunk; at Corinium/Cirencester the old amphitheatre was turned into a defended settlement. Notably, there is no evidence of systematic destruction of towns from east to west coasts as Gildas implies happened during the major Saxon revolt of the 440s. At the same time, long-abandoned Iron Age hill-forts were reoccupied, mostly in southern England (e.g. Cissbury in Sussex and Cadbury-Congresbury in Somerset), and coastal fortresses such as Tintagel may have served as lookouts for raiders as well as secure landing-places for traders. The evidence of eastern Roman imports at south-western 'port' sites such as Tintagel argues for continued trading links with the Empire into the sixth century, but there is no British literary evidence of the link and on the Roman side only a confused reference to a divided Britain by Procopius around 550.

Some time in the first half of the fifth century the ditches of the Wansdyke across northern Wiltshire and Avon were probably dug as a form of defence (against the Saxons in the upper Thames valley?). The date and contiguousness of the eastern and western sections of this apparent defensive work are unclear. The most impressive post-Roman defensive work was at Cadbury Castle, as excavated by Leslie Alcock in the 1960s, where a large first-century BC/AD hill-fort was reused some time in the fifth century. Major timber construction work was found indicating a substantial hall as well as new ramparts, with the name hinting at the 'fort of Cador', a king of the Dumnonii around 500. Alcock was keen to claim the builder as 'King Arthur', who was cited in local tradition as the occupant by John Leland in the 1540s, and argue that the site's proximity to the Fosse Way enabled a mobile cavalry force based here to operate along the Roman road-system against Saxon attackers across Britain. Other reuse of hill-forts included Danebury in Hampshire, logically protecting an area under threat from raiders along the Test valley from the traditional landing-site of the West Saxon invaders in the 490s/510s, and Cissbury in west Sussex near the landing-site of the warlord Aelle at Selsey in 477 (?).

The forts were presumably used as refuges for the local inhabitants in time of war and as military bases for British forces. Given their remoteness from the areas of 'Germanic' archaeological finds in the fifth century, we have only Gildas' word for it that the areas in question were subject to Germanic raids and that the forts were thus used as anti-'Saxon' bases. More likely, there was inter-kingdom British warfare after the end of centralised administration (around AD 410) and smaller kingdoms fell victim to better-resourced and better-led neighbours. It is still speculation to suggest that the British owed their fifth- to sixth-century success against 'incomers' and their ability to campaign across wide areas to survivals of the Late Roman military cavalry, which were still being bred in pastoral areas – probably by large estates in the Cotswolds and by tribal military units such as the Votadini in Lothian. This is a logical assumption, and would explain the way in which 'Arthurian' battle-sites are scattered across Britain; but the latter may be due to the popularity of the relevant legends among the 'heroic' warrior-society of sixth- to ninth-century Britain. The Late Roman emperors had substantial forces of 'Companion' cavalry attached to their entourages – the title 'Count' comes from this word, as the Emperor's trusted 'companions' were placed in command of important posts. The local landed gentry, who bred horses on their estates (for hunting as well as the army) and included young nobles with equestrian skills, were certainly the core of a local cavalry resistance to Germanic invaders in the Auvergne around 470, so logically this could have happened in

Britain too. It is possible that an elite body of trained cavalrymen were at the basis of the myth of the 'Knights of the Round Table', but the lack of contemporary British literary evidence has led sceptics to savage the idea as unproven.

Due to the absence of coinage or literary records we do not have the names of local rulers in the kingdoms or cities of southern Britain. Unlike the embryonic Welsh kingdoms, they did not leave long-lasting 'states' that could maintain memories of their origins but were absorbed into the new Germanic kingdoms. The post-410 kingdoms of the Cantii (Kent), Regni (Sussex), Durotriges (Dorset), Belgae (Hampshire), Dobunni (Cotswolds), and East Anglia can be assumed to have existed and have had 'royal' leadership after the Roman administrative structure collapsed, but their leaders are unknown. (One ninth-century Welsh source mentions a 'Gwangon' as the king of the Cantii around 450, dispossessed by Hengest.) The insecurity of civil strife or raids from the Germanic tribes on the Continent may not have been as large-scale and catastrophic as indicated by our only near-contemporary source, the sixth-century monk Gildas (see below), but there was little survival of functioning towns for the Anglo-Saxon kingdoms to take over in the seventh century. The only important post-Roman towns which survived into the Germanic kingdoms were old 'tribal' administrative capitals – London (Londinium), Canterbury (Durovernum), Chichester (Noviomagus), Winchester (Venta Belgarum), Dorchester (Durnovaria), Exeter (Isca Dumnoniorum), and Lincoln (Lindum). Were these primarily administrative centres, mercantile emporia, or both when the 'Germanic' leadership took them over?

It is not adequate to argue that a return to rural life as the complex Roman economy collapsed was the sole cause of this decline of urban life, without any major impetus of violence or insecurity. But without long-distance trade, money, or a centralising administrative system there was little reason to maintain the structure of town life. 'Kings' in the post-Roman centuries, Briton and 'German' alike, usually lived on their rural estates, consuming food-rents from their vassals for their courts and war bands – as the Frankish kings did in Gaul. They travelled around their lands rather than remaining static in towns for two pressing practical reasons – to show themselves to their subjects and to eat up produce on their estates. Gildas undeniably exaggerated his picture of urban destruction for the purposes of polemic and had limited skills (or interest?) as an historian as we would now think of the term. His picture of a wholesale abandonment of town and farmed countryside alike to the wild beasts in the mid-late fifth century does not reflect reality (see section on the evidence of agriculture). But if there had been a mostly peaceful transition from post-Roman to 'Saxon' kingdoms, with minimal destruction or dislocation, more of post-Roman society – including its languages – would have survived in southern Britain. Both towns and aristocratic Christian Church leadership by the indigenous nobility survived into the new Germanic order in southern Gaul, where Germanic settlement was limited and their sixth-century political control not accompanied by major demographic change. So why was the southern British situation so different if there was only 'peaceful acculturation'?

The 'Celtic' British language was superseded by early Anglo-Saxon from the Continent in these areas – an indication, as with the triumph of French in ruling circles in England after 1066, that an alien ruling class had taken over and imposed their own culture. Unlike after the Norman Conquest, there is no evidence in the terminology used by all classes – e.g. in law – of a major survival of the old, pre-conquest language, let alone its eventual revival. This would indicate that Old English, derived from the Germanic dialect in use by the new arrivals, was used by all classes.

In France the Frankish tribes were able to take over an extant civic and religious administration of the conquered provinces, based on Roman towns which had a line of bishops (mostly from wealthy landed families) from the fifth to the seventh century. Existing Christian society survived with the eventual emergence of a dominant language derived from the Romans' Latin. In the more Romanised areas of southern France the ruling landed elite survived, if now exercising power via the Church rather than civic office as declining trade and the plague of 542 diminished the towns. There is no indication of that in Britain where the pagan Germanic leadership of the new kingdoms needed to be converted from Rome or Ireland not by an existing local British Church. St Augustine in Kent in 597 found no existing Catholic community worth mentioning, though it is possible that there was a degree of urban or Christian continuity at Canterbury. The major civic and trading centre of southern Britain, London, significantly saw the abandonment of the existing urban settlement in the City for a new seventh-century trading centre at the 'Aldwych' ('Old Wick', i.e. settlement) further up the Thames. The only major south-eastern Roman towns to be taken over as 'capitals' – or rather chief royal residences – of the new rural kingdoms were Canterbury, Winchester (after a break in the sixth century) and Lincoln.

Rulers After the End of Roman Government

Traditionally the independent cities and tribal polities are supposed to have owed some shadowy form of allegiance to a supreme ruler, subsequently referred to as a 'High King'. The absence of a functioning coinage system and of contemporary documentation means that the authenticity of later legends cannot be proved, though it would appear from the vague account of Gildas around 545 that the local authorities – civic or tribal – were able to organise a successful defeat of the initial Saxon raids in the 410s. There was certainly no mass-withdrawal of Roman troops in 410, with it not even being clear that the famous letter from Emperor Honorius telling the Britons to defend themselves was addressed to Britain rather than 'Bruttia' in southern Italy. Most of the forces stationed in Britain, as listed in the *Notitia Dignitatum* of around 400, presumably followed the usurper Constantine III – the third new local ruler in a year in Britain – as he sailed to Gaul in 407 to drive out a massive Germanic invasion and never returned.

The defeat of Constantine in the Rhone valley by the Western Empire's military leader Constantius (III) in 411 would have led to those still in his service being incorporated in the Imperial army, probably in Gaul. But local militia in each 'civitas' and province and a small amount of troops presumably remained, and would have passed under the control of local civic leaders and tribally based 'kings' – or even a super-tribal military commander appointed to coordinate campaigning, a 'Count of Britain'.

Conceivably the legends may reflect the emergence of a supreme military authority, as R. G. Collingwood speculated in the 1930s. They may even be correct to link the personnel involved in this military leadership to the line of the former commander in Britain who proclaimed himself Emperor in 383, Magnus Maximus, or to the settlements of Britons in Armorica (Brittany) under his rule. But many modern historians would prefer to maintain that the whole phenomenon is an invention of later writers seeking to establish an 'authentic' early precedent for later rulers governing most of Britain, most notably after the creation of the Anglo-Saxon kingdom of England in the tenth century and under the Anglo-Normans. Writers such as Geoffrey of Monmouth used contemporary terms for their pseudo-histories, rather than ones that could have been preserved intact by memory since the fifth century – such as constantly giving the main divisions of the 'ancient' kingdom as twelfth-century ones, such as the Duchy of Cornwall. But the Armorican/Breton settlements – though important for an Anglo-Norman historian to play up, given Breton participation in the Norman Conquest – was a logical source of experienced military leaders to aid the British civic authorities after 410. This tradition may be authentic.

Religious Sources on the Early Fifth Century – Germanus and Patrick

There is no reference in the contemporary hagiography of St Germanus of Auxerre, who visited Britain to combat the 'Pelagian' heresy in 429 (?) and dealt with civic officials at a site presumed to be Verulamium (St Albans), to the identity of the current authorities in Britain. The controversialist theologian Pelagius, apparently a student in Rome in the later fourth century (possibly in law), had turned against the oppressive and unjust secular order of society and denounced the selfish greed of the rich in *De Divitiis*. He inaugurated an early fifth-century 'heresy' that sought to deny the necessity of Divine Grace for salvation and promote the idea that Man could achieve his own perfection and conquer sin. He thus undermined the role of the clergy as intercessors with God, which led to a major confrontation with orthodox thinkers in the 400s. He was always called British (or Irish). Having been active in Rome itself and amassed a number of articulate followers with his attacks on social injustice, he was forced to flee to Africa after the sack of the capital in 410 and clashed with the most prominent exponent of the orthodox viewpoint, Augustine of Hippo. Eventually Augustine's party persuaded the Papacy to condemn the heresy, but it continued to be active as far east as Palestine into the 420s.

The heresy was apparently strong in Britain as well, assisted by a bishop called Agricola, and rest of the local Church lacked the will or ability to combat it. Its opponents called on the Gallic bishops for help around 428, evidently lacking any sympathetic secular ruler to suppress the heresy. They recommended the vigorous Germanus, a former military commander ordained as Bishop of Auxerre in 418. (The story is testified to by one of the Gallic Church's most zealous Catholic writers, the chronicler Prosper of Aquitaine.) Apparently the Pelagians had rich and well-connected supporters in urban Britain, probably including civic leaders, who Germanus had to counter – traditionally by carrying out miracles at a martyr's shrine (probably Verulamium/St Albans, where the remains of the most famous victim of the Diocletianic persecution were venerated.) Despite his supposed success in Britain he had to return again in the early 440s, and 'Pelagian' ideas survived in St David's South West Wales well into the sixth century. It has been speculated that Pelagius' denunciations of wealth influenced the extreme asceticism of some British and Irish hermits – including St David. The civic authorities who Germanus dealt with somewhere in the south-east lacked a military commander to tackle the Irish and Pictish invaders. (Notably, these were not Saxons.) They had to call on the experienced saint to rally their army and lead it against an army of raiders in a successful ambush in hilly country, perhaps eastern Powys near Llangollen. There were a number of dedications of churches in the region to 'St Garmon', who is presumed to be Germanus though he could be a similarly named fifth-century saint connected to the Isle of Man. The battle was known as the 'Alleluia' victory from the British bishops' rallying call which apparently put the enemy to flight, though the non-military hagiographer probably omitted the actual circumstances in which an ambush took place and the shouting was only part of an organised attack on surprised raiders.

At some time in this period St Patrick returned to his apparently peaceful home in western Britain some years after being carried off aged sixteen as a slave by Irish raiders, probably to Leinster. He subsequently decided to join the Church and take the Gospel to his former captors; later biographers seeking to show his links to the prestigious leaders of the Gallic Church connected his training to bishops Amator (d. 418) and Germanus of Auxerre. Patrick's return home cannot be dated as precisely as the first visit by Germanus, as Patrick's dates are disputed. He was active in Ireland for about thirty years – the Annals of Ulster says sixty years to his death in 493, but this is less likely – and his mission followed the less successful one around 430 by Palladius, the Papal adviser who had recommended Germanus for the British mission. The account of Patrick's mission given in Gallic sources by Prosper of Aquitaine, dating it around 431, is near-contemporary and probably accurate apart from patriotic pro-Roman 'playing up' the involvement of the Papacy and its advisor Palladius to the detriment of the bishops of Britain and Gaul. Patrick's kidnapping around twenty years earlier would thus seem to be datable to around 405–10.

Possibly Patrick's mission was the Irish part of a 'two-pronged' Catholic missionary offensive from Gaul, the British part being Germanus' mission. The assumption of nineteenth-century scholars that the '493' date for his death is wrong and that he died in 461/3 has been challenged by some who would date him later or even argue that he has been muddled up with Palladius, the latter's 430s missionary activities being assigned to Patrick who only arrived later. His early hagiographers claimed that he lived to Moses' age, i.e. 120.

It has been suggested since the eighth century that there were in reality two missionary Patricks, explaining how he could be active around 430 and according to some sources have died around 490; his relics were alternatively located at Armagh or Glastonbury. But it is clear that his home area was not affected by social chaos or major raids when he returned from captivity. His *Confessio* notes that he came from near 'Banevem Taburniae', which his early Irish biographer Muirchu says was identifiable as the town of 'Ventre'. This has been tentatively identified as Venta Silurum, i.e. Caerwent in Gwent. An alternative theory links him to the kingdom of Strathclyde, to whose king Ceretic he sent an indignant protest around 459 after Strathclyde raiders had kidnapped some of Patrick's converts from north-eastern Ireland.

Post-Roman Authorities

According to Germanus' biographer Constantius (around 480) there were clearly some high officials at the time, based in surviving Roman towns. There were also bishops, if ineffective ones, as late as the saint's second visit around 445, and a secular official called Elafius hastened to greet him as he arrived. There were presumably 'kings' as well, mostly in the more rural 'tribal' areas of the north and west, although only later Welsh legends give details of Germanus' conflict with 'Vortigern' and his involvement in the death of the tyrant 'Benli' (probably at 'Moel Benlli' in Clywd). The later Welsh genealogies provided details of the men then supposed to have been ruling in the fifth century, the ancestors of later dynasties, though the details of their supposed orderly 'father-son' descent need not be taken as totally accurate. Some names will have been forgotten. Some kingdoms may have retained their old pre-Roman aristocracy from whom the new dynasts descended – the Raglan Castle manuscripts, if genuine, suggest this for Siluria – but others may have been no more than opportunistic war-leaders who seized control. The polemic *De Excidio Britanniae* written by Gildas a century later, our main but problematic source for events in fifth-century Britain, is fond of abusing fifth- and sixth-century British kings as 'tyrants' and magistrates as corrupt and oppressive, ruling an immoral people who deserved divine wrath. But this picture implies that there was a formal government structure in the 'kingdoms' to be misused by its holders. The names of some fifth-century rulers in the later genealogies, such as 'Triphun' – 'Tribune' – of Demetia/Dyfed, suggest that they held power by virtue of some Roman office, or at least sought to justify their rule by assuming a regular title to cover their usurpation.

Infuriatingly, Gildas does not name those who led the successful resistance to the Saxon attack of 410/11 and thence ruled until the emergence of the 'superbus tyrannus' (taken to be a sobriquet for 'Vortigern', the 'over-king'). This is a reminder that he was not seeking to write history but a polemic castigating sin, and accordingly left out facts which were irrelevant. (This has impact on the question of the existence of 'Arthur', his most famous omission.) Lacking any other contemporary source, our earliest literary account of the era is that of the historian generally known as 'Nennius' in the 820s – or whoever later amended his surviving manuscripts. He claimed to be using extant books, and thus only citing existing records not inventing details, but modern work on his political aims suggests that he was consciously seeking to present a glorious British 'past' for his sovereign Merfyn of Gwynedd to emulate and so not an 'objective' historian. Nennius, in contrast to Gildas, has a large section on 'Arthur' but scarcely mentions Gildas' hero Ambrosius Aurelianus (possibly as the 'last of the Romans' was of less political use to the kings of Gwynedd than 'Arthur'). His *Historia Brittonum* has its own problems, which will be dealt with in the section on 'Arthur', and his reliability has been savaged in recent years by David Dumville and others. After him we come to the later ninth-century *Anglo-Saxon Chronicle* and the tenth-century Welsh *Annales Cambriae* and genealogies – all written long enough after the fifth century for major errors to have emerged. But there may be some truth behind the assertions in later centuries that the main fifth-century rulers to claim a super-tribal authority were:

Constantine, later called 'Fendigaid' ('The Blessed')

He was supposed by one version to be the son of Magnus Maximus (r. 383–8) by his second, British wife, Helen 'of the Hosts', daughter of Eudaf Hen (see section on Ergyng) and remembered in legend as supposed originator of the 'Sarn Helen' military road in Wales. As Maximus' eldest son Victor (executed by his father's conqueror Theodosius I in 388) was old enough to have an independent role as co-emperor at Trier in the mid-380s, Victor is likely to have been born before Maximus served in Britain after 368 and therefore not to be the son of Maximus and Helen but of Maximus' first wife, the elusive 'Ceindrech'. (Maximus was a Spaniard by birth and the name sounds Celtic, suggesting that Maximus had two British wives, but it may be invented or garbled out of recognition from a Latin name.)

Constantine, with his Imperial name, would have been Victor's half-brother. It is possible that this Constantine, with his British mother Helen, was mixed up with Constantine 'the Great' by medieval writers – hence the legend that the latter's mother Helena was also British, whereas in fact she was the daughter of an Illyrian tavern-keeper. Maximus' younger children are mentioned, but not named, by Roman historians, as being left alone by Theodosius in 388 – which indicates that they were under-age and so no political threat.

An alternative tradition makes Constantine the brother of Aldwr (Aldroenus), ruler of Brittany in the early to mid-fifth century, and a descendant of Maximus' wife Helen's brother Cynan Meriadawc who established the main British colony there around the 380s.

According to later Welsh legends, probably those used by Geoffrey of Monmouth, he was called back from residence with his mother's brother's family in Armorica/Brittany after 410 to take over civilian rule in Britain, possibly in succession to his brother or half-brother Owain/Eugenius ('Owain Vinddhu' in the Welsh Triads, and a 'Dux Gewissae' according to Geoffrey of Monmouth). Nennius gives him a sixteen-year reign. He died or was killed by Saxons around 433. As 'Fendigaid', 'the Blessed', in Welsh legend he may have been the king Custennin/Constantine who ruled in Ergyng in South East Wales – the presumed realm of his mother's father Eudaf. He was also mixed up with a ruler of Dumnonia in the fifth century, and it is unclear if there was one Constantine who ruled in both Dumnonia and Ergyng or two men who were later confused with each other. One or other of the two Constantines – the one not the son of Maximus or Aldwr? – was the son of Erbin (see also section on Dumnonia) according to ninth-century genealogies of Gwent. In 1284 Edward I was shown his supposed tomb at Caernarfon – as Segontium, an important late Roman military post and possibly the site of Maximus' command in the years after 368. If the tomb was genuine, either Constantine died in Arfon (during a campaign against the Irish settlers that Cunedda of the Votadini was brought in to evict?) or a descendant like Ambrosius installed his remains there at a family base.

Constans

Constantine's son Constans was supposedly a monk who left the cloister on his father's murder and ruled briefly. He was murdered, allegedly by his successor Vortigern. This may be a confused memory of a more definitely historical Constans, who left his monastery in Gaul around 407 to assist his father Constantine III – a rebel against Roman authority, based in Britain and probably its military commander – in fighting Germanic tribal invaders there.

Vortigern

This was in fact a title meaning 'Over-King' rather than a personal name. His real name may have been Vitalinus, as suggested by the names which Nennius (around 829) gives for his father and grandfather. He had some link to the city of Gloucester as remembered by Nennius and other Welsh legends who claim his ancestor 'Gloiu' founded it. By the ninth century the kings of Powys regarded him as their ancestor and the son-in-law of Magnus Maximus (see Powys section). He supposedly succeeded in the consulship of Theodosius (II) and Valentinian (III), i.e. 425, and ruled until the first Saxon revolt in the 440s. He was reviled by later generations as 'Gwertheyrn the Thin', one of the three great 'betrayers of Britain' in the Triads, and Nennius in the early ninth century was equally hostile in making him the foe of St Germanus. Vortigern's support for the 'Pelagians' and/or opposition to the Roman Church may have been a factor in this attitude, given that Nennius' patron Bishop Elvodug of Gwynedd was currently enforcing the Roman computation of the date of Easter on the North Welsh Church. Or was Nennius, a Gwynedd bishop, reflecting his state's dislike of a hostile Powys king?

The catastrophic Anglo-Saxon revolt of the early 440s (?) was traced to Vortigern's disastrous policy of calling in the Germanic marauders as 'federates', mercenaries to fight the more dangerous Picts and Irish, and allowing himself to be talked into recruiting more and more of them by their leader Hengest. In due course they broke into revolt, ravaging the country. The fact that it was Vortigern's son Vortimer not him who led the British campaign against them implied that he probably deposed, or at least eclipsed, his father. Vortigern was recalled after Vortimer's death, recalled Hengest whose daughter Rowena he had married, and was captured and forced to surrender Kent by Hengest whose men massacred Vortigern's councillors at a truce meeting. He then fled to Wales as his enemy Ambrosius returned from exile, made his base at the hill-fort of Dinas Emrys in Snowdonia, and was killed in a fire during a siege at another hill-fort. This was on the lower Wye, in Powys, or in the Lleyn Peninsula, and may or may not have involved prayers for his destruction by his enemy St

Germanus. For a fuller account see the section on Powys, of which he was probably ruler from around 425.

Vortimer

Vortimer was Vortigern's son. According to the historical tradition preserved in the Nennius' *Historia* around 830, he led his father's troops to defeat the first Saxon assault in the late 440s (?), taking a more active role in resistance than his discredited father who had lost support for inviting the Saxons in and causing the crisis. The four main battles are cited as taking place at sites that have been tentatively placed in Kent, advancing from the River Darenth to Aylesford and then a battle on the Channel shore, thus presuming a campaign based in London to drive the invaders back to their bridgehead in Thanet which was supposedly thrice besieged. An unnamed battle that followed may have been a British defeat that saved Hengest's invaders, possibly the battle at Creganford (Crayford?) cited as a victory of Hengest's in 457 in the *Anglo-Saxon Chronicle*.

Whether Vortimer served as deputy to Vortigern then or as an independent commander, he either became associated with him as co-ruler around 450 or usurped the throne. He died soon after his victory, possibly poisoned by his Jutish stepmother Rowena on her father Hengest's behalf, leading to his father's recall. The Triads remembered him as 'Gwerthefyr the Blessed', and listed the removal of his body from its burial on the seashore at an unknown port – done to protect Britain – as one of the 'Three Unfortunate Disclosures of the Island of Britain', carried out by his father at the Saxon Rowena's request. (The model for the ritual burial to protect his people was possibly the legendary burial of King Bran 'the Blessed's head at London.)

Given the dramatic nature of the tangled story of Vortigern, Vortimer, and Rowena, it is possible that some Dark Ages British heroic poem or a Saxon saga was used by the compilers of the legend that Nennius in the ninth century and later Geoffrey of Monmouth used. (David Dumville thinks the Welsh took up a Kentish legend about Hengest's conquests.) Lacking the original sources, we cannot determine how much was embellished. But Vortimer's name is recorded independently of the Kentish story, as the father of a princess who married into the dynasty of Gwent. This man was regarded as the founder of the town of Wonastow in Gwent, and the site is a logical one to be given as a local sub-kingdom to the son of a king ruling over nearby Gloucester and Ergyng.

Ambrosius Aurelianus

Known as 'the last of the Romans' following Gildas, Ambrosius Aurelianus was the successful leader of British resistance to the Anglo-Saxons, probably in the 460s to 480s. Gildas refers to his parents having worn (Imperial) purple and been killed in the Saxon assault, which may refer obliquely to Constantine 'Fendigaid' as the last ruler before Vortigern and the son of Emperor Maximus. 'Purple' in the Late Roman terminology would normally indicate royal rank, though some writers have argued that it might mean only consular office. (This would however locate Ambrosius' father as a senator in Rome itself, and make it unlikely that such a man would be killed in the Saxon conflict in Britain. No known senators holding consular rank in the early fifth century had British estates.)

Later Welsh legend called Ambrosius, 'Emrys Wledig', Constantine's son and Maximus' grandson. The 'Wledig' title was given to senior royal/ military commanders – arguably 'overlords' of sub-rulers – who had achieved notable success, e.g. Cunedda, as well as more obscure figures. But it is uncertain in that case where the name 'Aurelianus' came from. Assuming that it was his surname, it would make it more likely that any link with Maximus was in the female line rather than direct male descent; the Aurelii were his paternal ancestors. The '-anus' nomenclature usually indicated an adoption, as when the Emperor Augustus was called 'Caesar Octavianus' which indicated that he was from the Octavii and had been adopted by his great-uncle Julius Caesar. Logically, therefore, Ambrosius could have been a member of the Aurelii adopted by a more distant relative, possibly Constantine 'Fendigaid'.

Another member of the Aurelianus family was father to the early sixth-century Silurian Celtic holy man, St Paul Aurelian, who seems to have come from Dumnonia, and a relative called Aurelius Cynan/Conan was ruling Gloucester in Gildas' time, around 545. Gildas indicates that the current descendants of Ambrosius had fallen off from his good qualities, which presumes that they (among them Cynan/Conan?) still had political power. There have been attempts to link Ambrosius to the Italian family of the 'Ambrosii', to which St Ambrose (Bishop of Milan 374–97) belonged, particularly as the latter's father was also an 'Aurelius', and recently to claim that his father was a Roman consul in Italy not a ruler in Britain. But in that case it is unclear what Ambrosius was doing in Britain in the 440s to 460s, given how unsafe the province was to visit. Though Gildas' reference to his parents wearing the 'purple' need not mean royal office in Britain this is the likeliest explanation of the term. No link to the Roman Emperor Aurelian

(r. 270–5), is likely as that great restorer of Imperial unity had no sons and came of low rural origins from the Balkans.

The *Historia Brittonum* (820s?) also dated the 'conflict between Vortigern and Ambrosius' to twelve years after Vortigern's accession, that is, presumably Vortigern's assumption of the 'High Kingship' in succession to Constans round 425/430. The conflict is linked to the battle between Ambrosius and 'Vitalinus' – taken by some commentators like John Morris as Vortigern's real name – at 'Guoloph' (Wallop, Hampshire?). It is assumed that due to his family background Ambrosius represented a 'Roman party', probably of southern British landowners with contacts to the Gallic nobility and the Roman authorities there, who opposed the western British 'hill-country' dynast Vortigern. By this reading, as 437 is far too early for Vortigern's overthrow – the Saxon revolt against him was in 441/2 according to the Gallic records – the 'Roman party' were defeated at Guoloph and Ambrosius was forced into exile. The appeal to the Roman authorities in Gaul for aid in 443, recorded in the *Anglo-Saxon Chronicle*, would have followed this defeat.

It is unlikely that all the events surrounding Vortigern's wars with the Picts, the invitation to Hengest and his mercenaries and their subsequent proliferation, the Saxon revolt, Vortimer's defeat by Hengest and subsequent death, and Vortigern's recall and capture at the 'Massacre of the Long Knives' before Ambrosius' return can be fitted into this short period of twelve years. John Morris and others have therefore posited an earlier conflict between Vortigern and Ambrosius before Ambrosius' successful invasion to seize the throne – possibly a revolt on Ambrosius becoming adult against his brother's supplanter that led to his exile, or that Ambrosius was the son of a second 'Ambrosius' who unsuccessfully led a revolt around 437. There is also the question of the connection of this 'pro-Roman' party to the mysterious appeal from Britain to 'Agitius, thrice consul' in Gaul for aid against the Saxons. Assuming this man to be Aetius, commander-in-chief of the Western Empire who was assassinated in 454, rather than the later Gallic general Aegidius, the appeal would have been sent in or after his third consulship in 446. But Gildas, the first to refer to it, does not make its date or context clear and even places it before 'Vortigern' called in the Saxons.

If this second Ambrosius wore the 'purple' as Gildas says Aurelianus' father did, he could be a Roman-appointed 'king' or governor in the Romanised south of Britain in the late 410s or 420s who was the opponent of the 'anti-Roman' Vortigern. But this second Ambrosius has left no record in Celtic tradition, where Ambrosius Aurelianus is unambiguously presented as the son of Constantine 'Fendigaid'. If there were two men called Ambrosius and 'Vortigern' fought the elder of them long before being expelled by the younger, why did this fact not survive to the ninth century? The link to Brittany may be less certain, as some etymologists have speculated that the word used for Brittany – the Welsh 'Llydaw' – was a mistranslation of an early Welsh term referring to Gwent. This latter placing would explain Geoffrey's account of the enigmatic 'Merlin Emrys' – if the latter was correctly assumed to be Ambrosius Aurelianus – being found in 'Glevisseg' (around Cardiff) by Vortigern's emissaries.

It is certainly more likely that Ambrosius did not return to rule in the British lowlands until more than twelve years after Vortigern's accession. The literary evidence, albeit first written down some centuries later and thus open to faulty memories or invention, would place Ambrosius' assumption of power at some time after the Saxon revolt, that is in the 450s at the earliest – whether or not this followed Vortigern's capture by Hengest at the 'Massacre of the Long Knives' and involved (as in legend) Ambrosius landing with a Breton army, possibly at Totnes, and burning Vortigern in a hill-fort. If Gildas' obscure reference to the Battle of Mount Badon, the culmination of the British/Saxon wars, can be interpreted as meaning that the battle took place forty-four years after the start of Ambrosius' Saxon campaigns it could suggest that the campaigns commenced around 470 (see section on 'King Arthur').

It might be suggested that Ambrosius was born around 430, exiled as a child around 435, returned to Britain in the late 450s or early 460s, and fought a Saxon war from around 470 (i.e. once he had consolidated his authority in Britain) to the 490s. Geoffrey is likely to be wrong in placing Ambrosius' death as within a few years of his return, as this brief a reign would not have been likely to make the major impact on British memory that Ambrosius did. The relatively long reign of the successful victor over the Saxons in Geoffrey's story should be attributed to Ambrosius rather than the obscure 'Uther Pendragon'. But there may be a genuine memory behind the story in Geoffrey of Monmouth's account that Ambrosius had to fight a war with Vortigern's son Pascent, a historical figure of early Welsh tradition recorded as ruler of the Builth area in southern Powys, and his Irish ally 'Gilloman'. Vortigern appears to have had a dynastic link with the ruling Ui Niall dynasty in Tara and a prince appears there with his name in the mid-fifth century, so they may have come to his son's aid.

It is possible, as John Morris suggests, that Ambrosius concentrated his campaigns in regions of southern Britain later lost to the Saxons and planted military colonies of veterans at strategic sites. There may be some connection between Ambrosius and various place-names containing the element 'Ambres-' in southern England, e.g. Amberley in Sussex and Amesbury in Wiltshire. The latter was 'Ambresbyrig' in a charter of 880 and was suggested as an estate of Ambrosius' by J. N. Myres, and it has been suggested that these sites could have been where the monarch fought battles, owned estates, or settled colonies of army veterans. Strategically speaking, Amberley in the 'Arun gap' in the South Downs was an ideal 'military colony' to watch for Saxon raiders trying to penetrate upriver into the Weald, as was Ambrosden, north-east of Oxford to deal with attacks on British areas of Buckinghamshire from the Saxon sites in the upper Thames valley. There are also some 'Ambres' place-names in Essex that could have been settled with troops guarding against raids from East Anglia, while Amberley in the lower Severn valley could guard the Gloucester area. Comparisons have been made with the local militia, based on landed estates and towns, raised by Ecdicius in the Auvergne in southern Gaul to tackle the marauding Visigoths in 469–70. There was a similar concentration of towns and estates in the Cotswolds, where the fortified towns of Bath, Cirencester, and Gloucester only fell to the Saxons in 577; it was possible that Ambrosius, linked by Welsh tradition with local Woodchester, could have raised a fighting force similar to Ecdicius' there.

The medieval story that Ambrosius erected Stonehenge as a monument to the British nobles killed by Hengest in the 'Massacre of the Long Knives' at the suggestion of Merlin, who brought the stones from Kilara Mountain in Ireland, is clearly fictional. Some scholars have argued that it is a garbled descendant of a genuine record of his erecting a monument, traditionally known as the 'Giants' Dance' and near a place called Caer Caradoc according to the Welsh *Brut Tyssilio* that Geoffrey may have used as a source. (If the name is accurate, the 'fort of Caradoc' presumably means a hill-fort remembered as used by Caratacus so it is likely to be somewhere in South or East Wales where the latter staged his resistance campaign against Rome.) Various sites have been suggested for this place, e.g. the stones on 'Mynydd y Gaer' above Pencoed in Glamorgan (by Baram Blackett and Alan Wilson) or those at Cerrigydrudion ('Stones of the Heroes') near Llangollen in Powys (by Steve Blake and Scott Lloyd). But the attributions of these sites as the place where the murdered nobles were buried may owe more to medieval guesswork than reality.

Ambrosius' headquarters is unknown, though it is possible that the garbled medieval Welsh legends – taken up by Geoffrey – linking the 'High Kings' to Winchester are a mistranslation of older documents or bardic stories placing them at a more geographically feasible town with the same Roman name of 'Venta', i.e. Venta Silurum (Caerwent) in Gwent. Some Welsh traditions also link Ambrosius to Woodchester in the Cotswolds, which would make sense in terms of the likely survival of Romano-British society there in the later fifth century. Similarly, if Aurelius Cynan/Caninus of Gloucester was Ambrosius' relative this would suggest a Severn valley/Cotswold connection.

Ambrosius is linked in legend to the enigmatic figure of Merlin, not least through Geoffrey of Monmouth referring to the latter as also being called 'Emrys'. Geoffrey's account of the fabled encounter between Vortigern and his would-be victim Merlin, the 'boy without a father' whose blood needed to be mixed with the mortar of his new hill-fort at Dinas Emrys, would seem to date it some time after the main Saxon revolt and before Vortigern's final overthrow, with the disgraced Vortigern already forced to flee lowland Britain and relocate to his Welsh heartlands. The core of the 'Merlin Emrys' story appears in Nennius (around 829), and was expanded by Geoffrey of Monmouth to include biographical material from the career of the sixth-century bard Myrddin (see below).

The boy called 'Merlin', illegitimate son of the daughter of a King of Dyfed, who Vortigern had seized at 'Campus Eleti' in Glevisseg (around Cardiff) and sought to sacrifice, subsequently advised Ambrosius and was thus datable to the mid-fifth century. He is thus of course too early to be the bard Myrddin, whose poems are preserved in the *Red Book of Hergest* (around 1425). This enigmatic and semi-Druidical figure is identifiable from his poems as a bard (a client of King Gwenddoleu of Caerluel/Carlisle, his sister's lover) who was involved in the Battle of Arderydd around 573. The site was probably 'Arthuret' near the Solway, and the battle involved a conflict between two coalitions of rival princes from the dynasty of Coel 'Hen'. Gwendolleu was defeated by his cousin Urien/Urbgen of Rheged, who thereafter was senior ruler of the North. The trauma of the battle caused Myrddin to have some sort of breakdown and flee into hiding, and he lived as a hermit in the Caledonian forests of southern Scotland with his pet pig for many years. He was known as 'Myrddin the Wild', and was possibly the same as the elusive 'wild man' and prophet Lailoken of southern Scottish myth who was drowned at Drumelzier. The latter certainly seems to have had Druidic connections, his 'triple death' being a staple of Celtic legend, and the hagiography of the contemporary Strathclyde saint Kentigern (around 1100) shows that in the mid-sixth century there were still Druids at the royal court in Dumbarton. Geoffrey changed the name Myrddin – the Celtic for 'Martin' – to the more suitable 'Merlin' because of the associations of the French word 'merde' in the then-dominant Norman-French tongue.

There may also be some truth in Breton legend that Ambrosius was brought up in Brittany after his father's death to save him from Vortigern, given the historical link between the British settlements in Brittany in the 380s and the Emperor Magnus Maximus, Ambrosius' supposed grandfather. Welsh tradition also maintained he was connected to Arfon in Gwynedd, where there is a hill-fort known as 'Dinas Emrys' which is the putative site of Vortigern's attempt to sacrifice him. As his possible grandfather Magnus Maximus may have commanded troops at Segontium/Caernarfon and his putative father Constantine 'Fendigaid' was buried there, it is possible that Ambrosius did inherit lands in Arfon and lived at Dinas Emrys before assuming the 'High Kingship' (as in Rosemary Sutcliff's novels).

Uther Pendragon

It is uncertain if he ever ruled or was the brother of Ambrosius as legend stated. It is certainly extremely unlikely that he could have ruled for a full fifteen years or so as 'High King' as claimed in the work of Geoffrey of Monmouth (and his Welsh or Breton source) without leaving some trace on recorded history, even in the obscure political situation of the 490s. It is now claimed that the name is a mistranslation of a Celtic honorific, 'the awe-inspiring Head Dragon', this being Baram Blackett and Alan Wilson's solution to the problem of his identity. The 'Uther Pen Dragon' – 'awe inspiring Head Ruler(?)' – who appears in the early medieval Welsh stories of the *Mabinogi* as Arthur's father is not even said to be a king but an enchanter (as in Triad 28). One of their heroes, Menw, is the 'servant of Uther' and in the twelfth-century *Dialogue of Arthur and the Eagle* the latter is the transformed Eliwlod, son of Madog son of Uthyr and nephew of Arthur (who is thus Uther's son).

'Uthr' is a Celticisation of the Latin name Victor, which was that of Magnus Maximus' eldest son and thus Uther's supposed great-uncle (see section on 'King Arthur'). Given this nomenclature, 'Uthr' could have been called after his uncle Victor. At the most, he may have succeeded to Ambrosius' authority in southern Britain for a brief period, possibly in the 490s. Efforts have been made to link him and his title with a 'Dragon's

Head' comet visible in the 490s, but this is highly speculative. In later Welsh literature Uther appears as the late fifth-/early sixth-century hero Arthur's father but not specifically as a king. Nennius' claim around 829 that many of the kings that fought under Arthur were 'more noble than he' might seem to imply that either his father was not a king or that he was Uther's illegitimate son. It is possible that the sobriquet 'Uther Pen Dragon' refers to him as a 'Wonderful/Wonder-Working Head', as in the story of the magical talking head of the deceased King Bran in the Mabinogi legends, and that he was only identified as a 'Head King' later. Was he assumed to be a king, erroneously, as he was Arthur's father? Further details are given in the section on Arthur under Silures/Morgannwg.

Arthur
See section under Glamorgan.

Constantine of Dumnonia
See section on that kingdom.

Geoffrey of Monmouth's garbled version of the sixth century names all of Gildas' five tyrannical' kings – Constantine, Maelgwyn of Gwynedd, Cuneglausus/Cynglas, Aurelius Caninus, and Vortipor – as 'High Kings' of Britain in succession. This is definitely non-historical, as the Saxon settlements had spread across most of eastern England by their time (around 540–50) and this included Geoffrey's British 'capital' at London. At best, one or more of them may have exercised authority over the British rulers of the West – the most plausible candidate is Maelgwyn, whose sobriquet of 'Pendragon' or 'Dragon of the Island' implies that he was recognised as a leader by other British rulers. Gwynedd was clearly the most powerful state of the mid-sixth century, though if Maelgwyn is to be counted as a sort of 'High King' in the 540s the same rank could be allowed a few decades later to his son Rhun, able to march his army as far north as the Pictish realm in support of his brother (?) King Bridei and thus presumably secured the loyalty of those kings whose lands he crossed in the north of Britain. If military leadership of a coalition of kings can be taken as implying some sort of rank as 'High King', then it should also be accorded to Urien/Urbgen of Rheged, who led such a coalition against the Angles of Bernicia and besieged their king on Lindisfarne around 589 before being assassinated by his rival Morcant.

Similarly, Geoffrey presents the last Celtic sovereign to reign in England before the Saxon conquest as Cadwaladwr of Gwynedd in the mid-seventh

century. The most that can be said about any truth behind this fiction is
that Welsh legend may have regarded Cadwaladwr as possessing some sort
of super-provincial authority over his fellow rulers within Wales in 655–82,
in succession to his far more powerful father Cadwallon (ally of Penda of
Mercia and ravager of distant Northumbria) in the early 630s. Any such
leadership of the Celtic princes by Gwynedd clearly ended in the later
seventh century as far as our limited records ascertain, so this may have
lain behind Geoffrey's story.

A Cautionary Note on the Literary Tradition of Post-Roman Britain

It should be pointed out that the contemporary archaeological evidence for
the post-Roman period is at variance with any picture of constant British/
Anglo-Saxon conflict. The literary sources seem to indicate the latter,
though of course they tend to dwell on the 'heroic' and the dramatic and
present the unusual as normal, in the same way that the modern media
does. The 'bigger picture' of development in the post-Roman kingdoms can
be seen from the archaeology, particularly the continuity of agricultural
patterns in the centuries between approximately 400 and 700. If the lands
that the Anglo-Saxons 'occupied' had really been systematically ravaged
and emptied of inhabitants, we would expect to see the abandonment of
Roman farming and a return to wasteland. Forests that had been cleared
in the Bronze and Iron Ages would have encroached on the settled land,
and had to be cleared again by the early Angles and Saxons. This is what
would be expected if we took Gildas' picture of wholesale slaughter and
the abandonment of land as an accurate description of life in fifth-century
Britain. However, the careful modern analysis of land use in these centuries
indicates that this was not the case, and that there was a great deal of
continuity and no notable increase of wasteland or forests. The work of
pioneering agricultural historians such as Oliver Rackham (*The History
of the Countryside*, Phoenix Press, 1986) indicates no 'regression' from a
stable, occupied countryside to wasteland and forest from around 400 to
600.

In certain cases across the country, the boundaries of Late Roman estates
can be found behind the limits drawn for new Anglo-Saxon parishes, e.g.
in the Cotswolds. This is less obvious than in Gaul/France, where there is
better written evidence from the surviving Latin-speaking Roman upper
classes into Germanic times; but it is quite conceivable that some or many

'Saxon villages' in southern England are really post-Roman Celtic in origin and there was less dramatic change in the countryside, apart from certain areas subject to major wars. Indeed, in the crucial area of the Cotswolds there is no record of any warfare until the West Saxon conquest of 577 – though the western Wansdyke near Bath seems to indicate a disputed frontier in that area in the fifth or early sixth century. The catastrophic decline of international trade across the ex-Imperial lands in the fifth to seventh century may have led to the abandonment of 'uneconomic' stone-built villas, whose physical structure could not be maintained, in favour of smaller wooden farmsteads, but not any dramatic wholesale burning of villas by plundering hordes of pirates (and/or rebel peasants?) as used to be taken for granted.

The discovery of burnt remains at certain villas is no proof that there was a systematic campaign of arson and plunder either by embittered peasants or piratical Germanic raiders, and the complex nature of the Late Roman international economy makes it more likely that rising political insecurity from the raids of 367 made the large villa-based estates unsustainable. They were thus gradually abandoned as maintaining the physical structure of the building became impossible, and smaller farm buildings were used instead on the same sites (as the survival of the boundaries of Roman estates into Anglo-Saxon land use would indicate). Indeed, it should be noted that there were fewer large, impressively decorated palatial villas in Britain than in Gaul, even in the prosperous fourth century, and nothing on the scale of Piazza Armerina in Sicily. The majority of rural estates were based on farms with small houses rather than places like Lullingstone and Bignor, and there were accordingly fewer large villas that were impossible to maintain without a complex infrastructure. Outside the south-east, villas were rare and most towns were small apart from administrative centres such as Eburacum/York; accordingly the change in lifestyle as the Late Roman economy collapsed would have been minimal.

The abandonment of the use of Celtic languages in the south and east of Britain was also long used as proof that the native populace had been driven out or reduced to serfdom. However, the modern investigation of English DNA across the country shows a larger degree of genetic continuity from Roman times – and indeed from the Iron Age – than this theory supposed. The vast majority of the population do not seem to have been affected by the turbulence and chaos depicted in the histories of the period, and the archaeology is in direct denial of what Gildas asserts. The question of DNA is however still unclear, with the latest investigations still showing that around fifty per cent of the current male population may have some 'Anglo-Saxon' blood that is genetically linked to that of north-western Germany, whence the literary tradition says that the new settlers originated. It is also suggested that there was a closer genetic link between the 'Celtic' tribes of pre-Roman Britain, the Celts of Gaul, and the Germans than originally believed, and that the distinctiveness of 'Celtic' and 'Germanic' blood by the fifth century was not enough for us to be able to claim all 'Germanic' DNA as resulting from post-410 settlement in Britain.

This is not to say that the literary evidence of contending kingdoms of Celtic Britons and Anglo-Saxons is wholly inaccurate. The dominance of Germanic names by the seventh century and the apparent disappearance of Celtic Christianity in southern Britain before the Catholic missionaries arrived suggests a new 'ruling class' whose terminology and culture were taken up across society. (However, it has been pointed out that some ruling classes and 'mass-invaders' have retained significant native geographical terminology, as the colonists did with Native American place-names in the US.) The Anglo-Saxon law codes significantly placed their societies' 'Welsh' inhabitants low on the stratified social scale, retaining a clear distinction between those people of native British descent and the dominant Germans – presumably by reckoning 'ethnicity' by patrilinear descent. The word used for the British inhabitants was interchangeable for 'slave' and 'foreigner' by the ninth century. This indicates the new rulers' opinions of the ancient inhabitants of at least some of the new kingdoms. But the archaeological evidence is a warning that the struggles within and between kingdoms do not seem to have led to the overwhelming instability and turmoil in society as a whole that was once supposed. The polemical purposes of particular writers, notably Gildas, need to be borne in mind when considering their accounts of events.

For further detailed discussions of these problems, see Petra Dark, *The Environment of Britain in the First Millenium AD*, and Francis Pryor, *Britain A.D.*

Welsh 'High Kingship' or 'National' Leadership After the Seventh Century

'National' leadership of the kingdoms in Wales does not appear to have existed in the eighth and ninth centuries, apart from a primacy of honour given to Rhodri 'Mawr' of Gwynedd from around 854 until he was killed by the Vikings in 878. The notion of a Welsh 'national' political and cultural identity was fostered in the *Historia Brittonum*, written around 830 in the kingdom of Rhodri's father, Merfyn 'Frych'/'the Freckled' of Gwynedd and probably authored by Bishop Nennius. This played up the roles of pan-British leaders in resisting the Saxons after the end of Roman rule, with 'Vortigern' as the villain and 'Arthur' as the hero. It was probably intended to draw a parallel with the aspirations of Merfyn to lead the Welsh against the Anglo-Saxons, in a 'national' revival after the recent Mercian ravages of Gwynedd and Powys. The book's concentration on pan-British leaders, not the minor kings of Gwynedd or Powys or Dyfed, followed the 'narrative' of Gildas around 540, who had concentrated on Vortigern and Ambrosius. But Gildas had stressed the self-deserved ruin of the feuding, petty post-Roman dynast; Nennius intended to pose a 'positive' message. The notion of a heroic line of kings of all Britain also emerged in early Welsh legends, e.g. Bran 'the Blessed' and arguably Emperor Maximus ('Macsen Wledig'). The founding king was supposed to be 'Brutus' around 800 BC, a Trojan prince from Italy. But neither Merfyn nor Rhodri claimed the literary title for 'over-ruler' – 'Wledig'. There was no attempt to restructure merged Welsh kingdoms into one state under Rhodri or the tenth-century Dyfed ruler Hywel 'Dda' – probably customary law was too strong. Rhodri, son of Merfyn and the heiress of Powys who ruled both Gwynedd and Powys in 854–78, also began the 200 years of union between Gwynedd and Powys after the last king of the latter, his uncle, fled to Rome during heavy Mercian attacks. This virtual doubling of the size of Gwynedd restored their primacy among the Welsh kingdoms, though even with the extra manpower the rulers of the enlarged kingdom remained in a subordinate position in their dealings with the surviving Anglo-Saxon kingdom, Wessex, in the joint resistance to Viking invasion (at least in the Saxon version of events preserved in their *Chronicle*).

The tenth century saw the emergence as a military power of the joint South Welsh kingdom of Dyfed and Seissylwg, now sometimes called 'Deheubarth', under its new royal line – a junior branch of the House of Gwynedd, founded by Rhodri's son Cadell. In 942 his son Hywel 'Dda', greatest of medieval Welsh lawgivers and King of Deheubarth since 905, secured the succession to Gwynedd after the death of his cousin Idwal ap Anarawd ap Rhodri. The major Welsh kingdoms were thus united dynastically for the first time, with all three (Gwynedd, Powys, and Deheubarth) under the rule of one man, but the needs of competing family members prevented the union from surviving and presenting a new power to rival the emerging English state across the border. Hywel was personally dominant among his large family and it is clear that he initiated policy, but he still had to nominally share power with his brothers while they lived and could not preserve a united kingdom by passing it on to one son.

On Hywel's death in 950, Idwal's sons Iago and Idwal reclaimed Gwynedd (with Powys), while Hywel's son Owain had to make do with Deheubarth. The union was however briefly restored by Owain's son Maredudd of Deheubarth in 986–99, following a round of feuding and coups among the royal family of Gwynedd, and was continued by Cynan ap Hywel of Gwynedd in 999–1005. It is possible that some informal agreement had been reached that preserved a united kingdom of Gwynedd and Deheubarth in 986–1005 by alternating its rulers from the two branches of the royal family, the descendants of Hywel and Anarawd; but if so it was not long lasting and it fell victim to individual ambition. In 1018 the killing of the kings of Deheubarth by a usurper enabled Llywelyn ap Seisyll of Gwynedd to pose as their avenger and remove the latter, restoring the union – but only for the five remaining years of his life.

Following another return to the two separate kingdoms from 1023, Gruffydd ap Llywelyn ap Seisyll of Gwynedd restored a union by military force for a brief period in 1044–7. Deheubarth revolted and installed his rival Gruffydd ap Rhydderch, but in 1055 he killed the latter and became king of a shakily united Wales for eight years. His attempts to rectify the frontier with England secured him rare advances for a Welsh dynast in regaining part of Herefordshire in 1056, but Earl Harold of Wessex launched a major campaign to destroy his power early in 1063 with a seaborne raid on his hall at Rhuddlan and kept his army in Gwynedd until Gruffydd's followers killed their leader to secure peace some months later. The realm that Gruffydd had created was broken up, with Deheubarth returning to the son of Gruffydd ap Rhydderch and the kingdom of Gwynedd/Powys being divided between the later ruler's half-brothers, Bleddyn and Rhiwallon ap Cynfyn. Bleddyn's family kept control of Powys until the English conquest, dividing Wales further, and after the death of Madoc ap Maredudd (seen as a 'national' leader, albeit more cultural than military, by his prestigious following of poets) in 1160 Powys spilt further into northern and southern halves.

This reverse was soon followed by the arrival of the Normans with their extra manpower and new military technology, giving the Kingdom of England a definitive military superiority over the Welsh, and the settlement of the land-hungry 'Marcher' lords on the frontier and their building of castles ended the Welsh hopes of an advance of the frontier which had seemed possible in the 1050s. They soon put the Welsh princes on the defensive through incessant warfare and campaigns into Wales to secure new lands while the princes continued to waste their manpower on feuding, and by the mid-1090s both Gwynedd and Deheubarth had lost large amounts of their most fertile land and were in danger of being overrun. The Anglo-Norman advance into Pembrokeshire in the south proved permanent, though the heroic efforts of Gruffydd ap Cynan and his vassals turned the tide in Gwynedd and removed the precarious new Norman settlements along the north coast. Thereafter, the best that the Welsh could hope for against superior English numbers, resources, and weaponry was for a powerful and determined leader to take advantage of those times when the English king was preoccupied elsewhere to depose or force submission from Welsh allies, regain marginal land from the English, and secure an advantageous diplomatic agreement with the latter's government – as Llywelyn ap Iorweth did in 1212–40 and Llywelyn ap Gruffydd in 1258–77. They stood no hope of survival when an English sovereign could attack them with his full military strength except by retreat into the mountains and waiting for the invader to give up waiting for their surrender and agree to terms, as when King John invaded in 1210, Henry III in 1242, and Edward I in 1277.

3

RULERS OF NORTH WALES (GWYNEDD)

Note on King Lists

These are heavily dependent on the genealogies later drawn up in the *Historia Brittonum* in the 830s. This is attributed to a bishop called Nennius, holder of the see of Gwynedd in the 820s – though even if he was the author and the book was compiled at that date, its genealogies reflected current political claims and dynastic mythology as much as a faithful record passed down by previous generations. Its extant version dates from some time after its latest historical entry in 957 and it is uncertain how much is 'original'. The other main body of genealogies were compiled at the court of Hywel 'Dda' of Deheubarth in the early tenth century (and are now British Library Harleian Mss. 3589 and at Worcester College, Oxford). As Hywel – a cadet of the dynasty of Gwynedd who ruled firstly Dyfed and later Gwynedd/Powys too – was the first sovereign to unite the Welsh kingdoms, he had his own reasons for commissioning definitive dynastic lists. The latter were neatly arranged to show his legitimate claims to his various kingdoms, and as such had a contemporary political end in view rather than being a 'neutral' transcription of existing lists for scholarly study. There are also pedigrees of early saints, both in hagiographies and in the *Bonedd y Saint* (National Library of Wales Mss. Peniarth 183), which make reference to their royal relatives. They are particularly valuable for the minor kingdoms of South Wales. No original documents of legal transactions survive, but there are a number of quotations or transcriptions in later work (e.g. the *Llandaff Charters* for Morgannwg) of arguable authenticity.

The Welsh kingdoms' genealogies from these sources are available in P. C. Bartrum, *Early Welsh Genealogical Tracts* (1966) and *A Welsh Classical Dictionary* (1993). The earlier parts of the genealogies, to the fifth century, are full of names unattested by other sources which may have been invented or at least garbled – and a multitude of links to Emperor Magnus Maximus that are less likely to be genealogical reality than a ninth-century (or later) reflection of a 'political' ancestry. Some genealogies, Gwent and Siluria in particular, are contradictory and cannot be used to establish a definitive dating. The names of the fifth and sixth centuries therefore are particularly remote in time from the extant documentation. There is no reason why earlier documents could not be copied accurately or lists remembered correctly, but it provides a note of caution – particularly over the habit of naming successive rulers in a simple father-son descent when the true genealogy may have been more complicated. (Notably, the genealogists made earlier Roman Emperors succeed by 'father-son-grandson' descent, which we know from Roman literary evidence is incorrect.) The approximate dates of early rulers can be drawn up by working backwards from the ninth century, assuming around thirty to forty years per generation and checking against other records and traditional stories to see which ruler of one kingdom was contemporary with which other rulers. But there is always a danger that the omission of one or more names in the lists that have survived, or an unremembered fact that one king gave birth to his son in his teens or his old age could have distorted the extant record.

Events from 682 (the death of Cadwaladr of Gwynedd, later supposed to have been the last Welsh king ruling in England by Geoffrey of Monmouth) are recorded in the *Brut y Tywysogion* ('Chronicle of the Princes'). The use of this date testifies to the work's purpose as a 'continuation' of Geoffrey's book; the main source appears to have been the monastic annals of Strata Florida Abbey. The original Latin version has been lost; there are surviving Welsh translations, the most important of which is in the National Library of Wales (Peniarth Mss. 20).

Princes/Kings of Gwynedd: the Fifth Century

The area was the ancestral land of the Ordovices and Deceangli at the time of the Roman conquest; the new post-Roman name of 'Gwynedd' was a Celticisation of 'Venedotia'. The royal House was descended according to the genealogies from Cunedda (Kenneth), a prince of the British tribe of the Votadini in what is now Lothian. He is supposed to have been called south by the British authorities – at a date 146 years before the time of 'Mailcunus', i.e. Maelgwyn of Gwynedd, who died in the plague of around 547, according to Nennius, writing in the 820s. He was brought in to reoccupy lands in North Wales lost to Irish settlers, and the archaeological evidence confirms settlement in Lleyn. If this is accurate, he would probably have been a protégé of the Western Roman Empire's regent Stilicho who is recorded as campaigning in Britain around 399 by his panegyrist Claudian. (The use of one body of non-Roman 'foederati' as allies to defeat another body of non-Romans on the frontier, giving them the latter's lands, was a common practice by the undermanned Roman army.)

An alternative date suggested on the basis of genealogies would put this at only 106 years, making it in the 440s. This fits better with the established genealogy giving only one generation between Cunedda and Catwallaun 'Longhand', who ruled around 500, but raises the question of which post-Roman ruler in Britain (Vortigern?) devised the strategy and could order or lure him south. If the earlier date is correct, Cunedda may have been a 'foederatus' (subject ally) of the late Roman Empire; historians have speculated that his grandfather Paternus' nickname 'of the red tunic' implies some sort of Roman military office. Two generations back from Cunedda certainly brings the date into the later fourth century, contemporaneous with Ammianus' record of the general Theodosius' reconstruction of a system of local rulers as Roman allies after the great 'barbarian' attack on Britain in 367. Medieval Welsh genealogists traced the dynasties of various parts of Gwynedd and the allied principality of Ceredigion to Cunedda's sons – 'Edernyion' was ruled by the descendants of Cunedda's son Edern, 'Rhufoniog' by Rhufon and his line, 'Dogfaeling' by Dogfael and his line, 'Ceredigion' by Ceredig and his line, and Pwlheli by Afloeg's line. The most 'senior' of the principalities, 'Meirionnydd', fell to Meirion (Marcianus), the son of Cunedda's predeceasing eldest son Tybion. It is uncertain if this is a correct memory of an actual division of the new kingdom among Cunedda's family in the fifth century or a 'post-facto' translation of political links established over generations into explanatory dynastic terms – it seems rather 'tidy' that the cantrefs of Gwynedd were all allegedly neatly parcelled out among Cunedda's sons and thence ruled by their direct descendants. Given the apparent relevance of the contemporary revival of Gwynedd in Nennius' writings (see the section on King Arthur), it is possible that the concept of a unitary Gwynedd parcelled out among Cunedda's family was invented to justify its 'reunification' by Nennius' patron King Merfyn. It has even been suggested that the 'tradition' of the division of Gwynedd among Cunedda's sons was created as late as the 1170s, to provide an earlier precedent for the current division among the sons of Owain Gwynedd.

Catwallaun 'Lawhir' ('Longhand'), the king of Gwynedd around 500, was remembered by the twelfth-century Welsh *Bruts* as the contemporary of 'King Arthur'. According to later stories he reoccupied Mon/Anglesey, which the Irish had settled. It is more likely that if he was indeed Cunedda's grandson the average dating of generations would make it probable that his grandfather was ruling in the 440s rather than the 400s, but the earlier date is possible.

Maelgwyn: the First Gwynedd Overlord?

Maelgwyn, one of the five rulers who Gildas castigated for his misrule in *De Excidio Britanniae*, died around 547 (549 according to the *Annales Cambriae* in the ninth century). The date is likely to be accurate, as he was a victim of the great plague which swept across the Roman Empire from 542 onwards and is independently recorded as decimating Ireland in the late 540s. (One theory would prefer the plague when Maelgwyn died to be the recurrence of the first outbreak, from 555 onwards.) This enables us to approximately date other rulers; he was regarded as the most powerful ruler of Britain in his time, the 'Head Dragon' ('Pendragon') or 'Dragon of the Island' (Britain or Mon?). The title is probably connected to the use of the dragon as a symbol on the Welsh kings' battle standards, deriving from its origin as a Late Roman standard. By the twelfth century Geoffrey of Monmouth could cite the red dragon as the British symbol in his story of the white and red dragons found fighting in a pool at Dinas Emrys by 'Merlin'.

'Maglocunus' was castigated by Gildas as greatest of the rulers of his day but also greatest in evil, and was the subject of the longest of his diatribes. A patron of pagan bards according to the later legends of Taliesin but allegedly educated as a boy at the school of St Illtud at Llantwit in Morgannwg around 500, he murdered his uncle to gain the throne. This was presumably his father's brother Owain 'White-Tooth', ruler of Clwyd, though the precise term used may mean 'mother's brother' and so refer to another man; he also killed assorted other minor rulers, presumably in unifying the chieftaincies of Gwynedd. He later murdered his nephew in order to marry the latter's wife. Gildas accused him of having once abdicated to become a monk and then returned to secular life, suggesting that he did 'repent' of his crimes at one point and that Gildas' animosity was partly due to exasperation at him abandoning religion. He also accused Maelgwyn of drinking wine pressed from the grapes of the Sodomites, which probably implies homosexuality and certainly a reputation for unbridled sexual license.

His chief court was apparently at Degannwy, and the fact that his younger son Bridei (known to the locals as 'Brude mac Maelchon', the latter name being unique in Pictish annals) probably became king of the Picts has been used to suggest that he also married into their royal house. Maelchon is probably Maelgwyn, though this is not certain. His younger contemporary Taliesin the poet, who was remembered in medieval legend as coming to his court as a young man and confounding his pagan bards, accused him of 'treachery to the race of Arthur' in a poem of debatable authenticity.

One 'Triad' makes him the chief elder of Arthur at his West Wales court at Menevia (St David's), presumably before he succeeded to the throne of Gwynedd. Accordingly he has been linked to the controversies about the real 'King Arthur' and suggested as the latter's chief rival for pre-eminence in Wales. According to the Welsh Laws he was raised to be over-king by an assembly of the chief men of Wales, with authority over the subordinate rulers of Dinefwr (i.e. Dyfed) and Cerniw (i.e. Gwent). But it is possible that the dating of later 'memories' of Maelgwyn's rule over Wales makes the evidence unreliable; the extension of the kingdom's power over Wales in the thirteenth century led to contemporary writers backing up its claims by arguing that they were only reviving the power of Maelgwyn.

Maelgwyn's uncle Owain, as the most powerful North Welsh ruler around 500–520, has been cited as one candidate to be 'Arthur' (see further under section on Morgannwg) by Martin Keatman and Graham Phillips (*King Arthur – the True Story*, 1992). It is supposed that his fortress was 'Dinarth' on the Clywd coast – due to which the owner of this fort might have been nicknamed 'Arth'/Artos ('the Bear'). But there is no clear evidence that he was so called and thus came to be referred to by later writers under that name which was then turned into 'Arthur'. The 'Bear' after whom Dinarth was named could have been any one of a number of its occupants over centuries. There are plenty of 'Arthurian' sites in Gwynedd, not least the locations of his execution of the rebel and/or raiding Caledonian prince Huil ap Caw at Ruthin.

Owain's son Cynglas is described by Gildas as 'the tawny butcher' and 'the charioteer of the Bear's stronghold'. But that is not proof that this stronghold was Dinarth near Llandudno, though it is likely – or that Arthur was therefore the King of Gwynedd rather than its occasionally visiting overlord or ally. Cynglas may have been connected to Dinarth either as the king (or the king's heir) of the Clwyd region or as a prince serving the stronghold's chieftain who was not a relative. Lords had a custom of sending their sons to serve fellow chieftains, sometimes as effective hostages; it is not certain that Cynglas was charioteer to his royal father 'Arthur' (i.e. Owain) rather than to his father's senior sovereign or colleague.

The Sixth and Early Seventh Centuries: Rhun to Cadwallon

The most powerful king in northern Britain, Maelgwyn may have managed to have his son Bridei made king of the Picts; his other son Rhun 'Hir' ('The Tall'), who was illegitimate, succeeded Maelgwyn's immediate heir Cynglas around 550. Rhun's mother was the daughter of the enigmatic Avallach or Aballach, possibly 'the' Avallach who was recorded in literary legend as owning the island off the west coast (Bardsey?), which later became known as 'Avalon'. Under that name it was supposed to be the seat of a sisterhood of holy priestesses (a common 'Celtic' practice for islands) who carried off the wounded 'King Arthur' there after his last battle at Camlann around 539; their leader was supposed to be Arthur's sister Morgan. Rhun kept up his father's military prowess, and led an army via the Pennines or York all the way to Pictland (to assist Bridei?) around 560, in an expedition of rare geographical extent for the 'Dark Ages' but logically possible on the Roman roads. It suggests good logistics. This is supposed to have also been to overawe his immediate northern neighbours, the princes of Rheged in Lancashire, e.g. Eleutherius/Elidyr, the father of the later poet Llywarch 'Hen', who had recently raided Arfon. This man is supposed to have been killed or dispossessed by Rhun. But military leadership among the northern Britons seems to have passed to Rheged by around 580, and little is known of Rhun's immediate successors, his son Beli and his grandson Iago. The latter was possibly assassinated according to the Triads, or else was killed at the Battle of Chester by the expanding Anglian power of Northumbria under its unifier Aethelfrith around 616. Edwin of Northumbria, an exile in Gwynedd after his family was driven out of Deira on its annexation by Aethelfrith of Bernicia around 604 but its enemy once he had regained his kingdom, seems to have used his conquest of Rheged and acquisition of a fleet to subdue the Isle of Man and later Anglesey – a stark indication of Gwynedd's decline under the un-warlike Cadfan around 620.

Cadfan, who died around 625, was buried at Llangaladwr on Mon/ Anglesey, and called 'the wisest and most renowned of kings' on his monument. Around 628/9 Edwin invaded Anglesey, either by land or by sea, and drove Cadfan's son Cadwallon to take refuge on nearby Priestholm and then flee to Ireland. He may have overrun the coastal strip from Flint to Bangor too.

Probably Edwin's earlier exile in Gwynedd meant that he had studied its army and commanders and knew how to defeat them. In a subsequent revival of North Welsh fortunes, the ferocious Cadwallon could return from enforced exile in Ireland some time around 630 and expel Edwin from Gwynedd. He was remembered in later poems as winning fourteen great battles for Britain, presumably against both British and Anglian enemies, and probably defeated Edwin at the battle of Digoll in Gwynedd. He then invaded Northumbria, possibly aided by the local British kingdom of Elmet in the southern Pennines (subdued by Aethelfrith or Edwin) as he fought in the land of Dunaut, its former king. He defeated and killed Edwin in autumn 633/4 at the Battle of Hatfield Chase near Doncaster, and ravaged Deira; Edwin's cousin Osric managed to claim the kingdom but was later killed in battle by Cadwallon also. Edwin's Christianity clearly mattered less to Cadwallon than the ancestral rivalry of Briton and Angle for control of the North; his near-genocidal ravaging of his foe's lands was denounced by Bede.

Ravaging as far as Bamburgh in Bernicia, he was the last British ruler to achieve military supremacy in northern Britain. His solution for the Northumbrian problem seems to have been outright massacre rather than building up a permanent coalition of restored local sub-kings that could have lasted, though Bede's hostile account may have exaggerated due to the 'Roman' Christian monk's dislike of the Celtic Church. But although he managed to defeat and kill the outmatched new king Eanfrith of Bernicia, son of Edwin's late enemy Aethelfrith, the latter's brothers Oswald and Oswy returned from exile on Iona in the Hebrides, probably with military backing from the Scots of Dalriada. After Cadwallon was killed by Oswald at the Battle of Heavenfield near Hexham in 634/5 the military power of Gwynedd was ended. The usurper Cadfael ap Cyffedw, regarded as 'low-born' in the tradition of the Triads, took over instead of Cadwallon's probably young son Cadwaladr, and took a more junior role in his alliance with the new Anglo-Saxon power on his frontier, Cadwallon's old ally, the pagan warlord Penda of Mercia.

Probably Gwynedd was militarily exhausted by Cadwallon's wars. It was Powys under Cyndylan which was Penda's main ally against Oswald.

Cadfael was killed in or expelled after Penda's defeat at the Winwaed (near Leeds?) by Oswy of Northumbria in 655; his participation in this campaign shows his maintenance of Cadwallon's anti-Northumbrian stance.

Cadwallon's son Cadwaladr was then restored, and must have had some degree of prestige beyond his frontiers as he was later remembered by the medieval Welsh (and Geoffrey of Monmouth or his source) as the 'last king of the British' before their complete eclipse by the Saxons. The unhistorical Geoffrey even had Cadwallon and Cadwaladr reigning in London, albeit precariously.

After Cadwallon: Eclipse and Revival

It is a mark of the decline of Gwynedd and/or the poor state of our sources that we cannot be clear of the dates and genealogy of its kings in the later eighth century. Cadwaldr was probably too young to rule when his father was killed in 633/4, and died around 682 when he was probably around fifty-five to sixty. His son, the long-reigning Idwal 'Iwrth' ('the Roebuck', probably a physical description of his appearance), was succeeded around 720 by his son Rhodri, who was succeeded by Caradog ap Meirion. All that is clear is that Mercia continued to be a formidable foe, though the construction of 'Wat's Dyke' on the northern frontier in the early eighth century may indicate serious raiding at times from Gwynedd. The kingdom was fortunate not to be the main target of the autocratic Offa, who again concentrated on defending not expanding the Mercian kingdom, but the absence of records may hide a number of Mercian attacks in the mid-eighth century. The stability of the state was not affected in any case, and it had a series of long-lasting rulers such as Idwal and his son Rhodri 'Molwynog' (d. around 754). The latter's successor was not his son – under-age at his death? – but a prince of the ruling line of Rhos in eastern Gwynedd, Caradog ap Meiriaun, possibly descended from Cynglas. Given his location and his name (an echo of the legendary anti-Roman hero Caratacus), he and his father may have made a reputation as the 'front-line' leaders against Mercian attacks and/or have raided Mercia, causing the Mercians to construct the defensive 'Wat's Dyke' from Flint southwards. Whether the sharing of the rule of Gwynedd between two dynasties in the mid- to late eighth century was harmonious or not can only be guessed; by around 800 it had led to warfare between them.

Cynan ap Rhodri and Hywel ap Caradog seem to have been engaged in a fierce struggle for the kingship around 800, with the latter the survivor.

There were also major Mercian invasions by Offa's successors Coenwulf (796–821) and Coelwulf (821–3), with a battle at Degannwy around 797 and ravaging of the heartland of the kingdom in the early 820s. Following the extinction of the main line of the dynasty, in 825 (?) Hywel ap Caradog was succeeded by his late co-ruler Cynan's daughter Essylt's son by Gwriad, Merfyn 'Frych' ('the Freckled'), from the presumed line of Llywarch 'Hen' on the Isle of Man. Not coming from the ancestral Gwynedd dynasty, Merfyn may have needed to assert his role as a legitimate Welsh leader by reviving enthusiasm for the legendary past Welsh successes of 'Arthur's era – or have had a wider understanding of Gwynedd's role than his feuding predecessors. His alleged ancestor Llywarch 'Hen's heroic poetry about the pan-British warlords Urien and Owain of Rheged may also have inspired him. Merfyn was the probable patron, even the instigator, of the writing of the first extant Welsh 'history', Bishop Nennius' *Historia Brittonum*, in the late 820s. The work may have served as much as propaganda for the expansionist claims of the new dynasty as heirs of the great hero-kings of the past, particularly 'Arthur', as an accurate transcription of earlier documents. This at any rate is Oliver Padel's theory. Notably, the book left out Maelgwyn and almost all of the history of Gwynedd itself and concentrated on the legendary history of the 'pan-British' kings like Vortigern and Arthur – a template for Merfyn to follow?

The recent Mercian successes made it especially important to revive the power and pretensions of Gwynedd to emulate its glory in the early sixth century. But if Nennius was directed by his sovereign in what he wrote, the king's intention was to promote 'British' rather than narrow Gwynedd patriotism, as the deeds of the royal line of Gwynedd were not played up in the book. Possibly Merfyn did not feel comfortable having the line he had replaced, that of Maelgwyn, eulogised? Or did the Church dislike Maelgwyn as a patron of Druids and a possible homosexual?

Merfyn's son Rhodri 'Mawr' ('The Great') succeeded his father in 844 and inherited Powys, weakened by repeated Mercian assaults, from his maternal uncle Cyngen around 853. He married into the royal line of Ceredigion/Seissylwg which duly passed to his sons, indicating a renewed effort for Welsh unity in the face of attacks from Vikings as well as Saxons. He defeated the first major Viking attack on Anglesey in an internationally celebrated battle in 856, killing their leader Gorm, but still faced attacks from Mercia and in 865 king Burghred's army penetrated along the coast to Anglesey. Luckily the invasion of eastern England by the Viking 'Great Army' in 865–6 forced Burghred to abandon his campaigns, and in 875

Mercia was split in two and its eastern half settled by the Vikings. At the end of his reign Rhodri had to flee to Ireland when the Vikings of Dublin returned to Anglesey in 877, and gathered mercenaries to retake his kingdom. He was killed by Mercia's new king Ceolwulf II, a Viking nominee so probably acting in co-ordination with them, in a new attack on his return in 878.

Rhodri's sons, led by the senior Anarawd, defeated the Mercians heavily in 880/1 on the River Conwy. They shared the kingdom, but with Anarawd ruling most of the heartland, including Anglesey and Powys; Merfyn died in 904 and Cadell, ruler of Ceredigion and Seissyllwg to the south-west, in 909. The Mercian preoccupation under 'Ealdorman' Aethelred and his wife Aethelfleda, Alfred's daughter, on regaining their eastern lands taken by the Vikings, then ended the threat from the east until the establishment of the newly united Kingdom of England led to a permanent danger from a far stronger neighbour across Offa's Dyke. Anarawd even entered into alliance with the new Viking kingdom of York in the 880s. He attempted to overrun Dyfed and Morgannwg in the early 890s, but faced invasion from the Danes in East Anglia with a major raid in 894. The Viking army currently operating in south-eastern England against King Alfred of Wessex penetrated to Shropshire on a raid in 893, being besieged by the local militia at Buttington Walls, and a second raid led to the Vikings seizing Chester, a useful fortified town with river access for their ships, and ravaging the nearby part of Gwynedd. Anarawd tried to assert his power over the South Welsh rulers, but was forced to recognise their new protector, Alfred, as his overlord, and allegedly to accept re-baptism. The succession of Anarawd's brother Cadell to Dyfed by marriage in 905 however opened up the new kingdom of 'Deheubarth' to close alliance with Gwynedd by peaceful means. The main threat was now from Wessex, which under Alfred's son Edward 'the Elder' merged its forces with Mercia's to reconquer the 'Danelaw' of eastern Mercia and East Anglia in 914–18. On Aethelfleda's death in 918 Edward was to dispossess her daughter Egwynn and merge the two kingdoms, creating a new Kingdom of England.

The Tenth and Eleventh Centuries:
Sporadic Welsh Unity and the English Threat

Anarawd's son Idwal succeeded in 916 to face the threat of a permanent merger of Wessex, Mercia and the Danelaw, and in 918 he was probably one of the Welsh kings who obeyed a summons to visit the victorious

Edward at the Mercian capital Tamworth; he certainly recognised him as his overlord (according to Saxon sources).

The Danish kingdom of York now submitted to Edward too in 919, and he set up a base at Chester to counter raids from the Vikings in Man and Dublin and overawe the Norse settlers in Lancashire and Cumbria. This implicitly threatened Gwynedd too. Idwal was forced to meet the new king of united England, Edward's son Athelstan, at Hereford in 926 to delineate the Anglo-Welsh frontier and was his tributary ally. He was required to attend Athelstan's court, visiting Exeter in 928, King's Worthy (Hampshire) in 932, and Winchester and Nottingham in 934, and in the latter year assisted him against the Scots. Also at court twice at Dorchester to witness charters in 935, he prudently stayed out of the Viking-'Celtic'/Scots coalition against Athelstan in 937, and so avoided its crushing defeat at the unknown site of 'Brunanburh' in 937; its leader, Olaf Guthfrithson of Dublin, was as great a threat to Gwynedd as to England. Athelstan's death in 939 led to Olaf retaking York and temporarily the eastern Midlands, but Idwal avoided helping him against the new king Edmund. He finally attacked Edmund in 942 after the latter had regained the Danelaw, possibly missing his best chance; did he wait until the dangerous Olaf was dead and the new Viking rulers of York were less of a threat? Presumably acting as an ally of the latter against the Anglo-Saxon kings from Wessex, Idwal miscalculated; he was defeated and killed with his son Elisedd. His other sons Iago and Idwal were expelled from Gwynedd and the throne passed temporarily from the senior line to Hywel of Deheubarth, son of Rhodri 'Mawr's younger son Cadell and now the temporary unifier of most of Wales.

On Hywel's death in 950 the throne returned to the main line in the person of Iago ap Idwal, son of Hywel's predecessor. He technically ruled with his younger brother Idwal Ieauf until the latter's murder in 969, their feuds continuing to weaken the kingdom. The two brothers invaded Deheubarth in 952, and in retaliation Hywel's sons raided Gwynedd in 954 but were defeated at Llanrwst in the Conwy valley. Idwal's son Hywel continued the feud; both rivals were forced to attend their overlord Edgar of England at Chester in 973 when the latter is supposed to have made his Celtic vassals row him on the Dee. Having temporarily expelled Iago in 974, Hywel finally removed him in 979; both factions had been using Viking mercenaries. Hywel succeeded in killing Iago's son Custennin (Constantine), but failed in his efforts to overrun Deheubarth in the early 980s despite the aid of 'Ealdorman' Aelfhere of Mercia. He was killed by the English in 986. His brother Cadwaladr was then killed by his cousin

Maredudd of Deheubarth, who imposed the second union of the kingdoms from 986 to 999; Hywel's son Cynan maintained the union from 999 to 1005 before the two kingdoms split again. Possibly Maredudd reached an agreement with Cynan sooner than hand his unified kingdom on to his closer relatives, his late brother Einion's sons, due to a family feud.

Gwynedd then passed to Llywelyn ap Seisyll, an intriguing character in that he was the only 'outsider' – not in the direct male line of descent – to secure the throne. He was supposedly the grandson of Elisedd, a younger son of Anarawd, and was married to Maredudd of Deheubarth's daughter Angharad. He ruled Gwynedd for eighteen years, and for the last five (from 1018) Deheubarth too after killing the usurper Aeddan. In 1022 he saw off an obscure invader, Rhain ap Maredudd. Iago ap Idwal ap Meurig then took the throne when Llywelyn died in 1023, and was succeeded by Llywelyn's son Gruffydd, the most successful of the Welsh dynasts since Hywel 'Dda', in 1039.

Gruffydd now drove his predecessor's son Cynan into exile in Ireland. He was strong enough to defeat the English heavily at Rhyd-ar-Groes near Welshpool in 1039, killing Earl Leofric of Mercia's brother Edwin, and in 1044 to impose the final union of the two kingdoms, killing his rival Hywel ap Edwin of Deheubarth in a battle at the mouth of the River Teifi. He then faced Gruffydd ap Rhydderch, probable ruler of Glywysng in Glamorgan, in a war for Deheubarth, and called on his new ally Earl Swein of Hereford (eldest son of the English chief minister, Earl Godwin) for help.

Swein ravaged his enemy's lands in 1046, but got into trouble with King Edward for seducing the Abbess of Leominster on his return from the campaign and was exiled; instead Edward appointed his half-French nephew Ralph of the Vexin to rule Herefordshire. Gruffydd's impressive and warlike rule of all Wales was interrupted by his rival Gruffydd ap Rhydderch's seizure of Deheubarth from 1047–55, but he reconquered the latter and killed his rival. He followed that up by regaining the part of Herefordshire west of the Wye from the English in 1055 by defeating Earl Ralph, who had brought in Norman knights to build castles and had been teaching his levies to fight on horseback in the Norman fashion – before the 'Norman Conquest' made such actions routine. But the English cavalry ran away from the Welsh, and Gruffydd won the battle and proceeded to a spectacular sack of Hereford. The following year he killed the new bishop Leofgar of Hereford in battle, and was able to force the English 'strongman' Earl Harold Godwinsson, brother of his ally of the 1040s Earl Swein, to cede Ewias to him. This first official re-annexation of lost Welsh territory by force – Offa had probably abandoned some Mercian settlements in Radnor to the Welsh in the eighth century – was the greatest Welsh military triumph for centuries, and when King Edward's ineffective nephew Earl Ralph of Hereford died in 1057 Harold had to take over the defence of the earldom in person.

Gruffydd countered the House of Godwine by an alliance with their rival Earl Aelfgar, Leofric's son, ruler of East Anglia in 1051–7 and of Mercia in 1057–62 (?), whose daughter Edith he married – probably in the late 1050s. He helped the exiled Aelfgar to force his way back into his earldom when he was exiled on two occasions with military assistance, first in 1055 and then in 1058. On the first occasion Leofric failed to intervene after Gruffydd's success at Hereford and thus forced the king and Earl Harold to allow his son's restoration; on the latter occasion Aelfgar fled to Gwynedd and joined up with an army of Hebridean Vikings. But then Gruffydd faced a sustained attack by Harold which started in midwinter 1062–3 with a raid on his headquarters at Degannwy. Given the lack of any intervention from his ally Mercia, his father-in-law Aelfgar had probably died and Harold was seeking to destroy him as a threat to the Godwinsson family. He was eventually driven into the mountains by superior English numbers, with Harold's brother Tostig bringing Northumbrian troops into Gwynedd too, and was killed in August 1063 by one of his followers, Cynan ap Iago (a dynastic rival?), as Earl Harold ravaged Gwynedd in a prolonged English campaign. His head was purportedly put on the prow of Harold's ship as it sailed back to the royal court at Gloucester. His widow Edith, probably not more than twenty at the time, was later married by his nemesis Harold in 1066 to cement an uneasy alliance between Harold, now King of England, and her brothers Earls Edwin of Mercia and Morcar of Northumbria; Gruffydd and Edith's daughter Nest married a Norman baron around 1075. Edith had a son or twins by Harold, born posthumously after their father's death at the Battle of Hastings as Edith sheltered from the Norman invasion at Chester. Her subsequent fate is unclear but she may have died in Spain in the 1080s.

Gruffydd was the most successful Welsh ruler since the sixth century in territorial terms, but proved unable to resist English military superiority even under the pre-Norman kingdom. On his death Earl Harold imposed the rule of his half-brothers Bleddyn and Rhiwallon to the joint kingdom of Gwynedd and Powys. They were the sons of Angharad, daughter of Maredudd of Deheubarth (d. 999) so they had a claim to that kingdom too, and the obscure noble Cynan ap Gwerstan; Bleddyn was married to

Haer, daughter of Cilinn ap Yplaidd, a landowner in Eifionyd. Bleddyn killed Gruffydd's two sons when they attempted to overthrow him at the Battle of Mechain in 1070, but was betrayed and defeated in battle (and either killed then or murdered later) by Rhys ap Owain, a rival contender for Deheubarth, in 1075. His eulogy remembered him as generous, just, and not self-seeking unlike most of the other current princes. The throne was seized by an 'outsider' of dubious lineage, the princeling Trahaern of Arwystli.

Trahaern defeated and evicted his rival Gruffydd ap Cynan (born around 1055), a descendant of Iago ap Idwal and son of Cynan ap Iago by an Irish Norse princess, Ragnhild of Dublin, who had briefly ruled Lleyn in 1075 but been driven out due to local anger at his plundering Viking mercenaries. Trahaern was killed at Mynydd Carn in Pembrokeshire in 1081 when the latter returned from Ireland and joined forces with a claimant to Deheubarth, Rhys ap Tewdr, at St David's under the auspices of the bishopric. They challenged Trahaern's ally Caradog ap Gruffydd ap Rhydderch, who Trahaern aided. The vacant throne passed to Gruffydd ap Cynan, but Trahaern's family retained the rule of Arwystli.

The Norman Conquest and Resistance: Gruffydd ap Cynan and Owain Gwynedd

The Norman barons of Cheshire under Robert of Rhuddlan, cousin and lieutenant of William I's Earl of Chester, Hugh d'Avranches, had been active in Gwynedd's coastal strip since around 1073 when Robert built Rhuddlan Castle and secured rule of the lower Conwy valley. Gruffydd ap Cynan had sought his support in 1075, but they had then fallen out and Gruffydd attacked Rhuddlan. They now invaded the main part of Gwynedd in 1081. Gruffydd ap Cynan was captured at Corwen and imprisoned by Hugh at Chester Castle for up to a decade, and the Normans conquered most of the coastal territories as far west as Caernarfon in the early 1080s. Coastal castles were erected on a strip of territory as far west as opposite Mon/Anglesey and much of later Flintshire was incorporated in the earldom as two new English 'hundreds'. An English 'borough' was founded at Rhuddlan and a first castle at Caernarfon, and in 1092 an Anglo-Norman clerk, Hervey, became Bishop of Bangor. Much of the local church's lands were taken for the abbey of St Werburgh, Chester. Imprisoned at Chester for years, Gruffydd eventually secured his release as client ruler of Anglesey around 1091 and was able to kill Robert of Rhuddlan in a sudden 'strike' with three warships against his castle in July 1093. Seeing the raiders carrying loot back to their ships, Robert furiously charged down onto the beach with a couple of men to recapture it and was overpowered and killed; his men had to watch as the raiders then cut his head off and stuck it on the prow of their warship. Gruffydd joined in a revolt on the mainland in 1094, but had to flee to his mother's homeland, Ireland. A second exile followed his brief return in 1098 as William II's 'Marcher' vassals, the Earls Hugh of Chester and Hugh of Shrewsbury invaded, but after the Normans clashed with King Magnus of Norway's fleet over Anglesey and the Earl of Shrewsbury was killed by an arrow fired from a longship into the Norman ranks on the beach the invaders retreated. Gruffydd was able to return.

In the 1100s he regained most of his ancestral lands on the mainland as well, as his main foe the new Earl of Shrewsbury, Robert de Belleme, fell foul of the new King Henry I for backing his brother Robert of Normandy in the 1101–2 civil war and was dispossessed. Gruffydd found it politic to submit to the invading Henry in 1114, but remained practically independent. The Earldom of Chester passed from Hugh to his son Richard, who was drowned with Henry's son William in the 'White Ship' disaster in November 1120; the Welsh then attempted to regain the lands lost to the Earldom but were driven back in 1121 by the new Earl, Hugh's sister's son Ranulf 'le Meschin' (d. 1129). Under the latter's son Ranulf 'le Gernon', poisoned in 1153, the earldom became enmeshed in the civil war of 1138–53 between King Stephen and the Empress Matilda and Gwynedd had a respite from attack. But its church remained under threat of the legal supremacy claimed by the archbishopric of Canterbury over all Wales; in 1120 the new Bishop of Bangor, David 'the Scot' (Irish or Scots?), was consecrated at Westminster. Gruffydd meanwhile lent support to the major Welsh rebellion against the Anglo-Noman settlers in Deheubarth in 1136 after Henry I died, his daughter Gwenllian having eloped with their leader Gruffydd ap Rhys (who Gruffydd had earlier given sanctuary in Gwynedd but tried to hand over to Henry I) some time around 1113–15. The latter was seeking his father-in-law's aid in 1136 when Gwenllian was killed attacking the settlers at Kidwelly/Cydweli Castle.

Also killed in action against the Anglo-Normans, in 1132, was Gruffyd's eldest son and heir Cadwallon – whose name indicates his father's desire to revive the memory of the kingdom's greatest war-leader from the seventh century, conqueror of Northumbria.

Gruffydd died in 1137 aged over eighty, the longest-lived ruler in medieval Gwynedd. He and his second son and successor Owain Gwynedd (born around 1100) were the most powerful rulers of Welsh-governed Wales, and seemed to have restored Gwynedd to its ancestral power – provided that they avoided a direct clash with the more powerful Kingdom of England, aided by the English civil war in the 1140s, and a bardic revival took place. Owain even managed to fully annex all the sub-principalities linked to Cunedda's sons' families, Meirionydd and the eastern lands of Clywd, and during the 1140s took over parts of Powys. In 1150 he defeated Madoc ap Maredudd of Powys, his daughter Susanna's husband, at the Battle of Ewloe/Coleshill and took the cantref of Ial from him, holding it until King Henry II made him return it in 1157. He secured Ceredigion, in revolt against its Anglo-Norman lords since 1136, for his brother Cadwaladr who gradually took over the kingdom from its northern frontier with Gwynedd. Cadwaladr also took Gwynedd troops to aid the Marcher (Chester and Gloucester) forces of Empress Matilda, cousin and rival claimant to King Stephen's throne, at the battle of Lincoln in 1141. Stephen was captured but had to be released after a revolt drove Matilda out of London and her brother Earl Robert of Gloucester, greatest of the Marcher lords, was captured to force an exchange.

Cadwaladr murdered his neighbour Anarawd of Deheubarth, Gwenllian's stepson, who was about to marry their sister, in 1143 – presumably to weaken the threat from Deheubarth to take over Ceredigion, to which both kingdoms had claims. He faced revolt in Ceredigion so Owain exiled him. He fled to Ireland and fought his way back into Ceredigion with an army of Irish mercenaries, and Owain had to accept his return to prevent a costly civil war. Owain had recently lost his eldest illegitimate son and designated heir, Rhun (called after the great sixth-century ruler), in battle (1142). He now sent his eldest surviving illegitimate son Hywel (whose mother was Irish) to assist the ruler of Deheubarth, Cadwaladr's victim and Anarawd's brother Cadell, to besiege Carmarthen and retake Llansteffan in 1146 and Wiston in 1147, reconciling the two kingdoms (implicitly at Cadwaladr's expense). In 1150–1 Hywel drove Cadwaladr's son Cadfael out of his lands in Ceredigion and imprisoned him but was later expelled. After Cadwaladr's second exile in 1152 Cadwaladr took refuge with the future Henry II, now fighting Stephen and probably well disposed to the Gwynedd prince for his help to Henry's mother Matilda. Succeeding to the English throne in 1154 and reviving royal power, Henry forced Cadwaladr's restoration on Owain in an expedition in 1157 and made him hand back Oswestry and Whittington Castles which he had taken from the English around 1146.

Meanwhile the Anglo-Normans were able to set up a new bishopric at St Asaph, held by nominees of the Archbishopric of Canterbury, which claimed religious suzerainty over all the Welsh bishoprics in 1143, the first bishop being Gilbert. But Owain kept its holders – including the Marcher historian of Wales' legendary past, Geoffrey of Monmouth, in 1151–5 – from actually residing there into the 1160s.

The 1157 English invasion of Gwynedd saw Henry's main army, joined by Madoc ap Maredudd of Powys, ambushed in the forests near Hawarden; the king was nearly killed. His fleet's landing on Anglesey was repulsed, but his weight of numbers told and Owain was forced to surrender hostages and the disputed eastern cantref of Tegeingl. Henry constructed new castles at Basingwerk and Rhuddlan to protect his gains, and in 1163 Owain had to journey to Woodstock near Oxford to do homage to his new overlord. Henry was still ambitious to extend his rule, but his massive overland march into Mid Wales to gain more territory in 1165 proved a weather-hampered failure with the threatened rulers rallying around Owain's leadership at Corwen. Even Rhys ap Gruffydd of Deheubarth, Owain's nephew, came to aid him, and Henry's troops floundered in heavy rain in the forests and could not reach Corwen.

After the English had retired Owain regained Basingwerk and Rhuddlan. His leadership of the Welsh princes was even acknowledged by the English whose legal documents referred to him as 'prince of the Welsh', senior to the other princes of Powys and Deheubarth. Nor could the Archbishopric of Canterbury, held from 1162 by the aggressive ex-chancellor Thomas Becket, force Owain to accept its nominee as the Bishop of Bangor; when Becket refused to consecrate Owain's choice, Arthur, Owain had him consecrated in Ireland instead and kept the English candidate out of Gwynedd. Owain died on 28 April 1170, aged around seventy; his power and reputation were unparalleled for a post-1063 ruler of Wales but his achievement (like that of Rhys of Deheubarth later) was hampered by his lack of a sole, unchallenged heir.

The division of Gwynedd between Cadwaladr and Owain's large family on his death in 1170 led to a further bout of inter-family strife. Owain had at least two sons by his first wife, Gwladys, the eldest being Iorweth, who was married to the daughter of Madoc ap Mareudd of Powys, and two more by his own cousin, Cristin, daughter of Goronwy ap Owain, plus assorted bastards who had rights to lands too under Welsh law. Owain's eldest illegitimate son, the poet Hywel, was exiled by his half-brothers Dafydd and Rhodri (the sons of Cristin), collected an army from Ireland to invade, and was killed by them in an ambush at Pentreath in Anglesey, allegedly at the instigation of their mother Cristin. His death, and that of his seven foster brothers, the sons of Cynfor, was lamented in a famous poem. Maelgwyn, one of Owain's illegitimate sons, received the heartland of the kingdom, Anglesey, but was expelled in 1173 by his half-brothers Dafydd and Rhodri, followed by the oldest surviving brother Iorweth 'Flatnose' of Arfon. The latter may never have ruled any lands (due to physical infirmity?) despite some observers, e.g. the clerical historian Giraldus Cambrensis, calling him Owain's only legitimate son; the Church regarded Owain's marriage to Cristin illegal, and Dafydd and Rhodri thus ineligible for the throne, as they were cousins.

The identification of an obscure, younger and landless illegitimate son of Llywelyn, Madoc, with the supposed founder of a 'Welsh colony' in the south-eastern U.S. is sixteenth-century; no contemporary records refer to him. The first, mid-sixteenth-century account only calls him a 'voyager', not naming his destination, and a contemporary later Triad refers to him as one of three voyagers who sailed off to unknown places with his followers. It was the Elizabethan 'magus' Dr John Dee who furthered the 'Welsh colony' theory to give legal grounds for Elizabethan claims to America. (The precise identification of the 'Welsh Indians' with the Mandans on the Upper Missouri was only made in the 1790s, following claims that a Welsh missionary had been able to understand their native language; the cultural revivalist 'Iolo Morgannwg' enthusiastically joined in the cause.) Eventually the conflict stabilised with the rule of Owain's sons by Cristin, Dafydd in east and Rhodri in west Gwynedd, the River Conwy dividing their lands. Dafydd married Emma de Laval, half-sister of Henry II.

The Career and Overlordship of Llywelyn 'Fawr'

Dafydd, marrying Henry II's half-sister as a royal ally with a grant of lands in England, even temporarily deposed Rhodri, until the latter escaped from prison and managed to regain Anglesey and Arfon. Dafydd, the more powerful of the brothers, was heavily defeated in battle on the lower Conwy by two nephews late in 1194 and forced to hand over lands to them. The more dynamic of the two, Llywelyn ap Iorweth, was apparently already in rebellion against Dafydd in his mid-late teens, in 1188, according to Giraldus. He defeated Rhodri, who had already been driven out of Anglesey by his nephews (the sons of Cynan) in 1191 and had had to seek Viking help to return, in two battles in Anglesey in 1194 and thence ruled part of the west. He defeated and reduced Dafydd to nominal co-rulership in a battle on the Conwy in 1195 and imprisoned and exiled him in 1197/8, driving him and his family into England as refugees to live on the lands Henry II had given them at Hales in Shropshire. (Dafydd died there in 1203.) He then set about removing his other relatives from their domains, aided by the death of his main rival Gruffydd ap Rhodri of Anglesey and Arfon in 1200. His eviction of his cousin Maredudd ap Cynan from Lleyn in 1201 and Meirionydd in 1202 completed his triumph, and in 1201 the English government recognised his current possessions and allowed the supremacy of Welsh law in them. He was also aided by the military eclipse of his powerful neighbour Gwenwynwyn of Powys, defeated by royal Justiciar Geoffrey FitzPeter at Painscastle in 1198. In 1202 he attacked Powys again, though decisive victory was prevented by the troops of the cantref of Penllyn refusing to aid him; he deposed their lord, Eliseg, in retaliation.

Llywelyn, who came to regard himself as 'Prince of Wales' as the senior ruler among all the Welsh dynasts, restored the pre-eminence that Gwynedd had held under Gruffydd ap Llywelyn in 1055–63, seizing part of Powys as King John deposed its ruler Gwenwynwyn in 1208 and also taking back Ceredigion to impose client-rulers. As of 1226 his elder, illegitimate son Gruffydd was his viceroy in southern Powys, later being superseded by his younger son and heir Dafydd. But he lacked his eleventh-century predecessor's full control of Wales as he could not either regain the south coast from the Anglo-Norman settlers or depose the remaining rulers of Deheubarth and Powys. Nor did his marriage to Joan (Siwan), born around 1190, the illegitimate daughter of King John and a certain Clementia, and a formal treaty of vassalage (1205) mean that John would allow Llywelyn to build up an unchallenged position in Wales.

His marriage brought him into Marcher politics when his unfaithful wife had an affair with the Baron of Brecon and the 'Three Castles' of the upper Monnow valley, William de Braose, who Llywelyn captured in 1228 and 'invited' to his court as an ally. William was required to hand over Builth to Llywelyn, who thus gained a valuable foothold on the upper Wye. He was found in compromising circumstances with Princess Joan in Llywelyn's bedchamber in February 1230 and was executed in a famous scandal, later turned into a Welsh-language play, *Siwan*, by the 1930s author Saunders Lewis. Joan was retained as Llywelyn's wife, and died at Aber on 2 February 1237; her husband founded a nunnery at Llanfaes in her honour. One daughter, Helen, was married off to Earl Ranulf of Chester's heir John 'the Scot' (d. 1237) and after he died was forced by Henry III to marry an English baron, Roger de Quincey. Another daughter, Gwladys (d. 1251), married Roger de Mortimer, Lord of Wigmore, and was the ancestress of the later Mortimers who became Richard II's heirs and as such posed a threat from 1399 to the House of Lancaster. One of her descendants, Edward IV, took the English throne in 1461. A third daughter, Margaret, married (1219) the nephew of Joan's later executed lover William de Braose, John de Braose, whose father and grandmother had been murdered by King John so he was nicknamed 'Tadody' ('the Fatherless'). The girls were thus used to further Llywelyn's dynastic links to major Marcher families. One of Llywelyn's other daughters by either Joan or a mistress, Angharad, was married to a junior member of the Deheubarth dynasty, Maelgwyn 'Fychan', who succeeded his father to Ceredigion in 1230.

Gwynedd at the height of its power under Llywelyn 'Fawr' was still unable to repel a sustained English assault on the lowlands by John. The king was concentrating on England and Ireland after losing almost all his Continental lands to Philip Augustus of France in 1204, and his restless presence loomed large over his vassals. Llywelyn loyally aided him against King William 'the Lion' of Scotland in person in 1209, but faced his suspicion – probably over links to rebellious Marcher lords such as William de Braose of Brecon, father of his later ally. After De Braose fled to Ireland in 1209 John pursued him there, while Earl Ranulf of Chester and Bishop Peter des Roches invaded the coastal lowlands of Gwynedd. Llywelyn, who was building new castles in stone in the English style (most notably at Dolwyddelan in the upper Conwy valley) had to pull down his new castle at Degannwy and retire into the mountains. John then invaded in person in 1211. Llywelyn had to take refuge in his mountain fastnesses as John occupied the Conwy valley, and relied on the English running short of time and supplies to secure a reasonably favourable treaty through Joan's mediation with her father. He handed over the lands east of the Conwy but retained the heartland of Gwynedd, as his grandsons were both to be forced to do (1247 and 1277). He was lucky in that a challenge from his cousin Owain failed in 1212; John could not invade again that year due to fear that his mutinous barons would seize him during the planned campaign, and the English barons' revolts kept John preoccupied thereafter. Pope Innocent absolved Llywelyn from his oath to the king, who was currently under a Papal interdict, in 1212. Already in 1212 he could enter into some sort of pact with the other princes of Wales whereby they recognised him as their superior, and negotiate on their behalf with John's enemy Philip Augustus of France.

Having reclaimed the disputed Perfeddwladd, the 'Four Cantrefs' east of the Conwy, in 1213 while John faced invasion from the Pope and France, he used the confrontation between John and his barons in 1215 to resume his authority in central Wales and lead a large army South into Deheubarth, one of whose feuding rulers, Rhys 'Gryg' of Cantref Mawr, had arrived at his court asking for help against his nephews and the English. A mild winter enabled him to retake Ceredigion and overrun the major English castles of Cardigan and Carmarthen, along with Gower. The following year the contending princes of Deheubarth (Rhys, his brother Maelgwyn, and their nephews) were summoned to a meeting at Aberdyfi/Aberdovey where Llywelyn imposed his own division of their lands as their overlord. He granted custody of Swansea Castle to Rhys on his authority in 1217. He also concluded a treaty with John's foe, King Philip Augustus of France, in his role as overlord of all the Welsh – a strategic alliance to be repeated by Owain Glyndŵr after 1400.

Gwynedd's period of greatest authority among the other Welsh princes (1212–40 and 1258–77) notably coincided with English preoccupation elsewhere, and depended on the personal prowess and power of the two Llywelyns rather than any permanent acceptance by the other Welsh princes of legal and military subordination to any ruler of Gwynedd. But in the youth of Henry III Llywelyn 'Fawr' was temporarily able to build up as much dominance over Wales as was practicable for a realm much weaker in resources than its English neighbour, and could even have one son – his son by John's daughter, Dafydd, not the elder Gruffydd – recognised as sole heir to avoid a repeat of the civil wars after 1170.

In defiance of Welsh custom he chose to avoid the division of his lands between his legitimate and illegitimate sons, and secured Papal approval in 1222 for following the Europe-wide practice of inheritance solely by his legitimate son, i.e. Dafydd. The Welsh lords were duly summoned to assemblies in 1226 and 1238 to swear fealty to Dafydd. Gruffydd was given two cantrefs in the early 1220s, took an army to help drive the Earls of Pembroke out of Ceredigion in 1223, and became his father's sub-ruler of annexed southern Powys (Gwenwynwyn's former lands) in 1226, but was imprisoned at Degannwy from 1228–34 and as of 1238 was only allowed to rule Lleyn.

The civil war in England in 1216–17 gave Llywelyn the chance to seize the territories of his enemy Gwenwynwyn in southern Powys in 1216, and in 1217 he made a major progress through South Wales unopposed, receiving the submission of Swansea and marching through Deheubarth as far as Haverfordwest. His subsequent treaty with the regency government of England at Worcester in March 1218 granted Llywelyn the custody of Cardigan and Carmarthen Castles for the king's minority and recognised his annexation of southern Powys in return for his fealty. The two castles, and Montgomery, were regained by the English in 1223 as the newly adult Henry and his principal South West Wales Marcher lords, the Marshals of Pembroke, turned their attention to restoring their local power. But the aggressive new Earl of Pembroke (1219), the ex-regent's son William, and his brothers Richard and Gilbert all died young, and for much of the late 1220s and early 1230s they were at odds with the king's government and in semi-revolt so they lacked royal aid to tackle Gwynedd. Llywelyn's strong position in central and southern Wales remained intact for his lifetime, and the English sought his help in ordering lords such as Rhys 'Gryg' of Cantref Mawr to return disputed territories in 1220. One of these areas, Gower, was handed over to Llywelyn's new son-in-law (1219), John de Braose, Lord of Bramber in Sussex, of the senior line of the Lords of Brecon, whose family retained it throughout the thirteenth century.

When he executed William de Braose early in 1230 the latter's lands passed to his daughters (Builth to Dafydd's wife), and King Henry granted Brecon and thus the most powerful southern Marcher estates to his senior minister and commander Hubert de Burgh, who had successfully defended Dover Castle against the French in 1216. In retaliation Llywelyn used the convenient deaths of two major Marcher earls who held the main estates in South West and South East Wales, Pembroke and Gloucester, to join in a revolt by their tenants and by the local princes – who had to seek his permission to break the peace with the English first. In June–July 1231 he retook Montgomery, Radnor, Hay, Brecon, and other central Marcher castles and then moved on south to Neath and west to retake Carmarthen and Cardigan, reasserting his power in the south, while the inexperienced Henry moved up the Wye to retake Painscastle but then stayed inactive there for weeks. A truce was finally arranged with the English at Brocton in Shropshire in March 1234, and renewed in June the following year at Myddle – as it turned out, permanently.

Llywelyn was left supreme within those lands held by the Welsh rulers, and in 1234 the English government relied on him to return some lands in northern Glamorgan seized by local rebels. He tied his Welsh junior princes to him by bonds of fealty and by requiring legal suits to appear in his courts. The difficulty – apart from the lack of any historical tradition or legal precedents to back up these initiatives – was that Llywelyn's supremacy rested on personality rather than long-recognised rights and he had restive junior princes, particularly in Powys. He sought to play up the supposed tradition of primacy by Gwynedd in Wales with promotion of the overlordship of his ancestor Maelgwyn within Wales in the sixth century. As of the late 1230s he was weakening after a stroke in 1236 and his wife's death in 1237, and it is probable that the oaths taken to his son Dafydd in October 1238 implied that the latter was now effective co-ruler.

'The early genealogy', from Egerton Phillimore's 'The Annales Cambriae and Old Welsh Geneaologies from Harleian Mss. 3589', in *Y Cymmrodor* vol. IX (1888), pp. 141–83:

Guozcein – Cein – Tacit – Patern – Aetern – Cunedda – Einiaun Girt – Iauhir – Calgolaun (i.e. Catwallaun) – Mailcun (i.e. Maelgwyn) – Run – Beli – Iacob – Catman (i.e. Cadfan) – Catgalluan (i.e. Cadwallon) – Catgualart (i.e. Cadwaladr) – Iutgual (i.e. Idwal) – Rotri – Cynan –Eithil (i.e. Eissylt, daughter) – Mermin (i.e. Merfyn) – Rotri (i.e. Rhodri 'Mawr').

The earlier names, to Cunedda, are those of the rulers of the Votadini under Roman rule; presumably 'Tacit' is the Roman name 'Tacitus'.

Name	Date of accession	Date of death/ dep.	Years reigned
Cunedda	*c.* 400/440?		
Einion 'Yrth' ('the Impetuous')	Mid-fifth century?		
Catwallaun 'Longhand'	Later fifth century?	*c.* 500?	
Owain 'Dangwyn'	*c.* 500?	*c.* 520?	*c.* 20?
Maelgwyn ('the Tall', 'Pendragon')	*c.* 520?	*c.* 547	*c.* 25?
Cynglas ap Owain (sub-king of 'Rhos' since 520s)	*c.* 547	*c.* 552?	*c.* 5?
Rhun ap Maelgwyn	*c.* 552?	*c.* 580?	*c.* 28?

Beli	*c.* 580?	?	
Iago ap Beli	End of sixth century	*c.* 616?	
Cadfan ap Iago ('Wisest of Kings')	*c.* 616?	*c.* 625	*c.* 9?
Cadwallon ap Cadfan	*c.* 625	633/634	8/9
Cadfael	633/634	November 655?	*c.* 21?
Cadwaladr ap Cadwallon	655/656	682?	26/27?
Idwal 'the Roebuck' ap Cadwaladr	682?	715?	33?
Rhodri ap Idwal	715?	754?	39?
Caradog ap Meirion	754?	798?	*c.* 44?
Hywel ap Caradog	798?	825?	*c.* 27?
Cynan ap Rhodri	?	816?	
Merfyn 'Frych' ('the Freckled')	825	844	19
Rhodri 'Mawr' ('the Great')	844	878	34
Anarawd	878	916	38
Idwal 'Foel'	916	942	26
Hywel 'Dda ('the Good') (ruler of Dyfed; son of Rhodri's son Cadell)	942	950	8
Iago ap Idwal (with brother Idwal Ieuaf to 969)	950	979	29
Hywel ap Idwal Ieuaf	979	985	6
Cadwallon ap Idwal	985	986	1

Maredudd of Dyfed (grandson of Hywel)	986	999	13
Cynan ap Hywel	999	1005	6
Llywelyn ap Seisyll	1005	1023	18
Iago ap Idwal	1023	1039	16
Gruffydd ap Llywelyn ap Seisyll	1039	Spring 1063	23/24
Bleddyn ap Cynfyn	Spring 1063	1075	12
Trahaern of Arwystli	1075	1081	6
Gruffydd ap Cynan ap Iago ap Idwal (i)	1081	1081/1082	*c.* 1

Norman Conquest.

Gruffydd ap Cynan (ii)	*c.* 1091	1137	46?
Owain Gwynedd ap Gruffydd	1137	28 November 1170	33

Partition of Owen's dominions between his sons and his brother Cadwaladr.

Cadwaladr (Ceredigion 1136/–43, 1143–52; co-ruler from 1157)	December 1170	1172	1/2
Maelgwyn of Anglesey	December 1170	1173 (dep.)	2/3
Iorweth of Arfon	December 1170	1173 (dep.?)	2/3
Cynan of Meirionnydd	December 1170	1174	3/4

Rhodri of West Gwynedd (i)	December 1170	1190	19/20
Rhodri of West Gwynedd (ii)	1193	1194?	1?
Dafydd of East Gwynedd (Rhos/ Rhufuniog)	December 1170	1195 (dep.)	24/25
Llywelyn 'Fawr' ('the Great') (Prince of Wales)	1195 (East)	11 Apr 1240	45
	1191/1200 (West)	11 Apr 1240	40/49
Gruffydd of Anglesey (son of Rhodri)	1190 (West)	1200 (dep.)	10
Maredudd ap Cynan of Lleyn & Meirionnydd	1174	1202	28
Dafydd ap Llywelyn	11 Apr 1240	26 Feb 1246	5 years 10 months
Owain ap Gruffydd	26 Feb 1246	June 1255	9 years 4 months
Llywelyn ap Gruffydd (Prince of Wales)	Mar 1246 (West)	11 Dec 1282	36 years 9 months
	June 1255 (East)	11 Dec 1282	27 years 6 months
Dafydd ap Gruffydd	Autumn 1277 (East)	April 1283	5 years 6? months
	December 1282 (West)		4 months

English Conquest.

Owain Glyndŵr (Prince of Wales)	16 September 1400	*c.* 1411	*c.* 11

The Final Years of Gwynedd

The last Princes of Gwynedd/Wales were closely connected to current English politics, not least from Llywelyn Fawr's marriage to King John's illegitimate daughter Joan. Their son Dafydd succeeded on 11 April 1240 when Llywelyn died aged around sixty-seven. His elder half-brother Gruffydd was superseded. Dafydd had been recognised as heir by all the principal men of Wales, who Llywelyn required to do fealty to him at Strata Florida Abbey in October 1238. (He had intended a full ceremony of homage, but Henry III protested that this was illegal as he was a royal vassal.) Dafydd arrested and imprisoned Gruffydd and his eldest son Owain either before or after their father's death, but Gruffydd's wife Senena escaped to England and persuaded – and paid – Henry III to intervene on the prisoners' behalf. Dafydd was Henry III's nephew but was still rudely treated as an ordinary vassal not a sovereign prince at his post-accession meeting with Henry at Gloucester in May 1240 – even his knighting there emphasised his dependence on his patron. He had to restore Gruffydd and Owain to their lands, but the former was promptly removed to England as a hostage. His lack of power was shown up as his father's dependents and enemies mockingly reasserted their power, the Marshal family (Earls of Pembroke) seizing Cardigan and the mid-Marches baron Roger Mortimer, Dafydd's cousin, seizing Maelienydd and Gwerthyrion in southern Powys. A royal military campaign into Gwynedd saw Dafydd submitting to a new treaty at Gwerneigron (29 August), and in its confirmation later in London was required to give up Degannwy, Mold, and the eastern section of Gwynedd to England to curtail its power. Dafydd had married (1229) Isabella de Braose, daughter of the William de Braose who his father had executed in 1230 for adultery with Dafydd's stepmother Joan and Eva Marshal, daughter of the English 'regent' of 1216–19 William Marshal, Earl of Pembroke, but they had no children. Gruffydd, deported to the Tower of London as an English hostage in 1241 to be used against Dafydd if the latter displeased Henry, died on 1 March 1244 when a rope gave way as he was trying to climb down from a window in the White Tower. This led to a major revolt by angry Welsh tenants of the Marcher lords, from which Dafydd was able to regain some territory.

Gruffydd's eldest son Owain succeeded Dafydd when he died, aged under forty, on 25 February 1246 at Abergwyngregyn. He was forced to surrender as Henry's new lieutenant of Cardigan and Carmarthen Castles, Nicholas de Molis, led a royal army north from Carmarthenshire along the coast right to the new English fortress on the Conwy at Degannwy that summer (a template for Edward I's attack in 1277). Owain had to surrender much more territory to Henry – the entire 'Perfeddwlad' east of the Conwy – in the Treaty of Woodstock in April 1247.

The most effective resistance against the encroaching English (whose power was now enforced by the creeping extension of the remit of the king's courts) was from Owain's younger brother and co-ruler Llywelyn 'the Last'. Already a semi-autonomous dynast in Dyffryn Clywd in Dafydd's later years, in 1250 he secured a secret alliance with Gruffydd ap Madoc of northern Powys, and in 1252 allied with Maredudd ap Rhys 'Gryg' and Rhys Fychan of Deheubarth. If they stood by their promises they could widen any war with Henry, whose relations with his barons were deteriorating over his rash promises to aid the Pope in taking over Sicily and his favouritism for his French relatives so England might be distracted from an assault. Owain was defeated in battle at Bryn Derwin and deposed by Llywelyn in 1255. The latter regained most of the 'Perfeddwlad' from England late in 1256, and exploited Henry's troubles with his barons to improve his position. He stalled Henry's invasion in 1257, gained his acceptance of Gwynedd's reconquest of lands that Henry had handed back to Gwynedd's Welsh and English Marcher rivals in 1258, and was recognised as 'Prince of Wales' by an assembly of the senior Welsh lords called to conclude a treaty with the Scots in March 1258. He then seized Builth (with the cantref of Gwerthyrnion) from the Mortimers in 1260, took over Cedewain (on the upper Severn in northern Powys) when its ruler Owain ap Maredudd died in 1261, and in November 1262 accepted the opportunity of an attack by locals on the new Mortimer castle of Cefnllys in Maelienydd to overrun that territory too. Maelienydd was annexed to Gwynedd; in the north the royal castles of Diserth (August 1263) and Degannwy (September 1263) fell and in December 1263 Gruffydd ap Gwenwynwyn of southern Powys submitted. Llywelyn now allied himself with the baronial coalition led by Henry III's brother-in-law Simon de Montfort, Earl of Leicester, in 1263–4, and sent his troops to capture Bridgnorth for De Montfort (June 1263) and in 1264 to compel royal garrisons at Montgomery and Worcester to surrender to the earl. Usefully for him, the earl had taken control of the Earldom of Chester from Henry's aggressive heir the Lord Edward. He thus secured enhanced recognition and legal status from his ally, then in control of the captive Henry, in the Treaty of Pipton (near Hay-on-Wye) on 19 June 1265; the Montfort regime was luckily in need of his help as a Marcher revolt had just broken out, joined by Henry's heir Edward who had fled from Montfortian captivity at Hereford to join the Mortimers at Wigmore. Llywelyn's conquests were recognised, as was his title of 'Prince of Wales', and he was promised more useful border castles such as Hawarden, Ellesmere, and Painscastle; in return he was to pay £20,000 over ten years. If the English side failed to carry out the terms – which was quite likely if Earl Simon was overthrown or Henry died and the aggressive Edward took over – Llywelyn was excused from his obligations.

The Montfort entourage, with the king in tow, needed Llywelyn's help to deal with the Marcher rebellion raised by Edward and was in danger of being trapped west of the Severn, and when Earl Simon tried to sail from Newport to Bristol Edward's men burnt his ships in the Usk; eventually he was able to slip across the Severn near Worcester. Llywelyn was left exposed after Simon's defeat and death at Evesham days later but the restored royal regime was so weak they had to confirm his arrangement with Simon at Montgomery on 25 September 1267. His title and his control over all but one of his vassals were confirmed, provided that he paid fealty and homage to Henry, and he retained most of Maelienydd and Elfael – and the claims of his dispossessed brother Dafydd to a share of his lands were to be resolved by impartial, Welsh arbitrators by Welsh law and not by the king's men. He was able to enforce his control over restive vassals like Maredudd ap Rhys of Deheubarth, who was imprisoned and forced to hand over castles in 1259 as punishment for abandoning their alliance although in 1267 the English succeeded in keeping Maredudd as their vassal, not Llywelyn's. Gruffydd ap Gwenwynwyn had to acknowledge Llywelyn as his – hereditary – overlord in late 1263, as did Maredudd of Machen in South Wales in 1269; in 1269 Llywelyn supervised a division of northern Powys among rival heirs and in 1273 he built a new castle (Dolforwyn) in annexed Cedewain in southern Powys, threatening Gruffydd ap Gwenwynwyn's 'capital' at Pool.

Edward I clearly awaited his chance to reverse this and reduce Llywelyn's lands and status to that of Dafydd, as he was to do in 1277; Llywelyn's continued efforts to marry Simon's daughter Eleanor (probably arranged in 1265) in the 1270s showed his sense of honour but could not have been better calculated to arouse Edward's distrust. Eleanor's brothers, in exile in France like her, had murdered Edward's cousin and close aide Henry in Italy in 1271, and when they sent her by ship to Wales she was intercepted and taken to the English court as a prisoner. Nor was Llywelyn helped by his treacherous brother Dafydd, who had already been exiled once for plotting (1263), was restored to his lands in 1269, but in 1274 joined Gruffydd ap Gwenwynwyn to plan his brother's murder. They were discovered and fled to Edward, while Llywelyn seized their lands. He had also refused to attend Edward's Coronation in 1274 to do homage or to turn up to a meeting with the king at Chester in 1275, probably fearing arrest but enraging Edward. In spring–summer 1277 a massive English invasion was co-ordinated with one army marching across northern Powys to the Bay of Cardigan, a second taking the usual route west from Chester to the Conwy and Caernarfon, and separate local Marcher campaigns reducing Llywelyn's castles in Cedewain and Builth and forcing the princes of Deheubarth to submit. The prince, a refugee in the mountains of Arfon with his lowland possessions overrun, was forced to submit and in the Treaty of Aberconwy was reduced to the status of vassal prince of west Gwynedd and forced him to return lands to his dispossessed brothers, Owain and Dafydd (the latter in Rhos and Rhufoniog, east of the Conwy). Their other brother, Rhodri, had his claims bought out.

This time, taking no chances, the methodical Edward started building a string of massive new castles in the occupied lands (firstly at Flint, later at Rhuddlan, Aberystwyth, and Hawarden), left his foe the homages of some minor north Powys princes for his lifetime, and started to use English-law courts to put pressure on the autonomy of local Welsh law and its princely guarantor. The courts of the royal bailiffs extended their jurisdiction over the locals, while the 'Perfeddwlad' east of the Conwy was controlled by the royal Earldom of Chester; captured ex-princely castles remained under royal control. Even Llywelyn was forced to appear before the new royal judges as an ordinary litigant; as with the dispossessed or vassal princes of south-central Wales, the lesson was emphasised that Edward was in full legal control of all of Wales. It is likely that Edward used a legal dispute between Llywelyn and Gruffydd ap Gwenwynwyn over who owned the Gwynedd/Powys border cantref of Arwystli to 'tighten the screws' on or even provoke Llywelyn, as the case – now under the jurisdiction of his courts – was repeatedly delayed and dubious manoeuvres occurred. But Llywelyn was not guiltless either, as he secured local Church agreement that his earlier claim of overlordship over Gruffydd ap Gwenwynwyn was still legal, so he may have planned to depose him again.

Llywelyn was allowed by Edward to marry Eleanor de Montfort at Worcester Cathedral on 13 October 1278 with the king in charge of proceedings as overlord, but she died in childbirth in 1282. An attack by Dafydd on English-occupied east Gwynedd and his capture of Hawarden Castle on the night of 21 March 1282 sparked off another round of warfare, apparently co-ordinated with risings in central and South Wales where Llywelyn ap Gruffydd Maelor of northern Powys attacked Oswestry and some princes of Deheubarth retook Aberystwyth, Llanmyddfri and Carreg Cennen. The cautious and realistic Llywelyn was probably forced unwillingly into a war which he was likely to lose by Dafydd, who had a history of such gambles, but the Welsh had early successes despite Edward's inevitable advance to the Conwy valley and the revolt spread south to Mid Wales. After rebels there defeated Gilbert de Clare, Earl of Gloucester, at Llandeilo Llywelyn moved south to aid them, while the king's forces in the north recaptured Ruthin and Denbigh (September), Roger Mortimer put down the rebellion in the Montgomery area, and in the south the rebel castles were recaptured by Robert Tiptoft. Archbishop Peckham of Canterbury attempted to mediate as Edward prepared his forces to move in on Arfon, but all the king would offer Llywelyn was land to the value of £1,000 in England – his principality was now earmarked for confiscation.

Llywelyn was campaigning in the upper Wye valley when he was killed on 11 December 1282 at Irfon Bridge, Cilmeri. The exact circumstances are unclear but he was facing a local Marcher force under his cousin Roger, 2nd Lord Mortimer of Wigmore – who had only just succeeded his father Roger, usually on friendly terms with Gwynedd. The hiatus in local leadership following Roger senior's death probably enticed Llywelyn to intervene, while he had 'breathing space' in Arfon as the king's men had met with disaster as they attempted to construct a bridge of boats from occupied Anglesey to the mainland to invade. Llywelyn was ambushed with a few companions while separated from his main force by English troops under John Giffard of Bromfield who caught him by surprise by crossing a nearby ford; possibly there was a 'trick' offer of a truce to lure him into a false sense of security. But his identity was not recognised in the confusion so he was not 'targeted' personally; his body was only identified next day and Mortimer sent his brother Roger, Lord of Chirk, to present the Prince's head to Edward I.

The weight of resources on Edward's side meant that even Llywelyn would have been lucky to escape outright conquest once the English king returned to the fray and his successes in 1282 were bound to be reversed. Instead, it was Dafydd who was forced into flight into the mountains and was captured hiding in a cave in April 1283, being publicly executed at Shrewsbury as a traitor to the crown of England. To the victorious Edward there was no question of Dafydd being an independent prince; like the executed Bruce brothers later in Scotland, he was a treacherous vassal to be treated with contempt. A chain of huge coastal castles, the largest on the legendary site of Maximus' fortress at Caernarfon, were constructed for Edward by his Savoyard master-mason to hold Gwynedd down – and are ironically now major tourist magnets. New English-style fortified boroughs were created on the coast with Welshmen banned from residing there, both at older settlements such as Caernarfon and Conwy and at strategic new sites such as Beaumaris (1295).

After Dafydd's execution Edward I had his sons imprisoned for life in Bristol Castle and kept in secure cages at night (they were still there thirty years later), and deported Llywelyn's infant daughter Gwenllian (his own cousin) to the distant East Midlands nunnery of Sempringham so that she could not marry and beget further challengers to his rule of Wales; she died in 1337. The male heirs of Gwynedd were now represented by the descendants of Llywelyn's disinherited younger brother Rhodri. His son Thomas, living at Tatfield in Surrey, died around 1363. His son Owain 'Lawgoch' ('Red Hand') provocatively took service with the French during the Hundred Years' War so that they could use him as their candidate if they invaded Wales. Gathering a collection of exiles and utilising bardic prophecies of the recovery of the lost realm of the 'Trojan' Britons to the treacherous Saxons, he secured money and men from Charles V of France in 1372 but was forced to help him attack Guernsey first. He was then sent to aid the Castilian fleet at La Rochelle. He was murdered by an English agent to pre-empt another attack in 1378.

Rulers of Meirionnydd

A sub-kingdom of Gwynedd throughout its history. Ruled by a line of kings descended from the eponymous Meirion, allegedly the grandson of Cunedda. The only definite dates connected with these obscure rulers are the deaths in battle of Idris, Brochmael, and Cynan; the mountain of 'Cader Idris' was called after the former.

Name	Date of accession	Date of death/ dep.	Years ruled
Meirion	Late fifth century		
Catgualart	Early sixth century		
Gwrin 'of the Ragged Beard'	c. 530?		
Gwitnoth	560s?		
Gueinoth	Later sixth century		
Idris	?	632 (k.)	
Sualda	632	c. 645/650?	
Brochmael	c. 645/650?	662 (k.)	
Owain	662	?	
Iutnimet	Late seventh century		
Brochmael II	Early to mid-ninth century?		
Cynan	?	880 (k.)	

Other Sub-Kingdoms of Gwynedd

Rhos

The easternmost 'cantref', modern northern Clywd. Cynglas, the son of Owain 'White-Tooth' and cousin of Maelgwyn, succeeded the latter in Gwynedd around 549 but his family do not appear to have been able to maintain this claim to the main kingdom. Cadwal may have been killed at the Battle of Chester against Northumbria around 616.

Name	Approximate date
Cynglas (see Gwynedd)	c. 520? to c.550?
Maig	c. 550?
Cangun/Aeddan	c. 580?
Cadwal	c. 600/10?
Idgwyn	c. 616?
Einion	c. 650?

Rhufon	*c.* 680?
Meirion	*c.* 710?
Caradog	<754? to 798?

If Caradog is the ruler who died around 798, there may be one or more generations missing from the extant genealogy.

Dunoding
The southern area of Gwynedd, around Harlech.

Name	Approximate date
Dunaut	*c.* 450?
Eifion	*c.* 480?
Dingad	*c.* 510?
Meurig	*c.* 540?
Eifion	*c.* 570?
Isaac	*c.* 600?
Pobien	*c.* 630?
Pobdellw	*c.* 660?
Eifion	*c.* 690?
Brochwael	*c.* 720?
Eigion	*c.* 750?
Ieunawl	*c.* 780?

There were also obscure traditional sub-kingdoms of Gwynedd, ruled by other younger sons of Cunedda, which may or may not have been historical entities of the fifth and sixth centuries. The tenth-century genealogies composed at the time of Hywel Dda (now Harleian Mss. 3589) include the realms of Princes Afloeg (ruling northern Lleyn, west of Caernarfon), Dunod (ruling southern Lleyn and the Pwllheli-Porthmadog area), and Rhufon (ruling western Clywd); they may be no more than eponyms created from the names of 'their' principalities (Afloegion, Dunoding, and Rhufoniog). Another prince, Dogfael ap Cunedda, the 'founder' of Dogfaeling (southern Clywd), was supposedly the father of 'Glast', whose junior branch ruled the 'land of the Glaestings'.

This territory has been linked to the distant Glastonbury in Somerset, as William of Malmesbury (around 1125) referred to that town as founded by

'Glast' of the line of Cunedda. But how old and how reliable this tradition is is unclear; it would seem unlikely. The line of Glast ruling Dogfaeling may have taken over part of northern Powys in the 620s following the death of Powys' king Selyf ap Cynan at the Battle of Chester around 616.

4

RULERS OF MID WALES (POWYS)

The land of the 'Pagenses', that is, the rural district dependent on a Roman 'civitas'. The genealogy given for the line of Vortigern would seem to indicate that this city was Gloucester, the Roman 'Glevum'; but Viroconium, principal town of the Cornovii tribe, pre-Roman inhabitants of the West Midlands, may also have been the main urban centre in the fifth century. The Cornovii retained enough of a local administrative identity under the Late Empire to supply a military unit of their name to garrison Newcastle-upon-Tyne in the *Notitia Dignitatum* of around 400.

The genealogy of its rulers is preserved not only in the extant manuscripts but in a rare archaeological monument, the 'Pillar of Eliseg' near Llangollen set up in the ninth century by the last of the original dynasty, Cyngen/ Concenn (possibly faithfully re-stating an original eighth-century version). The genealogical list in the inscription, as recorded by the antiquarian Edward Lhuyd in 1696 before it became difficult to decipher, traced their line back to Vortigern, his wife Severa, and his father-in-law Magnus Maximus. After unrelenting pressure from Mercia even at a time of Viking raids, Cyngen abdicated and fled to Rome and Powys was absorbed into its stronger neighbour, Gwynedd, under Cyngen's nephew Rhodri 'Mawr'.

Note on Vortigern and Wales

This is a nickname rather than a personal name, translating as 'the overlord' or 'over-king' in concurrence with later Welsh tradition (used by Geoffrey of Monmouth and Arthurian writers) that regarded him as the senior ruler in Britain about a generation after the departure of the Romans in 410. His original name may have been in Latin 'Vitalis' or 'Vitalinus', the later Welsh genealogies and Nennius giving the former as his father's name, and in later Welsh tradition he was known as Gwerthyrn 'the Thin' or 'of the Repulsive Lips' (perhaps because he spoke Saxon). There may have been a connection with Gloucester, to which his supposed ancestor 'Gloiu' is connected, with Nennius in the *Historia Brittonum* calling him the son of 'Guitaul' (Latin 'Vitalis'), son of 'Guitolion' ('Vitalinus'), son of 'Gloiu' of Gloucester. Geoffrey of Monmouth gives the post-Roman Archbishop of London as 'Vitalinus', who if he was real may have been another relative – a member of the main aristocratic dynasty of Gloucester would be a logical candidate for senior office, the Gallic Church being dominated by such provincial nobles.

The Welsh genealogies also give an unlikely link to the rebel third-century Emperor Carausius (alias 'Casnar Wledig'): but this list may have been no more than a list of rulers in origin, not a genealogy.

It is possible that the Late Roman rural district – 'pagus' – (of the Cornovii?) governed from Gloucester or Viriconium did include the lands around Builth, and that Vortigern or his father held some sort of authority there. According to Nennius he succeeded as king (of Powys, Builth or southern Britain?) in the consulship of Theodosius (II) and Valentinian (III), that is 425, and invited the Saxons to Britain four years later. He was in dread of the Romans and 'Ambrosius' at the time as well as the Irish and Pictish raiders – the dates make it unlikely that 'Ambrosius' was Ambrosius Aurelianus, active around the 460s, unless this statement is an indication that he feared Ambrosius' dynastic claim even when his rival was a youth. The notion that he feared the Romans has been used as a hint that Vortigern was supporting the anti-Catholic 'Pelagian' heretics in Britain, people whose doctrinal challenge to the Bishop of Rome's authority was to cause the authorities to send St Germanus over to Britain on a proselytising mission in 428/9. It is noticeable that Vortigern, the main secular authority in Britain at the time of Germanus' visit, offered him no known support against the 'Pelagians'.

Vortigern was the ruler of Powys and the lands around Builth, later descending through his family and called 'Gwertheyrnion'; he was supposedly married to Severa, daughter of Emperor Magnus Maximus (d. 388), according to the genealogy written on the eighth/ninth-century 'Pillar of Eliseg'. According to the legends which Geoffrey of Monmouth and the twelfth-century Welsh compilers of assorted *Bruts* used, he usurped the throne of his nephew Constans as 'High King' of Britain by murder. (See section on the fifth century in Britain for his career as 'High King'.) Hounded by St Germanus out of Gwerthyrnion during the saint's second mission to Britain, he took refuge somewhere in North Wales – at Dinas Emrys in Arfon according to Geoffrey of Monmouth or his source. Vortigern sought to construct an impregnable fortress there. The foundations kept crumbling, and he was advised by his (Druid?) 'magicians' to sacrifice a 'boy without a father' and mix his blood with the mortar to secure the foundations. His men duly found the young 'Merlin' being addressed by his playfellows as fatherless in South Wales, kidnapped him, and was advised by him of the true cause of the problem – the two dragons, white and red (i.e. the symbols of the Saxons and the British), fighting in a pit beneath the site. He had to abandon his project and find another refuge; he was either forced into exile in Brittany or was killed in a fire at a besieged hill-fort (in Lleyn?) as Constans' brother, Ambrosius Aurelianus, took over Britain. (The *Red Book of Hergest* prefers a site in Gwent for the fire, following Geoffrey of Monmouth). There is a strong case for his presence (and death?) at Nant Gwertheyrn in the Lleyn area of Gwynedd, Nennius recounting that he fled to the 'left-handed part' of Wales – which must be the opposite region to Dyfed which was known as the 'right-handed part' ('dexter pars'), hence 'Deheubarth'. A saint with a similar name to Vortigern appears in Brittany, from which some have argued that he fled there; this may be coincidence.

John Morris has suggested in *The Age of Arthur* that the surprise appearance of a name similar to Vortigern's in eastern Irish genealogies in the fifth century, 'Fortchernn', confirms hagiographic tradition that the ending of Irish attacks on Britain around 430 involved a treaty whereby Vortigern's daughter married the son of an Irish ruler, possibly 'High King' Loeghaire. It is also a moot point what attitude Vortigern, as the superior dynastic authority in southern Britain at the time of St Germanus' missionary visit in 429, took to him and his campaign against the 'Pelagian' heretics. The originator of the doctrine, Pelagius, is presented as a Briton (or possibly Irishman) and the heresy as present in Britain and requiring the Roman Church to send Germanus over to argue with its adherents. But the contemporary *Life of St Germanus* only refers to its hero dealing with civic authorities at an unnamed town with a shrine, probably Verulamium (St Albans), rather than a ruler – and he later leads the Britons successfully against Irish raiders in hill-country without reference to local kings.

Later tradition has Germanus as a foe of Vortigern, praying for the tyrant's punishment before his fortress is consumed with fire (presumably during his second visit to Britain, around 445). Local traditions link Germanus to the Llangollen area, a possible site for his ambush of the Irish raiders, and to St Harmons ('Harmon' or 'Garmon' deriving from 'Germanus') near Rhaeadr.

Vortigern's son Pascent is supposed to have succeeded to the rule of at least part of Powys, based on the area around Builth where a minor line of rulers of his family continued to rule the cantref of 'Gwerthyrnion'. The preservation of his name in their genealogy suggests that the dynasty there actively sought to stress their superior lineage to that of the main line in Powys. Part of Powys may have been ruled for a time by Vortigern's son Categirn, a prince whose name was known to Nennius. The rule of the main kingdom of Powys was seized by the humbly born Cadell, founder of a new dynasty and posited in the hagiography of St Germanus as that holy man's slave-born candidate for the throne of an unknown king called 'Benli'. Benli, whether or not confused with Vortigern, was a tyrant whose fortress was burnt by fire from heaven on the prayers of Germanus according to Nennius; the site of his burial was at 'Foel Fenli' on Maes Mawr in the hills of Clywd.

Germanus' biographer Constantius states that Ambrosius, Vortigern's successor as 'High King', gave part of southern Powys – the Builth area – to his foe's son Pascent. Some part of Vortigern's lands may have descended to an obscure prince called 'Riocatus' ('King of Battles'), apparently Pascent's nephew. The latter was a friend of St Faustus, Bishop of Riez in Gaul in the 460s, who is probably the man who Nennius portrays as Vortigern's youngest son by an 'incestuous' marriage to his (step-?) daughter.

Sixth and Seventh Centuries: First Period of Regional Greatness?

Claims have been made that the references to Powys (or the south-eastern section of Gwynedd ruled by Owain 'White-Tooth' and Cynglas) as the 'White Land' in later Welsh literature indicate that it can be considered a candidate for the original of the 'Grail Kingdom' of legend or Arthur's kingdom. There are assorted Arthurian place-name connections, such as Arthur's traditional fostering by Ynyr (the original of 'Sir Ector') at Caer Gai near Lake Vrynwy, but there is no tradition of Arthur in the dynastic genealogies. More prosaically archaeological evidence shows that the probable 'capital', the former Roman city of Viroconium, continued to be inhabited to at least around 500 and had major building work in wood done into the sixth century. It would thus have been an important centre during campaigns against the Saxons, and was known in Nennius' *Historia* around 829 as 'Caer Guricon'. The construction of large wooden buildings there (one a hall for a ruler?) long after eastern British towns had fallen into disrepair might indicate an authority capable of co-ordinating a mobile cavalry force that would be able to use the Roman road system to strike at will against foes of the Britons throughout the island. After the decline of Viroconium, possibly as trade collapsed due to the great plague recorded for 547/9 or after encroaching Angles in the Midlands made the roads unsafe, the kingdom's principal royal residence in the later sixth century seems to have been the hill-fort of Mathrafal, safer in the hilly country to the west. Possibly the hill-fort at the Wrekin was refortified to serve as another strong point to guard the middle Severn valley, and it may be the elusive royal residence of Cyndylan in the mid-seventh century, 'Pengwern'.

By the later sixth century the ruler of Powys appears to have been Brochfael 'of the Tusks' (does this refer to his prominent teeth or to a boar's tusk or seal's tusk helmet?). He was son of Cyngen 'the Renowned' and St Tudlywystl, one of the many holy daughters of King Brychan of Brycheiniog, and a contemporary of Morgan of Morgannwg. His elder son Cynan 'of the White Shank' was supposed to have been a tyrant; according to later hagiography his younger son was St Tyssilio (d. 640), patron saint of Powys, a devout young man who refused his father's orders to do military service and trained as a monk at the monastery of Bangor-on-Dee instead. After Cynan died his widow Gwenvywyr wanted to secure her role by making Tyssilio become king and marry her, but he refused and fled to Gwynedd to join his fellow ex-student St Beuno (d. 640), founder of the Lleyn monastery of at Clynno Fawr. Later he was able to return to Powys and founded a monastery at Meifod, which became the kingdom's principal monastic centre and royal burial place.

Selyf ap Cynan, son of the ambitious queen, ruled in the early seventh century and was apparently killed by Aethelfrith of Northumbria at a crucial battle near Chester around 616. This disaster saw the Anglo-Saxons finally break through the north-west Midlands to the sea around the Dee estuary with a major victory at Bangor-on-Dee and kill not only the king but a troop of monks from the monastery praying for his victory; according to Bede Aethelfrith said that their action made them combatants. This disaster is supposed to have cut off the rulers in Wales from their kinsmen in Cumbria, though no settlement of Angles in Cheshire for the early seventh century has been found so it may have been more gradual. It is probable that from this time Powys lost control of most of any lands (possibly the old Cornovii territories) held east of the Severn valley, and that the kingdom was temporarily divided into a northern and a southern half with Eiludd (ap Cynan or ap Glast?) and Cyndrwyn ruling them respectively. If Eiludd was the son of Glast as one genealogy has it, he was from the royal line of the Gwynedd cantref of Dogfaeling, not from Powys, and so may have taken over the nearer region of Powys as the strongest local ruler after the military disaster at Chester. Cyndrwyn's lineage is uncertain so he may have been a 'usurper' too, suggesting a period of chaos in the 620s; Selyf's son Manwgan's domain is uncertain but was clearly restricted. The Welsh poetry of the era has at least one prince, Morfael, continuing to rule around Lichfield into the 640s or 650s.

In the mid-seventh century, another subject of Welsh literature was Cyndylan of Powys, ruler at Pengwern (the Wrekin or Shrewsbury?) and probably of southern Powys. He was the son of Cyndwyrn and ally of the emerging new Anglian warlord Penda, ruler of Mercia (most of the Midlands) from around 626 and a pagan but a foe of Northumbria. Cyndylan's exploits in battle against the English were hailed by the poets, the most famous poems on him being attributed to Llywarch 'Hen' though it is unlikely that that Rheged prince was still alive in the 640s or 650s. The *Canu Cyndylan* refers to his men as the 'heirs of Arthur'. Probable brother of Morfael of Lichfield, he appears to have been an ally of Penda of Mercia against Northumbria in the 640s and may have fought at the Battle of 'Maes Cogwy' or 'Cocboy', probably Oswestry, in 642 when King Oswald of Northumbria invaded the region to be killed – and ritually dismembered – by Penda. The location of the battle on or within the Powys frontier logically implies that Oswald was attacking Powys as well as Mercia. Cyndylan appears to have been killed around the mid-650s (possibly with Penda at the Battle of Winwaed, when the Mercian king was ambushed en route home from an invasion of Northumbria by its king Oswy). Penda was later supposed to have married Cyndylan's sister Heledd, and their story was revived for a Welsh-language rock opera in the 1990s. At this point in the mid-650s Mercia gained control of the upper Severn valley, though it is uncertain if the famous poem attributed to Llywarch 'Hen' referring to the desolation of Cyndylan's abandoned court after his death is contemporary. David Dumville ('Sub-Roman

Britain: History and Legend', in *History*, 1977) would prefer to ascribe the *Marwynad Cyndylan*, the posthumous lament for Cyndylan, to the ninth century, but J. Rowland's 1982 thesis 'A Study of the Saga Englynion' (University College of Wales, unpub.) argues for its contemporary composition. The poem does not make it clear that Cyndylan's realm around the Wrekin was lost to Mercia after his death, but this is a logical assumption.

Decline and Obscurity

The kingdom of Powys survived in the uplands to the west, but descended into such obscurity in the eighth century that we cannot be certain who reigned at what point or how potent a threat it remained to Mercia by the time that Offa 'the Great' constructed his famous 'Dyke' to delineate the frontier. From the genealogies, it would seem that Beli ruled in the first half of the seventh century and his son Gwylog in the second half; the latter's son Elisedd ruled in the early eighth century. He was remembered as regaining lands lost to the English, probably around 740 to 760 from his great-grandson's dates and logically at the time that Powys' local foe Mercia was distracted with the murder of its aggressive, ruthless king Aethelbald (r. 716–57) and the overthrow of his successor Beornred by the even more formidable Offa 'the Great'. Eliseg may have constructed the first 'Pillar of Eliseg' in the Vale of Llangollen, a national religious centre since the time of St Germanus around 430, to commemorate his victories; Cyngen later put up the extant Pillar (see below). Logically its commemoration of the descent of the Powys kings from Vortigern and Emperor Magnus Maximus, 'Macsen Wledig', was used as a rallying point in times of crisis from Germanic invasion such as that which had faced Vortigern and Vortimer. It may be that this Welsh revival was serious enough to induce Offa to construct a physical barrier against further raids along the frontier (and to abandon indefensible areas in Radnor). Offa certainly campaigned extensively in Wales, with a major campaign in 784 according to the *Annales Cambriae* and another at the time of the visit of a Papal legate in 786, but we do not know if his recorded penetration to Dyfed was preceded or accompanied by ravaging of Powys.

The reigns of Eliseg's son Brochfael and grandson Cadell (d. 808) are equally obscure. But in the third decade of the ninth century massive Mercian attacks on Powys resumed, with Coenwulf (d. 821), Ceolwulf, and

Beornwulf all raiding the kingdom. Ceolwulf marched right across it to Degannwy in Gwynedd shortly before his deposition, in 823, and claimed to have conquered it. As Mercian military power collapsed from 825 Cadell's son Cyngen restored the kingdom's independence if not its full power, but he still faced a raid from Mercia's temporary conqueror Egbert of Wessex around 830 and renewed pressure from the restored native dynasts later. There was also the question of the death by treachery of his elder son Gruffydd in 814, apparently due to the latter's brother Eliseg according to the *Annales Cambriae*; this presumably marked a dynastic feud and as Eliseg never succeeded as king he was presumably disgraced and exiled. Instead Cyngen's sister Nest was married to his neighbouring ruler, the new (825) king, Merfyn of Gwynedd, probably as part of an alliance against their mutual foe Mercia in the late 820s.

Their son Rhodri became the heir to Powys. In 853 a major invasion by the joint armies of Burghred of Mercia and Aethelwulf of Wessex (who had married his daughter to the former) saw Powys overrun again, and no known or successful efforts to help it by its powerful neighbour Rhodri of Gwynedd (Cyngen's nephew). If Powys had held out until the imminent Viking assaults on England after 865 it could have survived as an independent state, but the ageing Cyngen gave up the struggle, abdicated, and fled to Rome. He died there in 856. Presumably without closer relatives capable or willing to take the throne, he left his kingdom to his nephew Rhodri who merged it with Gwynedd. The two states were ruled together for the next two centuries.

Genealogies of early kings in the *Old Welsh Genealogies*, ed. Bartrum, nos. XXII, XXVI, XXX, XXXI; Vortigern's immediate family in the *Life of St Germanus*. Ancestors of the line of Vortigern, possibly dynastic connection with Gloucester:

Name	Date
'Gloiu'	fl. mid-fourth century?
Vitalis	fl. later fourth century?
Vitalinus	fl. *c.* 400?

End of Roman rule.

Name	Date of accession	Date of death/ dep.	Years ruled
Vortigern/ Gwertheyrn 'the Thin'	Early fifth century?	*c.* 455/460?	

At some point around 440/50, the story of St Germanus would also indicate an elusive king, 'Benli', who is not in the genealogies.

Name	Date of accession	Date of death/ dep.	Years ruled
Pascent (Builth)	*c.* 455/460?	?	
Cadell 'of the Gleaming Hilt' (new dynasty)	Mid-fifth century?		
Cyngen ap Cadell 'the Renowned'	Early/mid-sixth century?		
Brochwael 'of the Tusks' (ap Cyngen)	Second half sixth century?	*c.* 600?	
Cynan ap Broechwael 'of the White Shank'	*c.* 600?	*c.* 610?	
Selyf ap Cynan	?	616 (k.)	
Eiludd ap Cynan/Glast (North Powys?)	616?	?	
Cyndrwyn 'the Stubborn' (South Powys?)	*c.* 620?	?	
Beli ap Eiludd (North Powys)	*c.* 630/640?	?	
Cyndylan ap Cyndrwyn (Pengwern and South Powys)	*c.* 630/640?	*c.* 655/660?	
Gwylog ap Beli	Later seventh century?		
Elisedd	Early eighth century?		
Brochfael	Mid–late eighth century?		
Cadell	?	808?	

| Cyngen ap Cadell | c. 808 | 853 (abd.) | c. 45 |

Rhodri 'Mawr', Merfyn's son, succeeded his uncle Cyngen in 853 and ruled to 878.

Rulers of Later Powys: The Family of Bleddyn, a Dysfunctional Dynasty

The kingdom was restored under the half-brothers of Gruffydd ap Llywelyn ap Seisyll, Bleddyn and Rhiwallon ap Cynfyn. They were installed by Earl Harold of Wessex in 1063 as his vassals, breaking up Gruffydd's unified Welsh state, but from 1066 faced the new threat of heavily armoured and land-hungry Norman lords on their eastern borders. The new king's close companion William FitzOsbern became the Earl of Hereford, but was killed in battle in Flanders in 1071; he was succeeded by his son Roger de Breteuil, 1st Lord of Wigmore Castle near Ludlow. The new (or extended 1050s?) castle at Hereford went to King Edward's Norman follower Richard FitzScrob, Lord of 'Richard's Castle', and the new central Shropshire Lordship of Clun to Robert de Say; Ralph de Tosni acquired Clifford Castle, on the middle Wye near Hay. Around 1070 King William established Hugh d'Avranches at his new castle in Chester as its first earl and to the south Roger of Montgomery, 1st Lord of northern Shropshire, soon established a similar headquarters at Shrewsbury. Shropshire was the centre of the Anglo-Saxon rebellion of Eadric 'the Wild', a minor landowner and possible connection of King Ethelred's former earl, Eadric 'Streona' (k. 1016), who unsuccessfully attacked Hereford with Bleddyn's aid in 1067, fled to Powys, and in 1069 sacked Shrewsbury. He later submitted and served in William's invasion of Scotland in 1072; he was still supposed to haunt the Long Mynd centuries later as leader of the 'Wild Hunt'.

The middle Marches opposite Powys became the base for adventurous lords moving west into Radnor and up the Severn valley, building new 'motte-and-bailey' castles as they went. Earl Roger duly established his western base at a site on the upper Severn called Montgomery after his home in Normandy, and as early as 1073–4 exploratory raids were crossing the mountains into Dyfed. Bleddyn, having been left as sole ruler of Powys and Gwynedd by the death of his brother Rhiwallon at their victory over the sons of Gruffydd ap Llywelyn in 1070, was defeated by Hugh d'Avranches' raiding cousin Robert of Rhuddlan in 1073. He was murdered in 1075 due to treachery by his South Wales rival, Rhys of Deheubarth, but his eldest sons Madoc and Rhiryd managed to hang onto Powys as Gwynedd fell to other contenders. 1075 also saw Roger de Breteuil forfeit his earldom for joining in the 'Revolt of the Earls' against King William, apparently plotted at the wedding feast of the Earl of East Anglia; the Earldom of Hereford was left vacant and Wigmore passed to the loyalist Ranulf de Mortimer, founder of a famous Marcher dynasty. In 1093 Ranulf, Ralph de Tosni of Clifford, and Philip de Braose (primarily a Sussex dynast as Lord of Bramber Castle, but with lands in the Marches too) led the successful invasion of 'Rhwng Gwy a Hafren', the land 'Between Wye and Severn', which became Radnorshire under Marcher rule. (This was probably the obscure Welsh district of 'Cynllibiwg', 'Kenthlebac' according to the thirteenth-century Red Book of the Exchequer, which lay between Wye and Severn). The main Norman fortress was built at Radnor and owned by De Braose and his heirs.

Powys was subject to particularly bloody internal feuds under the sons and grandsons of Bleddyn ap Cynfyn in the early twelfth century, while weakened on the eastern borders by the establishment of new Norman 'Marcher' lordships based on castles such as Chirk, Oswestry, and Montgomery. Madoc and Rhiryd ap Bleddyn tried to annex Deheubarth in 1088 to recreate their uncle Gruffydd ap Llywelyn's united kingdom of the Cymry, but were killed when their victim returned from Ireland with Irish support; their brothers Cadwgan and Iorweth then took over the kingdom. Cadwgan assisted Gruffydd ap Cynan against the Normans in Gwynedd in 1098 but was driven into exile in Ireland with him; on his return the Normans accepted him as their vassal in Powys and Ceredigion. Iorweth joined his Marcher neighbour Robert of Belleme, son and successor of Hugh d'Avranches, in revolt against Henry I in 1102; he deserted him to win the king's favour but found that Henry preferred to build up his brother Cadwgan instead. Henry then imprisoned him in 1103–10. The forfeiture of the D'Avranches dynasty for the revolt of 1102 brought a new crop of Henry I's loyalists into the northern Marches, headed by Alan Fitz Flaald – ancestor of the Fitzalans and the Stewarts – as the Lord of Oswestry.

Cadwgan lost control of Ceredigion in 1109 amid rising chaos in Powys, spearheaded by his sons and the disinherited sons of his brother Rhiryd. The following year Henry, evidently despairing of his usefulness as a vassal, removed him from his remaining lands. Henry now restored Iorweth in the hope that he could restore order, but Iorweth was killed by Madoc ap Rhiryd in 1111. Cadwgan was restored only to be murdered by Madoc as well, at Welshpool a few months later. Henry I divided Powys between his son Owain and the murderous Madoc. Cadwgan's other sons were passed over; one of them, Morgan, proceeded to murder his sibling Maredudd in 1125 and showed unusual remorse for a prince of this murderous dynasty by going on pilgrimage to Jerusalem.

Owain proved a better ruler than his turbulent past as a plundering adventurer would have suggested. In 1109 he had famously abducted the heiress Nest, daughter of Rhys ap Tewdr of Deheubarth and wife of Gerald, castellan of Pembroke Castle, after attacking her husband in an isolated inland castle, probably Cilgerran. (They were the grandparents of the late twelfth- and early thirteenth-century historian Giraldus 'Cambrensis'.)

Gerald was driven to flee through a sewer, while the promiscuous Nest was believed to have been her kidnapper's accomplice. Owain put paid to one major threat by deposing and blinding Madoc (1113/14); Henry I invaded Powys and deported him in 1114 but felt confident enough of his reformed character to restore him the following year. Owain agreed to help the king put down the revolt in Deheubarth by Gruffydd ap Rhys ap Tewdr in 1116, but was ambushed and killed by a force of Pembrokeshire Flemings led by Nest's husband Gerald in 1116. Thereafter the revival of an independent South Wales principality in Cantref Mawr by Gruffydd, later extending into the lowlands, ended Powys' hopes of controlling this region. Owain's surviving uncle Maredudd (handed over to Henry as a hostage by his brother Iorweth in 1103 but escaped in 1108) had already ruled briefly as the English king's steward of Powys after Henry's arrest of Owain in 1114, and now succeeded as the senior among the remaining sons of Bleddyn. Despite his having to flee Henry's invasion of Powys and take refuge in Gwynedd in 1121, he succeeded in restoring stability to the turbulent kingdom. He won a crucial clash with Gwynedd in the Vale of Llangollen in 1132 and died later in the year, aged around sixty to sixty-five.

A 'golden age' followed under his son Madoc from 1132–60, with Powys the most prosperous kingdom in Wales (though militarily inferior to Owain of Gwynedd's realm in 1149–57) and its ruler the much-praised patron of a bardic revival. The poetic 'Arthurian' romance *The Dream of Rhonabwy* was compiled in his reign, presenting it as an era of pride and prosperity not seen since Arthur's time. Another major poet was Cynddelw, 'Byrdydd Fawr' ('the Great Bard') (d. around 1200), who composed Madoc's main eulogy in 1160. Madoc, married to Susanna, the sister of his predatory neighbour Owain Gwynedd, was a careful ally of the English Marcher Earldoms of Chester and Gloucester, and as such assisted Earl Robert of Gloucester with his campaigns on behalf of the latter's sister Empress Matilda against 'usurper' King Stephen in 1138–47. Stephen had invaded the Marches twice in the late 1130s to besiege Ludlow Castle and later to sack Shrewsbury, and was a potential threat. In 1141 Powys troops participated in the rebels' defeat and capture of Stephen at the Battle of Lincoln, but the king's wife Matilda held out with an army and later captured Earl Robert in an attack on the siege of Winchester, forcing Stephen's release. Madoc had less success against Gwynedd, losing the Battle of Ewloe/Coleshill to Owain Gwynedd in 1150 after which Gwynedd confiscated the border cantref of Ial. Madoc had to wait until his ally Earl Robert's nephew Henry II, Matilda's son, came to the throne in 1154 and turned on Gwynedd; he assisted Henry's invasion of Gwynedd in 1157 and received Ial back as a reward. His younger brother Iorweth also participated in the invasion, and received lands at Sutton in Shropshire as thanks for his services as an interpreter; Madoc would not give him any lands in Powys (to preserve its manpower resources intact for his own sons in the succession) so he moved there permanently.

The 1150s also saw the Welsh reconquest of the district of Maelienydd near Radnor, along with at least part of 'Rhwng Gwy a Hafren' (Radnorshire), by Cadwallon ap Madoc, great-grandson of his dynasty's founder Elystan Glodrydd (fl. 1010). Cadwallon secured the recognition of his principality from Henry II at Gloucester in 1175 and inherited his brother Einion of Elfael's lands too in 1176, but was murdered three years later by his Marcher neighbours the Mortimers of Wigmore.

After 1160: Division into North and South Powys

Powys was divided on the death of Madoc ap Maredudd at Lent 1160; his eldest son and probable heir Llywelyn was killed within weeks. His other sons Gruffydd 'Maelor' (d. 1191), Owain 'Fychan', and the illegitimate Owain 'Brogyntyn' (so called from his English estate at Pockington) took the north – Ial, Maelor Cymraeg, Maelor Sysneag, Mochnant Is Rhaeder, and Cynllaith, centred at Dinas Bran. His nephew Owain 'Cyfeiliog' (abdicated 1195) took the south (centred on the cantrefs of Mochnant Uwch Rhaeder, Ceirinion, and Cyfeiliog, with annexed Arwystli). He had been granted Cyfeiliog by Madoc in 1149 and founded the abbey of Strata Marcella on his lands; when he abdicated he became a monk there. The cantrefs of Penllyn and Edeirnion were detached from the north by their more powerful neighbours of Gwynedd, while the south ('Powys

Wenwynwyn') lost Mechain to a cadet branch. The River Rhaeadr served as the border between north and south. The weaker south was fought over between England and Gwynedd from 1240–77, but the latter was unlikely to prevail due to the greater resources available to the English Crown. Nor were its practical-minded rulers, hereditary foes of the line of Gwynedd and mindful of their earlier dispossession by Llywelyn 'Fawr' in 1208, likely to be loyal to the latter's heirs unless through fear and calculation of their – temporary – best advantages to accept Gwynedd supremacy.

The South: 'Powys Wenwynwyn' and the Line of Pool

The bold claims of Gwenwynwyn ap Owain Cyfeiliog, who succeeded to the south in 1195, as a national leader of the Welsh to retake lost territory from William de Braose, Lord of the upper Monnow valley and Brecon, met with a humiliating defeat at the Battle of Painscastle in 1198. He survived Llywelyn ap Iorweth's planned invasion in 1202 as the Gwynedd ruler decided in favour of a treaty at the last moment after Church mediation and the defection of the cantref of Penllyn, but in 1208 he tried to take advantage of the disgrace of his principal English Marcher rival, William de Braose (d. 1211), with raids on disputed lands. De Braose, a 'trusty' of King John believed to be his accomplice in the disappearance of the king's nephew Arthur in 1203, was forced to flee to his lands in Ireland, and John notoriously starved his wife Mabel and one of his sons to death at Corfe Castle, Dorset, in retaliation. But the Brecon lordship survived under De Braose's younger son, Reginald.

Having been summoned to the English court at Shrewsbury by the wrathful King John in 1208, Gwenwynwyn was deposed and his territories were briefly annexed to England. He was only restored in 1210 as a counterbalance to his enemy Llywelyn, having surrendered to humiliating terms of political and jurisdictional dependence; John presumably realised that without Gwenwynwyn's presence in Powys the English were unlikely to secure much of it from Llywelyn's attacks. Preferring the English to his main Welsh rival Gwynedd as his overlord, Gwenwynwyn's alliance with Llywelyn from 1212 did not last; in 1216 he was deposed by Llywelyn for allegedly plotting against him with John and his lands occupied by Gwynedd.

Southern Powys was incorporated into Gwynedd until Llywelyn's death in 1240, passing first to his elder but illegitimate son Gruffydd in 1226 and then to his younger son and heir Dafydd. It thereafter remained a dependent English client, its rulers regarding Gwynedd as the greater threat. Gruffydd ap Gwenwynwyn, restored to his lands by Henry III on strict terms of vassalage in summer 1240 and paying the king 300 'marks' for his father's lands in 1241, was a useful ally for the English Crown against Gwynedd. In 1244 he was one of only three major Welsh magnates to remain loyal to Henry in a rebellion that followed the accidental death of Gruffydd of Gwynedd at the Tower of London, and was besieged by his angry vassals at Tafolwen Castle until rescued by the English. He was duly deposed by Llywelyn ap Gruffydd for apparent disloyalty twice (1257 and 1274). In 1263 he was forced to accept Llywelyn as his overlord in the terms for peace. On the second occasion he joined Llywelyn's brother Dafydd in a plot to murder his overlord, probably alarmed at Llywelyn's recent construction of a new castle at Dolforwyn within his lands, and had to flee to England. He owed his restoration to Edward I's massive invasion of North Wales in 1277, and this time the balance of power shifted permanently to England and saved southern Powys from further attacks from Gwynedd. It became a prosperous vassal, under strict royal legal jurisdiction, whose Anglicisation and loyalty saved it from the depredations of Edward I until Gruffydd's death in 1286. An English trading borough developed at its lords' principal residence of Poole, and the dynasty ended up as English barons.

Gruffydd ap Gwenwynwyn married Margaret Corbet, of the Marcher line of Corbet of Caus (called after the founder's Norman home at Caux). His daughter Margaret married the local Marcher baron Fulke Fitzwarin of Whittington, scion of the family of a famous rebel/outlaw of King John's reign. His son Owain 'de la Poole', first 'Lord Powis' as an English baron, succeeded him in 1286 and endowed his four younger brothers with lands in 1290, with the proviso that if they had no heirs the lands reverted to his children. Two were priests so this occurred; the only brother to leave heirs was William, 1st Lord of Mawddwy. Owain died in 1293, leaving a three-year-old son, Gruffydd, second Lord Powis/de la Poole, who died in 1307. The latter's sister Hawise (d. by 1353) married John Charlton, ancestor of the lords Charlton, who duly acquired Poole/Welshpool Castle on their marriage in July 1309 and built the current Powys Castle. Summoned to Parliament as Lord Charleton in 1313, he was temporarily disgraced for supporting Edward II's rebel cousin Thomas, Earl of Lancaster, in 1321–2 and helped the baronial resistance to the king's unpopular and greedy favourite Hugh Despenser, new principal lord of the south-east Marches. He was restored to favour after the king was deposed in 1327, the successful invasion by Queen Isabella having been masterminded by his Marcher neighbour (and the queen's lover) Roger Mortimer who now became 'de facto' regent in 1327–30. Opposed as sole lord of the 'Powys Wenwynwyn' inheritance at times by his wife's uncle Sir Griffin (*sic*) de la Poole, he held the estates until his death in 1353 and they descended to his heirs.

In practice, the estates were incorporated into England in 1286. The lords had resided at their Anglicised new castle of 'Poole' at Welshpool even when independent, acting as much as Marcher lords as Welsh princes. The former Powys lands of Gwerthyrnion (Builth), taken over by Llywelyn of Gwynedd from the Mortimers of Wigmore Castle in the 1260s, were reconquered for England by King Edward in 1277 and incorporated into the royal lands; Llywelyn had also taken over the cantref of Cedewain in 1273 but lost it to England in 1277.

Powys

Name	Date of accession	Date of death/ dep.	Years ruled
Bleddyn ap Cynfyn (ruled Gwynedd)	Aug 1063	1075	12
Rhiwallon ap Cynfyn	Aug 1063	1070	7
Madoc ap Bleddyn	1075	1088	13
Rhiryd ap Bleddyn	1075	1088	13
Iorweth ap Bleddyn (i)	1088	1103	15
Cadwgan ap Bleddyn	1088	1111	23
Iorweth ap Bleddyn (ii)	1110	1111	1
Owain ap Cadwgan (i)	1111	1114	3
Madoc ap Rhiryd	1113	1113	2
Owain ap Cadwgan (ii)	1115	1116	1

Maredudd ap Bleddyn	1116	1132	16
Madoc ap Maredudd	1132	Feb? 1160	28

Southern Powys

Owain 'Cyfeiliog'	1160	1195 (abd.)	35
Gwenwynwyn (i)	1195	1208	13

Annexation by England, 1208.

Gwenwynwyn	1210	1216	6

Annexation by Gwynedd, 1216.

Gruffydd ap Gwenwynwyn (i)	Summer 1240	1274	34

Annexation by Gwynedd, 1274.

Gruffydd ap Gwenwynwyn (ii)	Summer 1277	1286	9

Northern Powys

Gruffydd Maelor ap Madoc (Maelor)	1160	1191	31
Owain ap Madoc (Cynllaith)	1160	1187	27

Madoc ap Gruffydd Maelor (Maelor: lands renamed 'Powys Fadog')	1191	1236	45
Gruffydd Maelor ap Madoc (Edeirnion)	1236	1269	33
Gruffydd Ial ap Madoc (Ial)	1236	<1269	<30
Madoc ap Gruffydd Maelor (Edeirnion)	1269	1277	8
Gruffydd 'Fychan' ('the Younger') ap Gr. Maelor (Ial and 1277 Edeirnion)	1269	1289	20
Llywelyn (Maelor)	1269	1282	13

Northern Powys

Gruffydd 'Maelor', senior ruler of the north, married Angharad the daughter of Owain Gwynedd and died in 1191. He was succeeded by his son Madoc ap Gruffydd Maelor (d. 1236), in whose honour the principality was renamed 'Powys Fadog'. He married Gwladys, daughter of Ithael ap Rhys of Gwent, assisted his uncle Llywelyn 'Fawr' in his southern campaign in winter 1215–16, and founded the abbey of 'Valle Crucis' ('Valley of the Cross') in the holy Vale of Llangollen. His domains were then split up among his five sons – Gruffydd 'Maelor' (II), Gruffydd Ial, Maredudd, Hywel, and Madoc 'Fychan'. The second Gruffydd Maelor, who married Emma Audley, was the senior; he backed Henry III against Dafydd of Gwynedd in 1240–1 and suffered attacks from the latter as a consequence and in 1256 was deposed by Llywelyn ap Gruffydd but fought his way back to power. He died in 1269, being succeeded by his sons Madoc (II) and Gruffydd 'Fychan'. All the time, the Welsh custom of joint inheritance by a ruler's sons kept the family inheritance divided and a diminishing amount of lands remained to each eldest son.

In 1277 Gruffydd's eldest son Madoc (II), an ally of Llywelyn 'the Last', was killed in Edward I's invasion; his younger brother Gruffydd 'Fychan' was allowed to succeed to his lands but was reduced to the rank of an English tenant, vassal to Edward I. The younger brother of the two Gruffydds, Llywelyn of Maelor, was among the first Mid Wales princes to defect to Edward, late in 1276, and duly retained his lands as a royal vassal. Fed up with being forced into costly litigation in 'rigged' courts by the English authorities, he joined in the 1282 revolt, probably at Dafydd ap Gruffydd's instigation, and attacked Oswestry on 22 March. He duly lost his lands at the English Conquest. Madoc's under-age sons, placed in the guardianship of Roger Mortimer of Chirk (brother of the man whose army killed Llywelyn 'the Last'), died in suspicious circumstances which were blamed on Roger (who was later deprived of his lands by Edward II on behalf of the Despensers).

Gruffydd Fychan's son Madog 'Crypyl', who succeeded as a minor in 1289 and died in 1304, inherited only half of Cynllaith and the Edeirnion property of Glyndyfrdwy, which passed to his descendants. Owain 'Glyndŵr' was either his grandson or his great-grandson.

Rulers of Builth and Gwerthyrnion

The sub-kingdom of Powys which remained with Vortigern's son Pascent and his descendants when Cadell's line took over the main kingdom; both St Germanus' biographer Constantius (around 480) and Nennius (around 829) testify to its separate existence and dynasty. Only Riocatus is known from outside (Gallic literary) evidence.

Name	Approximate date
Pascent	*c.* 460?
Riagath/Riocatus	*c.* 480/90?
Idnerth	Early sixth century
Paul	Mid-sixth century
Elaed	Late sixth century
Morvo	Early seventh century
Gwyddaint	Mid-seventh century
Pascent	Late seventh century
Gloud	*c.* 700?

The slightly different royal genealogy from the *Life of St Germanus*:

> Gliou – Vitalinus – Vitalis – Vortigern 'the Thin' – Pascent – Briacat – Meurci
> – Paul – Elaeth – Eldat – Moriud – Gwyddgant – Pascent – Theodore.

Gloud's daughter and heiress Brawstudd married Arthfael (Arthwys) ap Rhys, king of Morgannwg, who can be approximately dated from the latter kingdom's pedigrees to the early eighth century. The length of the pedigree between the first Pascent and Gloud and the time-scale thus agree with the idea of a father-to-son descent between them.

5

RULERS OF DYFED AND (TENTH-CENTURY) DEHEUBARTH

Pedigrees exist both in the Welsh documents – the Old Welsh pedigrees edited by Bartrum, Nos II, X, and XII – and in the Irish *Book of Ui Maine*.

The name 'Deheubarth' – 'dexter pars', 'right-handed part' – was a geographical term used for the new tenth-century united kingdom of Dyfed and Ceredigion/Seisslywg. It refers to the region as seen on a map, looking from Ireland.

This was historically the pre-Roman territory of the Demetae. But traditionally the ruling family of the post-Roman period, founded by Eochaid (an Irish name), was descended from the princes of the 'Deisi' in Leinster, Ireland, and were established as settlers in the fourth century. The existence of Irish 'ogham' stones in Pembrokeshire duly attest to a degree of use of the Irish language, implying some settlement. Some of the fifth-century rulers may have borne Roman names and titles, e.g. Tryffin ('tribune') and Aircol ('Agricola'). Aircol is supposed to have lived near Tenby (Dinbych) and to have been a foe of King Cynan of Powys; he may have been named after the first-century AD Roman general, who had completed the conquest of West Wales. His son Vortipor is uniquely referred to in an extant memorial stone at Castell Dwyran in two languages, in Latin as 'Voteporix' and in Irish ogham as 'Votecorigas'. He is called the 'Protictor' ('Protector') – a military rank of Palace bodyguards in the later Roman Empire. He was one of the five rulers castigated for his tyranny by Gildas around 545, who calls him 'greying', which would imply that he was

1. Maiden Castle, looking east. The archetypal Iron Age hill-fort.

2. Queen Boudicca. The Westmacott statue on the Thames Embankment at Westminster.

3. King Vortigern in his burning tower, from Peter of Langtoft's *Chronicle of England*. BL Mss. 20 A 11, folio 3. (British Library)

4. Deheubarth/Dyfed – Swansea Castle, ancient and modern.

5. Caernarfon Castle. (Bill Damick)

6. Kidwelly Castle. (Bill Damick)

7. Manorbier. (Bill Damick)

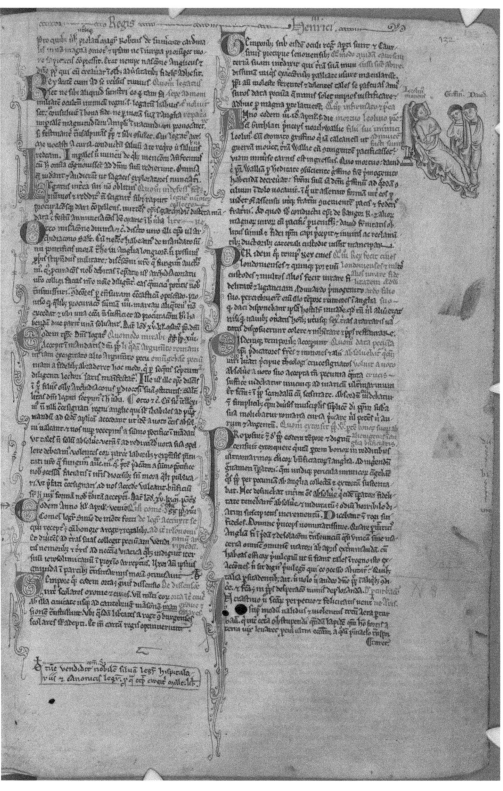

8. In the top right, Llywelyn 'the Great' on his deathbed, with his sons Dafydd and Gruffydd in attendance. Matthew Parr's *Chronicle*, CCC ms. 16, f. 132 r. (Corpus Christi College, Cambridge)

9. The main gate of Carmarthen Castle, crowded by the modern town, where Rhys 'Gryg' was fatally injured in 1234.

10. Hay Castle, guarding the middle Wye and the Marcher road into Deheubarth (plus bookshop).

11. Morgannwg – Llandaff Cathedral. Seat of the kingdom's see and rival to St David's.

12. St David's. (Bill Damick)

13. Ogmore (Ogwr) Castle – site of the enigmatic 'Ogmore Stone' referring to King Arthwys.

14. Pentre Meurig near Cowbridge. The seat of King Mouric?

probably over fifty by that time. Gildas also called him 'spotted with evil', probably an allusion to his grey-flecked hair but also possibly an indication that he was not as tyrannical as his fellow rulers.

The mid-late sixth century was also the era of the semi-legendary patron saint of the kingdom, David ('Dewi Sant'), an austere and stern hermit who lived on grass and water in the best traditions of self-denying holy men throughout the later Roman Empire and later founded a monastery at Menavia – St David's, site of his shrine. His actual career has been muddied by the political aims of his late eleventh-century hagiographer, Rhigyfarch, son of Bishop Sulien of St David's and a 'cheerleader' for the claims of the see to primacy over all Wales. In this aggressive polemical campaign, waged from 1115 by the new Anglo-Norman Bishop Bernard against the rival claims of the see of Llandaff (representing the kingdom of Morgannwg), it was claimed that the latter's Bishop Dyfrig had inherited the post-Roman 'archbishopric of Wales', based at Caerleon in Gwent. He then supposedly abdicated it at the synod of Llandewi Brefi in around 545 in favour of the holier St David, giving the latter's see – that of the kingdom of Dyfed – primacy over Wales. The existence of a see of Caerleon, the major Roman town in the region, is possible; an abdication of primacy over all Wales by its holders is very unlikely. But St David duly became the patron saint of Wales, and his shrine at Menevia became a prime object of veneration to the benefit of the kingdom of Dyfed. Historically, it is possible that the legends of David's aggressive austerity are accurate but if so they probably reflect the influence of austere Irish hermits, such as the settlers on the isolated rocky stacks of Skellig Michael in the Aran Islands under St Enda around 500. There was an isolated island monastery in contemporary Dyfed too, that of St Piro at Caldey Island, but it served as a base for missionary activity in Brittany (e.g. by St Samson, fl. around 486–560) so it was relatively 'outward-looking'. The contrast between the austere hermitage at Menevia, and any other actual as opposed to legendary foundations by David, and Caldey Island and the 'Romanised' estate monasteries of Morgannwg at Llancarfan and Llanilltud Fawr may imply a difference in religious tradition and zeal between the two kingdoms in the sixth century. The synod of Llandewi Brefi was also supposed to have been called to deal with a resurgence of Pelagianism in Dyfed, which might be connected to its monks' zeal for austerity – but this is only speculation.

Arthwys, grandson of Vortipor, is one of the candidates to be the 'original' for at least part of the legend of Arthur (see section on Morgannwg), but is probably dated too late for the timing of the campaigns that the war-leader of that name fought against the Saxons though some of his deeds may have been muddled with those of another, earlier 'Arthur'. His son and successor Nowy (Noah) is confused in some stories with a son of 'the' King Arthur, and was grandfather of the early eighth-century Powys king Elisedd. Nowy may have been the same man as the mysterious South Wales prince Llacheu ('the Glittering One'), alleged son of Arthur or Arthwys in later Welsh legends and the 'Triads'. Later hagiography made Arthur bullyingly try to intimidate St Padarn, founding holy monastic leader of Llanbadarn in Dyfed, into handing over a valuable tunic – the saint prayed for help, the earth swallowed him up, and he had to beg for forgiveness before he was released. Was this story connected to the king Arthwys of Dyfed?

In the mid-eighth century, under Rhain, Dyfed appears to have lost part of its northern territories – Ystrad Tywi – to the expanding kingdom of Ceredigion under king Seisyll. Logically the emergence of Seissyl's eponymous new realm, 'Seissylwg', was at Dyfed's expense and helped to weaken it, leaving it more exposed to Irish Sea Viking raids in the ninth century. There was also a threat of long-distance, temporary but damaging raids on Dyfed by the regional 'great power', Mercia, under King Offa. One invasion is recorded for 784 and there were probably others, though details are sparse; luckily after Offa's death in 796 Mercia seems to have concentrated its attacks on Powys and Gwynedd. But the Vikings now set up trading and raiding bases at Dublin and Waterford on the opposite shores of the Irish Sea, and seem to have terrorised Dyfed in the ninth century. Raids, and possible settlement along the south coast, probably caused or helped a political vacuum. No ruler is recorded between the death of Tryffin around 814 and Hyffaid ap Bleddri in the later ninth century, which may reflect an absence of surviving records or a more serious vacuum caused by the problem of Vikings. Did their settlement on the south coast include Swansea, 'Sweyn's Island'?

The Vikings may have used the Dyfed coast as a base for their attacks on Devon in the 870s, and in 878 Ubbe Ragnarsson, brother of the late Kings Ivarr 'the Boneless' of Dublin (d. 873) and King Halfdan of York (k. 877), launched an invasion of Devon from South Wales. This was meant to assist the warlord Guthrum, based in western Mercia, to overthrow King Alfred of Wessex, who had been caught by surprise at Twelfth Night at Chippenham and had fled to hide in the Somerset marshes at Athelney. Ubbe probably intended to take Alfred in the rear via Exmoor, as Guthrum's ally, but was killed by 'ealdorman' Odda of Devon at Cynwit (Countisbury?) and his famous 'Raven Banner' was captured. Alfred notably had a resident Welsh cleric for Dyfed, his later biographer Asser, at his court and probably knew about local matters from him; in the 880s the weakened South Welsh rulers successfully sought Alfred's patronage to fend off attacks from King Anarawd of Gwynedd and recognised Alfred as their overlord. In 914 the South Wales and Dublin Vikings operated a fleet in the Bristol Channel and took some senior clergy, led by the Bishop of Ergyng (south-west Herefordshire) hostage, and King Edward of Wessex had to intervene to ransom them. The local Welsh were powerless, and it was Wessex not Dyfed which evicted the Vikings from the Bristol Channel islands. But the unification of Wessex and Mercia by Edward in 918 brought a major new threat of invasion by the new 'Kingdom of England' to replace the Viking menace.

Revival and National Leadership: Hywel 'Dda' and his Heirs

The throne passed in the early tenth century to a junior branch of the dynasty of Gwynedd, when Rhodri 'Mawr's son Cadell deposed and executed Hyffaid's son Llywarch in 904. (The execution, by drowning, bore marks of ancient 'Celtic' ritual practice.) Cadell had married Llywarch's daughter Elen – possibly named after the semi-legendary Welsh wife of Emperor Magnus Maximus or after Constantine 'the Great's evangelising mother St Helen and so implying local Dyfed dynastic patriotic/religious enthusiasm. Due to this connection to Gwynedd, initialled by what amounted to conquest, powerful Dyfed rulers thereafter sometimes could lay claim to both thrones as Mareduud ap Owain did in 986. Cadell was succeeded to Dyfed in 909 by his son Hywel 'Dda', one of the greatest of early medieval Welsh rulers and the first to use his own coinage since Roman times. Younger son Clydog succeeded to Ceredigion, effectively as his brother's loyal junior; when another brother murdered him in 920 Hywel united the kingdoms. Hywel visited Rome as a pilgrim in 928, possibly in emulation of his apparent 'model' Alfred of Wessex, and ruled as a paragon of Christian kingship. He not only united Dyfed with Ceredigion/Seissylwg to the north but successfully pursued a claim to his paternal ancestors' Gwynedd, which he took over in 942. However even Hywel, the strongest ruler of his generation, found it expedient not to challenge the new Kingdom of England and attended Athelstan's court at Exeter in 928, King's Worthy in 932, Winchester and Nottingham in 934, and Dorchester (twice) in 935, witnessing charters as the king's vassal. He also accepted instructions to assist Athelstan against his fellow 'Celtic' Scots by taking part in the first English invasion of Scotland in 934, and loyally steered clear of the Viking-Strathclyde-Scots coalition which attacked Athelstan in 937. Around 945 he held a pioneering assembly of legal experts at Whitland in Dyfed to examine and codify the laws for the three kingdoms of Dyfed/Deheubarth, Gwynedd-Powys, and Morgannwg under his presidency.

The writing-up of the existing laws in this fashion, following Roman Imperial precedents, was organised by a jurist called Blegywryd, and represented an imaginative new legal/administrative plan for all Wales, a desire for justice (laws could now be cited accurately and looked up easily), and royal 'spin' with the King of Deheubarth as the guarantor of good government. This was combined with promotion of the cult of the True Cross at the church of Nevern in Dyfed, with the laying out of sites named after places in the Holy Land as a stimulus to devotion from pilgrims who could not go that far afield.

The union of all the Welsh kingdoms which Hywel established proved temporary and ended on his death in 950, his eldest son Owain succeeding to Deheubarth with the nominal co-rule of his siblings Rhodri (d. 953) and Edwin (d. 954) while the native line of Rhodri 'Mawr' under Iago and Idawl 'Foel' regained Gwynedd after a battle at Nant Carno in Arwystli. The two kingdoms fought a border war in 952–4; Hywel's sons invaded Gwynedd and reached the River Conwy but were defeated at Llanrwst. Owain's pretensions to 'national' leadership like his father were restricted to commissioning the *Annales Cambriae*, a chronicle of Welsh history since Roman times – although this had its flaws and its early section appears to have relied heavily on Irish Church annals. He abdicated in 986 and died in 988. His younger son Einion had been killed in battle in 984; his eldest son and successor Maredudd ap Owain (r. 986–99) restored Dyfed's rule of Gwynedd as joint king of both kingdoms later in 986 by killing the new king of Gwynedd, Cadwallon. When Maredudd died in 999 Gwynedd became the senior partner, as the union continued to 1005 under the latter's prince Cynan ap Hywel, Cadwallon's nephew. Possibly Maredudd reached an agreement with him to appoint him as successor in a 'rotating leadership' of the union to stop future wars, but this excluded his own nephews, Einion's sons – who had tried to invade Deheubarth in 991 and 994 and so may have been punished for this.

It was the Dyfed dynasty's turn to be excluded from rule in 999. On Cynan's death in 1005, Maredudd's brother Einion's sons Edwin and

Cadell succeeded to Deheubarth; they were challenged by an obscure prince, Aeddan ap Blegyrwyd, who deposed them in 1018. The union with Gwynedd was restored briefly in 1018–23 by Llywelyn ap Seisyll (the latter partly Dyfedian by descent, as son of Mareddud's daughter Angharad). He had taken over Gwynedd in 1005, and now drove Aeddan out of Deheubarth in 1018. Once again, the union was ephemeral and only lasted for the ruler's lifetime, as the obscure Rhydderch ap Iestyn, possibly a prince of Morgannwg not Dyfed, took over Deheubarth on Llywelyn's death in 1023. He was then driven out by Hywel and Maredudd, sons of Edwin, in 1033; Hywel became king of Deheubarth.

Llywelyn's son Gruffydd, new King of Gwynedd, attacked Hywel in 1039 and took over Ceredigion, and in 1041 defeated him again and took his wife prisoner. The English kingdom was distracted by the conflicts between the sons of the late King Cnut (d. 1035), and in 1042 the native claimant Edward (later called 'the Confessor') returned to the throne but, as someone who had lived long in exile, was unable to assert his power on the frontiers quickly. The aggressive Gruffydd attacked Hywel again in 1043 and this time drove him out; Hywel resorted to employing an fleet of Irish Vikings and invaded in 1044 but was killed in battle at the mouth of the River Teifi. Gruffydd now restored the union of the two kingdoms, but faced invasion of Dyfed by his rival Gruffydd ap Rhydderch (son of the ruler in 1023–33) in 1045–6. He employed the new earl Swein Godwinsson of Hereford, son of the English chief minister Earl Godwin of Wessex, to help him by marching his army to attack Deheubarth and ravage the pretender's territory in 1046. Swein was then disgraced for abducting (willingly?) the Abbess of Leominster and in 1047 Gruffydd ap Rhydderch took over all Deheubarth, but Gruffydd ap Llywelyn killed him and restored the union again in 1055.

It is not certain that Gruffydd ap Rhydderch (r. 1047–55) and his father Rhydderch ap Iestyn (r. 1023–33) were of the direct royal line of Dyfed; the extant genealogies differ over whether Iestyn was a son of Owain ap Hywel (r. 950–86) or a prince of the line of Morgannwg. Thus it is uncertain if Gruffydd ap Rhydderch's son Caradog, restored to parts of Dyfed by Earl Harold of Wessex when he overran Gwynedd and destroyed its power in 1063, claimed the kingdom on the basis of his Dyfed or Morgannwg descent. His rival Maredudd ap Owain ap Edwin was definitely from the line of Hywel Dda. Caradog raided the triumphant Harold's new Gwent hunting lodge at Portskewett near Chepstow in 1065, a personal insult which would probably have led to retaliation had the events of 1066 not intervened.

The Norman Conquest: 1066 to 1116

The Normans now took on the role of Earl Harold as the scourges of the Welsh, and the new King William appointed his old comrade William FitzOsbern as the Earl of Hereford to control the southern part of the Marches. He was killed fighting in Flanders in 1071 and his son was disgraced and lost the earldom for joining in a plot to depose the king in 1075. But restless and land-hungry Norman knights were moving forward to annex territory in South East Wales independent of 'high politics', and early settlers included Thurstan FitzRolf at Caerleon. Caradog seemed oblivious to the danger, and neither he nor his rivals thought of uniting against the new arrivals; meanwhile the Vikings were still a naval menace in the Irish Sea and in around 1073 they sacked St David's. Bishop Sulien (in office 1073–4?, 1079–86) was mostly resident safe inland at Llanbadarn Fawr. In 1067–8 a Norse/Irish fleet led by King Harold's refugee illegitimate sons Godwin and Magnus was operating in the Bristol Channel, but a Saxon revolt in Devon failed. Caradog, with local Norman help, killed Maredudd on the River Rhymney in 1072; the latter's brother Rhys ap Owain was attacked by Norman raiders in 1073 and 1074 and his only success was in trapping and killing King Bleddyn of Gwynedd/Powys in a surprise attack in 1075. If he hoped to expand inland into Powys, his gamble failed and the murder of a popular and just ruler led to widespread outrage. He was expelled by Bleddyn's self-proclaimed avenger Trahaern of Gwynedd after defeat at the Battle of Godwick in 1078, and was killed a few months later by Caradog. Their cousin Rhys ap Tewdr ap Cadell, descended from Hywel Dda's grandson Einion (d. 984), took over Deheubarth. He had to pay homage to King William, not called by contemporaries 'the Conqueror', and pay rent for his lands when the latter crossed his kingdom with an army en route to St David's in 1081. William may have set up the first Norman base at Cardiff Castle, a 'motte' within the walls of the old Roman fortress.

Rhys retained his kingdom, but the pressure from Norman encroachment redoubled from 1087 under the new king, William II, who had inherited lands around Gloucester from his mother Queen Matilda in 1083. Early settlers included Hamelin of Ballen at Abergavenny and his brother Winnebald at Caerleon. Rhys was temporarily expelled from his kingdom by the elder sons of Bleddyn, Madoc and Rhiryd, in 1088 but returned with a Viking fleet from Ireland – the usual resort of expelled Welsh princes – and killed them in battle. In 1091 a faction of nobles offered his crown to Gruffydd, son of Maredudd ap Owain, an exile in England; he invaded but was killed in battle at the mouth of the river Towy. But the victorious Rhys was himself killed in a skirmish with Norman settlers in Brycheiniog at Aberhonddhu in April 1093, probably assisting rebels against the new local lord Bernard de Neufmarche. By this date one Norman baron, Richard FitzPons of Clifford Castle in the upper Wye valley, had penetrated over the Brecon Beacons as far as Llandovery; their conquest of Brycheiniog seems to have followed the replacement of some west Herefordshire barons for rebelling against the new king, William II, in 1088. The new regional 'strongman', Bernard de Neufmarche, had been granted the castles of Ewias Harold, Durstone and Snodhill and was thus the immediate neighbour of Brycheiniog, ruling the 'Golden Valley'. Married to the daughter of Princess Nest of Gwynedd (daughter of Gruffydd ap Llywelyn ap Seisyll and Edith of Mercia), he appears to have overrun Brycheiniog in summer–autumn 1088; castles were built at Brecon and (probably) Bronllys. This posed a serious threat to Rhys ap Tewdr; would the fertile lands of the Towy valley be next? In 1093 Rhys apparently assisted a Welsh rebellion in Brycheiniog, and was killed attacking Bernard; a further local revolt was put down in 1094 as the Normans of Glamorgan came to Bernard's rescue and won a battle at Aber Llech. Castles were now built at Tretower and Crickhowell.

Dyfed was largely overrun by the Anglo-Norman barons after the death of Rhys ap Tewdr, with southern Pembrokeshire heavily settled and permanently lost. Arnulf of Montgomery, younger son of Earl Roger, set up a new lordship at Pembroke which proved permanent though his family were soon expropriated by Henry I as rebels. The castellanship of Pembroke was awarded by Henry I (around 1102) to Gerald of Windsor, new husband of Rhys ap Tewdr's daughter Nest who had fallen into Norman hands after her father's death and was probably one of Henry's many mistresses; they produced a large and famous family. (Their daughter Angharad's son by William de Barri was the historian Giraldus 'Cambrensis'.) A more insecure lordship was set up at Cardigan, where Arnulf and his father built a castle at Dingereint on the 1093–4 expedition but the lordship was only secured by Henry I's new nominee, Gilbert Fitz Richard de Clare, after 1110. Gilbert also founded castles in Ceredigion at Llanbadarnand Castell Gwallter around 1110. Henry also gave other new frontier lordships to his own men – Gower to Henry de Beaumont, Earl of Warwick (1106), Cydweli/Kidwelly to Maurice de Londres of Ogwr (Morganwwg), Cemais to Robert Fitz Martin, and Cantref Bychan to Richard Fitz Pons (Clifford). Bernard de Neufmarche kept the new lordship of Brecon until his death around 1125, but Henry required him to marry his daughter and heiress Sibyl to a royal 'trusty', Miles FitzWalter, the Sheriff of Gloucestershire. (Bernard's son was supposed to have been disinherited for an attack on his mother's lover.)

Miles (d. 1143) duly succeeded Bernard, and in the English civil war from 1138 backed the Empress Matilda against King Stephen; she made him Earl of Hereford in 1141. His son Roger, 2nd Earl of Hereford, held out against the resurgent Stephen as one of the semi-autonomous pro-Angevin barons in the Marches, but Matilda's son Henry II's accession in 1154 was followed by the eclipse of the family's power. When Roger (wounded?) had to retire to a monastery in 1155 Henry confiscated the earldom; Roger's brother Walter, Lord of Abergavenny and Sheriff of Gloucestershire and Herefordshire, took over Brecon but died on Crusade in 1160. These years also saw the Anglicisation of the kingdom of Deheubarth's see at St David's, under the king's nominee as bishop in 1115, Bernard (Queen Matilda's chaplain). He used the cult of St David and the claims in Rhigyfarch's 'Life' that David had become Archbishop of Wales to assert the primacy of his bishopric over that of Llandaff, and was fiercely resisted by the latter's new (1107) Norman Bishop Urban.

From this time onwards the kingdom of Deheubarth was matched against a group of permanent Anglo-Norman 'Marcher' lordships. The inner ring of lordships in southern Pembroke which were secure from attack, centred on the eponymous earldom and its headquarters at Pembroke Castle, included Wiston and Haverfordwest; the De Clare Earls died out in 1176 with Richard de Clare. Richard, 'Strongbow', was an ambitious adventurer who was invited to bring Anglo-Norman troops into Leinster to assist the exiled King Diarmait regain his confiscated lands from 'High King' Ruarhi Ui Conchobar in 1170, swiftly made himself the real power in his host's kingdom, and acquired a new domain as Lord of Dublin. As husband of Diarmait's daughter Aoife he then claimed the succession to Leinster (to which he was entitled under Anglo-Norman law) in defiance of Irish law which favoured her male cousins. He brought an anxious Henry II, who had originally allowed the expedition and marriage to go ahead, into local politics to curtail the growth of his power on two separate British islands; in 1172 Henry crossed Pembrokeshire en route to Dublin to reassert royal power over his alarmingly powerful vassal. Richard died in 1176; his and Aoife's daughter Isabel brought the earldom to her new husband (1189) William Marshal, paragon of contemporary chivalry and reputedly a model for Chretien de Troyes' Arthurian creation 'Sir Lancelot'. Marshal, a favourite of Eleanor of Aquitaine and her eldest son the 'Young King' Henry who was grudgingly trusted by his original foe Richard I, rebuilt

Pembroke Castle, had an uneasy relationship with the devious King John, and finally became regent of England in 1216–19 as he led the Angevin loyalists to drive out the boy-king Henry III's rival Prince Louis of France. Marshal's eldest son William regained Cardigan and Carmarthen Castles from Llywelyn 'the Great' of Gwynedd, thus controlling South West Wales, but had a difficult relationship with Henry and his ministers and had the two castles confiscated to curtail his vast landed power in 1226. He died in 1231; his brother and heir Earl Richard also clashed with the king over his opposition to Henry's power-hungry Poitevin kin, posed as leader of the 'national' English baronial resistance to the latter, and ended up in rebellion, being killed defending his Irish estates in 1234. Their younger brothers Gilbert (killed in a tournament in 1241), Walter (d. November 1245), and Anselm (d. December 1245), all died childless; their sisters divided up the Pembroke lands as co-heiresses and the unity of this landed bulwark of the Marcher lordships ended. The earldom eventually passed to Henry III's De Valence kinsmen. Beyond these secure lordships in Pembrokeshire was another group under sporadic Welsh attack, such as those of Cydweli/ Kidwelly (owned by the de Londres and then the Chaworths), Swansea and the southern Gower (the De Braoses and from 1230 the Bohuns), Talacharn/Laugharne (the De Brians), St Clears, and Cemmaes. There were also settlements of Flemings in Pembrokeshire. Carmarthen passed to and fro between the Welsh and the English, but was mainly under the control of the latter. Inland from Carmarthen, the centre of Deheubarth was relocated to the 'Cantref Mawr' based on Dinefwr.

National Recovery: Gruffydd ap Rhys and his Sons

The fortunes of Deheubarth were restored from around 1116 by Rhys' son Gruffydd (born around 1080?), who returned to overrun Dyfed in around 1113 and appears to have commenced his career as a guerilla chief in the interior hills of Ystrad Tywi. He went to Gwynedd around 1115 to seek aid from Gruffydd ap Cynan, but was reported to Henry I who sought his extradition; the Welsh king agreed but his namesake was warned in time and fled to sanctuary at the church of Aberdaron. Either now or later he married his second wife, Gruffydd ap Cynan's formidable daughter Gwenllian, mother of his younger sons Maredudd and Rhys. In spring 1116 he led what their opponents described as an unruly army of young troublemakers to burn Narbeth Castle, and thenceforward ruled inland 'Cantref Mawr' (with the ancestral 'capital' at the castle of Dinefwr). Henry

I called in Owain ap Cadwgan of Powys to destroy him, but the invader was killed by his 'love-rival' Gerald de Barri and Gruffydd held onto his inland territory, centred on the 'commote' of Caeo, apart from a brief exile to Ireland following an English attack around 1127.

During Henry's reign Gruffydd only ruled the remote inland hills and forests, and was unable to penetrate the coastal plains. But from 1136 he led a large-scale Welsh revolt across Dyfed following Henry I's death, although while he was seeking aid from his father-in-law Gruffydd ap Cynan his wife Gwenllian was killed (along with two sons, Morgan and Maelgwyn) as she attacked William de Londres, Lord of Cydweli and Ogwr, at Cydweli/Kidwelly Castle. Her memorable leadership of her husband's army, a 'first' for British/Welsh queens since Boudicca, and heroic death were remembered for centuries in local lore with the cry of 'Revenge for Gwenllian!' on battlefields, and the site of the clash was named 'Maes ('Field of') Gwenllian'. Coincidentally or not, her proto-feminist leadership of an army was to be repeated thrice in the next decade – by Empress Matilda and Stephen's Queen Matilda in England and by Duchess Eleanor of Aquitaine on Crusade. In one burst of Welsh success in 1136, Gilbert Fitz Richard of Ceredigion was killed in the Usk valley, a major Anglo-Norman-Fleming force was routed at Crug Mawr near Cardigan, and in 1137 Carmarthen was recaptured. Cardigan Castle held out despite a siege aided by a Dublin Viking fleet, but most of the lordship of Ceredigion returned to Welsh hands – only to be subsequently fought over by princes of Deheubarth and Gwynedd.

Gruffydd ap Rhys and his sons Anarawd, Cadell, Maredudd, and Rhys had a limited degree of success in regaining territory, and made little impact on the coast except in the Carmarthen region. Returning from Gwynedd with the promised aid after his wife's death, Gruffydd fought a largely successful campaign in Pembrokeshire in 1137 but could not overrun the south and later in the year he himself was killed in battle by the local Flemings. His eldest son Anarawd succeeded, killed the Fleming commander Letard in 1137, and had some success in regaining parts of Ceredigion with Viking help, but was killed in 1143 by the followers of a rival claimant, Cadwaladr of Gwynedd. His brother Cadell succeeded as senior prince in Cantref Mawr, and in 1146 he and his brothers Maredudd and Rhys (the latter, born around 1132, in his first campaign) succeeded in taking Llansteffan Castle, on the west bank of the Towy estuary downstream from Carmarthen. Wiston was taken in 1147 and Carmarthen itself in 1150, but Cadell abdicated in 1151 after being badly wounded in an ambush by the garrison of Tenby while out hunting. He left for Rome on pilgrimage in 1153, returned later to become a monk at Strata Florida Abbey, and died there in 1175. Maredudd now succeeded, and in 1153 regained both Ceredigion and Tenby (the latter with Rhys' help).

The youngest son, Rhys, started his career at the siege of Llansteffan in 1146 and took St Clears, the next castle west of Carmarthen, as his first independent command in 1153. He succeeded his brother Maredudd in 1155. Rhys ruled a virtually restored kingdom of Deheubarth, with southern Pembrokeshire and the Loughor-Gower region the main areas remaining to the English, but was easily outmatched by the manpower available to the new King of England as of 1154, Henry II. In 1156 he built Aberdyfi/Aberdovey Castle to secure his control of Ceredigion from Gwynedd. But in 1157 he was forced to submit as Henry invaded his lands and accept his reduction to being Prince of Cantref Mawr, the return of Ceredigion to its De Clare lords and Cantref Bychan to Walter Clifford, and abandonment of the royal title. Clifford now invaded Cantref Mawr, and Rhys drove him out and proceeded to retake Llandovery and Ceredigion; Henry invaded again in 1158 to force him to return them. In 1159 he attacked Carmarthen while Henry was overseas campaigning in southern France against Toulouse, but the king's half-uncle Earl Reginald of Cornwall, bastard of Henry I, landed with an army from Devon to relieve it and then unsuccessfully invaded Cantref Mawr with the Earls of Gloucester and Pembroke and the ever-hopeful claimant Cadwaladr of Gwynedd.

A further clash with the English and Rhys' capture of Llandovery during Henry's absence abroad in 1162 led to a third royal campaign the following year, and Rhys surrendered in Ceredigion and was deported to England. He was released after doing homage to Henry at Woodstock that summer. Forced to abandon his pretensions to a princely title and accept vassalage – hence his usual title, 'the Lord Rhys' – he nevertheless managed to retake most of Ceredigion in 1164 in an invasion after the local English authorities refused to do justice for the killing of his nephew and captain of the 'teulu' (household) troops, Einion ap Anarawd, by the De Clares. Only Cardigan held out. He regained most of the rest of inland Deheubarth when Henry was unable to suppress his next revolt in 1165, and retook Cardigan Castle which he then rebuilt as his principal residence. He also took over patronage of local Strata Florida Abbey, founded recently by settler Robert FitzStephen, and it became the burial place for his dynasty. He then joined Owain Gwynedd in his stand against the invading Henry at Corwen, and the bad weather frustrated the English army's attempts to penetrate the thick forests. Henry had to retreat and Rhys remained unchallenged, but the king blinded his hostage son Maredudd in revenge. In 1167 he aided Owain Gwynedd to take Rhuddlan, and in 1168 he marched into the upper Wye valley to demolish Builth Castle.

The English lords of the southern Marches, led by the De Clare Earls of Pembroke, now started building up new fiefs in Ireland from 1169 as Earl William, 'Strongbow', was invited to help the refugee King Diarmait of Leinster regain his throne and received his daughter in marriage. He and his Anglo-Norman allies duly started taking over Irish lands as they had done in Wales – and they appeared as much of a threat to Henry as did the Welsh lords. The king marched into the area to confront his own lords rather than Rhys in 1171, and went on to campaign in Ireland and remind his over-mighty vassals of his watchfulness and supremacy. En route Rhys met him at Newnham on the Severn to offer his submission and support and was guaranteed his lands in return for a rent of 300 horses and 4,000 cattle. He met Henry again en route home in 1172 at Laugharne, and was excused the horses still due. Under the eventual accommodation which Rhys reached with Henry during these meetings he ruled his lands as formally an English 'justiciar' or legal representative. He was practically independent and claimed the title of 'Prince of South Wales' though he never regained most of the coast. Securing control of Ceredigion from the De Clares, he managed to remove virtually all the inland English lords such as the Cliffords of Cantref Bychan and the FitzGeralds of Emlyn. Rebuilding Cardigan Castle as his principal residence in the English style (a practice of adapting the enemy's defensive strengths copied by the Gwynedd princes at Dolwyddelan) and funding Strata Florida Abbey, he also held a prestigious 'eisteddfod' at Cardigan Castle at Christmas 1176 to reinforce his role as the Welsh leader in the south and used literary propaganda, e.g. by his bard Gwynfardd Brycheiniog, to promote the cult of his kingdom's most famous religious figure 'Dewi Sant' as the patron saint of Wales, boosting Deheubarth's prestige in the process. Arguably he, rather than any princes of the divided Gwynedd or Powys, was the pre-eminent figure in 'native' Wales from around 1170 to his death in 1197.

Rhys however had a large and turbulent family, and faced feuding among his numerous sons in his later years. Married to Gwenllian, daughter of Madoc ap Maredudd (d. 1160) of Powys, he had at least four legitimate sons plus up to thirteen other children by at least five mistresses; his love-life was notorious. One daughter, Gwenllian, married Edynfed 'Vychan', the famous steward and senior counsellor of Llywelyn ap Iorweth in Gwynedd from 1215–46; their descendants were the Tudor dynasty and via this link Henry VII claimed the inheritance of Deheubarth (and used its heraldic arms) in his invasion of 1485. As a patron of international developments in monasticism, the outward-looking Rhys patronised not only the Cistercians (at Whitland) but the new Premonstratensian Order from France, giving them their first monastery in Wales at Tallylychau; but his confiscations of the endowments of older local Welsh houses ('clasau') to fund these ventures damaged them and emulated the actions of Marcher barons.

Rhys' shrewd judgement and determination to keep the peace with Henry, who had other preoccupations with his treacherous sons and with Kings Louis VII and Philip Augustus of France, delivered stability and peace for most of the 1170s and 1180s. His good relationship with the English monarchy continued, with Henry returning his hostage son Hywel (known as 'Sais', 'the Englishman', from his adoption of English manners) after long captivity. He aided Henry against the king's rebel sons in 1173–4 and took his army to Tutbury Castle (Derbyshire) to besiege rebels, and in 1175 he led a group of his South Welsh vassals (of Senghenydd, Breichiniog, upland Gwent, Elfael, Gwerthynion/Builth, and Afan) to the royal court at Gloucester to do homage (29 June). In 1177 he attended Court at Oxford and was granted part of Meirionydd, with Gwynedd being distracted by wars among Owain Gwynedd's sons; the furious sons of Cynan ap Owain attacked his lands in reprisal and Rhys married a daughter to their uncle and rival Rhodri. He also rebuilt Rhaeadr Castle in the upper Wye valley to boost his power there (1177). In 1184 he journeyed to Worcester to sort out Anglo-Welsh tension on the border, and in 1186 Henry's minister Ranulf de Glanville made a reciprocal visit to Deheubarth to deal with disputes between Rhys and the people of Herefordshire and Cheshire (a sign of the extent of Rhys' reach). In 1188 he acted as an enthusiastic host as Archbishop Baldwin of Canterbury toured south, then west, and finally North Wales to raise recruits for the Third Crusade, meeting him at Radnor. According to Baldwin's assistant Giraldus Cambrensis, who wrote up the tour and so gives us a 'window' into Rhys' realm as of 1188, Rhys wanted to take the cross himself but was dissuaded by his wife Gwenllian. His eldest illegitimate son Maelgwyn did take the cross, but never went on the Crusade as manoeuvres for the succession intruded.

The years of stability for Deheubarth ended permanently with Henry's death in July 1189. The latter's successor Richard was preoccupied with the Crusade, and new frontier disputes broke out with Rhys apparently alleging that the peace had been for Henry's lifetime and seeking to retake extra territory in the Carmarthen region, overrunning Laugharne. It was Richard's brother John, now married to the heiress of the Earldom of Gloucester so a recent addition to Marcher lords, who arranged a truce and invited Rhys to Court at Oxford. This time Richard failed to see him, so he went home and took St Clear's. Taking advantage of Richard's absence on Crusade and the resultant rebellion by John, Rhys and his warlike sons sought to extend their coastal territories and regained Kidwelly in 1190; a siege of Swansea in 1192 however failed. He also took Nevern, capital of the commote of Cemaes in Ceredigion, in 1191. But Rhys also faced trouble in his family from his impatient sons, and seems to have been persuaded by his eldest legitimate son and presumed senior heir, Gruffydd, to arrest Maelgwyn in 1189. Gruffydd handed Maelgwyn over to his wife Matilda's father William de Braose, the brutal and expansionist Lord of Brecon and Abergavenny, presumably to get him out of the way – permanently? – in the forthcoming struggle for the succession. Eventually Rhys secured Maelgwyn's release in 1192, but the two brothers remained at loggerheads. Maelgwyn also blamed his father for his ordeal, and in 1194 seized and imprisoned him; his and Gruffydd's younger brothers Rhys 'Gryg' ('the Hoarse') and Maredudd, possibly anticipating an immediate succession struggle and determined to oust Gruffydd from leadership, then seized Dinefwr. Luckily Rhys was released by an alarmed Maelgwyn and restored order, and in response to De Braose's aggressive rule as 'bailiff' of Carmarthen and Roger Mortimer's annexation of Maelienydd in 1195 launched a final offensive in 1196. Most of the Marcher castles in Radnorshire were taken, and Rhys' reign ended in a final burst of success for Deheubarth.

Division and Decline:
the Descendants of Rhys ap Gruffydd after 1197

On Rhys' death on 28 April 1197, aged around sixty-five, his princedom was split among his sons. He was buried at St David's Cathedral, but only after his body had been scourged as punishment for a recent 'outrage' (possibly an assault on Bishop Peter de Leia, builder of the present cathedral). Maelgwyn also underwent a scourging to gain Church support and offset his lack of legal recognition by the clerics as a bastard, in the manner of the way that Henry II had done penance for the death of Thomas Becket. The senior of Rhys' legitimate sons, Gruffydd, described by Giraldus as devious, succeeded to Cantref Mawr, but was soon under particular threat from his half-sibling Maelgwyn who gained Ceredigion. Maelgwyn, who was the most unscrupulous of the brothers, was under threat of disinheritance if Church law was followed as he was illegitimate – possibly accentuated by the recent removal of the 'illegitimate' claimant to Gwynedd, Dafydd, by his nephew Llywelyn ap Iorweth in 1195. He briefly deposed Gruffydd with the aid of Gwenwynwyn of southern Powys in 1198, and when his victim escaped and drove him out of most of Ceredigion he deserted to the new English king, John. The latter backed his return to Ceredigion as a royal vassal in 1199, and Maelgwyn handed over the crucial Cardigan Castle to the king's officials in an act regarded with fury by patriotic annalists. Meanwhile Gruffydd also secured his younger brother Maredudd's realm of Cantref Bychan in 1201, but died weeks later. Maelgwyn secured most of his lands, but their dispossessed brother Rhys 'Gryg' linked up with Gruffydd's sons Rhys and Owain. In 1204 the trio drove Maelgwyn out of Cantref Mawr, most of which fell to Rhys. Maelgwyn was also responsible for his men's murder of one of their excluded brothers, Hywel 'Sais', in 1204, but lost most of his remaining lands to William Marshal, Earl of Pembroke, later that year.

Rhys' continuing rivalry with his nephews led them to seek the patronage of Llywelyn 'Fawr', and in response Rhys backed John in the confrontation between Gwynedd and England in 1210–11. He received no territorial reward and eventually decided that Llywelyn was a safer ally after John's failure to invade Gwynedd again and preoccupation with the Church, France, and rebellion after 1212. Turning on his English ex-patrons after John's troops had assisted his local power with an expedition against Maelgwyn to Ceredigion in 1211 but set up new castles there too, he sacked Swansea in 1212. Maelgwyn supported whichever side suited his purpose at the time. Both Rhys and Maelgwyn eventually became loyal vassals of Llywelyn 'Fawr' of Gwynedd against King John and their rivals, Gruffydd's sons Rhys and Owain. In 1213 the latter two assisted an invasion of Rhys' lands in Cantref Mawr by John's most notorious mercenary commander, Fawkes de Breaute (who had rebuilt Aberystwyth Castle in 1211 to restore royal power in northern Ceredigion), and he had to flee to Llywelyn's court. He duly assisted the latter's southern campaign of winter 1215–16, when the large Gwynedd army used unusually mild weather to show its power across South Wales and to retake Carmarthen and Cardigan Castles. All the local Welsh princes queued up to submit to Llywelyn, who enforced a division of Deheubarth between them at a 'summit' at Aberdyfi in 1216. Rhys was secured in Cantref Mawr and Maelgwyn in Ystrad Tywi and Ceredigion, with Rhys (d. 1222) and Owain (d. 1235) ap Gruffydd restricted to minor principalities. In 1217 Llywelyn granted Rhys 'Gryg' the custodianship of Swansea Castle under his authority as overlord.

Despite the re-annexation of Swansea and local ravaging by Llywelyn's army in 1216 the princes of Deheubarth were unable to hold on to Gower/Gwyr, dominated by the castle of Oystermouth, which the 1216 expedition had seized from the De Braoses. Llywelyn agreed to hand it back to the latter in 1220. The English maintained a toehold on the coast east of the Towy estuary as well as holding out in southern Pembrokeshire. The powerful Marshal Earls of Pembroke, among them the regent of England Earl William, with his brood of aggressive sons, rallied the defence. His eldest son Earl William (d. 1231) recaptured Carmarthen and Cardigan from Deheubarth in 1223, and then allied himself to the dissident prince Cynan, son of Hywel 'Sais', who he granted the commotes of Emlyn and Ystlwyf as his ally against the senior princes of the dynasty. The Marshals retook the offensive in Ceredigion under William and his brother and successor Earl Richard (d. 1234); luckily Richard ended up in revolt against the royal government in 1233–4 so the family could not count on support from London. Instead Henry III, already prone to advancing Court 'trusties' at the expense of duly alienated regional warlord barons well before he faced major revolt in 1258, granted Cardigan (along with the 'Three Castles' of Skenfrith, Grosmont, and the White Castle in northern Gwent) to his chief minister and veteran general Hubert de Burgh. Hubert's military failure in 1228 (and the resultant southern campaign by Llywelyn ap Iorweth in 1231) complicated matters further. Rhys 'Gryg' recaptured Cardigan Castle in 1231. The Marshals and De Burgh failed to construct the large local South Wales fiefdoms which they had intended, the princes of Deheubarth survived their attentions – and in 1245 the Marshal line became extinct after the successive deaths of four brothers.

Rhys 'Gryg' died, aged around sixty, of wounds suffered in a failed attack on Carmarthen in 1234 and his lands passed to his son by Matilda de Clare, Rhys 'Mechyll'. After this and the eclipse of the Marshal dynasty in the early 1240s Owain's sons, particularly the eldest, Maredudd (d. 1265), were able to extend their rule over much of Ceredigion and to become one of the more successful surviving sub-dynasties of Deheubarth. The cantrefs of Iscoed, Gwynionydd, Caerwedros, Mabwynion, Anhuniog, and Mefenydd in southern Ceredigion were acquired by them, and Maredudd loyally supported Llywelyn ap Gruffydd, aiding his invasion of the south in 1256, and became his main South West Wales ally. But the tradition of dividing lands among all a ruler's sons prevented consolidation, and his territory was divided between his under-age sons Owain (d. 1275), Cynan, and Gruffydd in 1265. The younger two, surviving longer, and Owain's son Llywelyn were all loyal to Edward I in 1277 but joined in the 1282 revolt and were deported to England Llywelyn later got some of his estates – Yscoed and Mabwynion – back, but his uncles stayed in England under supervision to join the 'King's Welshmen' armed contingent at Court and served in Edward I's army in Flanders in 1297.

Maelgwyn died in 1230; his reduced principality duly passed to his son, Maelgwyn ('Fychan') ap Maelgwyn of Ceredigion (d. 1257), who married Angharad the daughter of Llywelyn 'Fawr' of Gwynedd. Rhys 'Mechyll' ap Rhys of Cantref Mawr (d. 1244) was succeeded as senior ruler by his brother Maredudd but his own son by Matilda de Braose, Rhys 'Fychan', inherited some lands too. In 1248 Rhys 'Fychan' joined in a revolt against the English, but his mother remained loyal and seized his castle of Carreg Cennen for the king; she was duly driven out by her son's men. Her daughter, Rhys 'Fychan's sister Gwenllian, married Sir Gilbert de Talbot, and their branch of the Talbots thereafter represented the descent from Rhys 'Gryg'.

The vassalage of these divided principalities of Deheubarth was sporadically enforced by both England and Llywelyn 'Fawr' and Llywelyn ap Gruffydd in the thirteenth century. Rhys 'Ieuanc' was installed by Llywelyn 'the Last' in 1257 to replace his pro-English brother Maredudd, but his brother fought his way back to co-rulership and had to be confirmed in his lands; Rhys held onto parts of Ceredigion. Maredudd had his fealty reserved to Henry III not Llywelyn in the Treaty of Montgomery in 1267, alone of local princes and probably at his request to have the king as guarantor that he would not be dispossessed again. The last princes ended up as clients of Edward I holding much-reduced lands. Rhys 'Ieaunc's son Rhys 'Wyndod' of 'Ystrad Tywi', Lord of Dinefwr, Carreg Cennen, and Llanmyddfri, was dispossessed of Dinefwr and other estates by Edward I 1277 for opposing the king's invasion; it became the main centre for English administration in the confiscated lands of northern Carmarthen. He was dispossessed of the remainder in 1282 for backing Llywelyn's revolt.

Rhys 'Gryg's other grandson Rhys ap Maredudd of Dryslywyn retained most of his estates for the moment and received much of his cousin Rhys' lands in Ystrad Tywi in 1282; he backed Edward in 1277 and 1282, but considered that the king had cheated on a promise to award him Dinefwr (the most prestigious dynastic centre of his line) in 1277. He was treated slightingly by the local English judges and castellans, particularly John Tiptoft, the new 'justiciar' of Carmarthen, and in response tried to argue that he should be legally subject to the Pembrokeshire district court instead. In 1287 he refused a summons to court in Carmarthen, and attempted to resist dispossession by a revolt; he seized Llandovery and Carreg Cennen Castles in July but was hopelessly outnumbered as a huge army was assembled at Carmarthen to tackle him. With the king in Gascony his brother Edmund, Earl of Cornwall, assembled around 2,400 men from the south-east Marches and Midlands, 1,000 locals under Tiptoft, and 5,600 under the Earl of Gloucester from Glamorgan, and on 13 August Rhys was besieged in Dryslwyn. After three weeks the attacking sappers undermined the walls, the chapel collapsed, and Rhys fled into the hills; he re-emerged to take Newcastle Emlyn in November after Earl Edmund's army went home but it was retaken in January 1288. He ended up a hunted fugitive, being caught in the Tywi valley in April 1292, taken to the king at York to be tried, and was executed on 2 June 1292. There was a rebellion in eastern Deheubarth in support of Llywelyn 'the Last' against Edward I in 1282, which saw the locals defeating their powerful English neighbour Gilbert de Clare, Earl of Gloucester and Lord of Glamorgan, at Llandeilo. But this was suppressed, as was a second rising in 1294–5.

Welsh version of early pedigree (Bartrum's pedigrees), not referring to the Irish descent:

> Maxim Gwledic (i.e. Emperor Magnus Maximus, r. 383–8) – Dimet – Nimet – Cloitguin – Clotri – Triphun – Aircol – Guoztepir/Gordebar (i.e. Vortipor) – Cincar/Kyngar – Peder – Arthwyr – Nowy – Cloten.

Alternative version from E. Phillimore's article in *Y Cymmrodorion*, 1888:

> Maxim Guletic – Nimet – Nimet – Gloitguin – Clotri – Triphun – Aircol – Guotepir (i.e. Vortipor) – Cincar – Pedr – Arthur – Nouogy – Cloten – Cathen – Catogocaun.

Obviously there are not enough generations between Maximus (380s) and Vortipor (540s) for a father-son descent; if this version is an accurate record it lists the rulers including several men of the same generation.

Dynasty of Dyfed from the Irish Settlements:

Name	Date of accession	Date of death/ dep.	Years ruled
Eochaid of the Deisi (Leinster)	Late fourth century?		
Corath	Early fifth century?		
Aed	Mid-fifth century?		
Tryffin 'The Bearded' (Tribune?)	*c.* 470/480?		
Aircol (Agricola)	*c.* 500?	*c.* 520?	*c.* 20?
Vortipor 'Protector' ('Gartbuir')	*c.* 520?	*c.* 550?	*c.* 30?
Cyngar	*c.* 550?		
Pedr (Peter?)	Later sixth century?		
Arthwyr (Arthur)	*c.* 600?		
Nowy (Nennue)	*c.* 625?		
Gwlyddien ('Cloten')	*c.* 650?		
Cathen	*c.* 675?		
Cadwgan	*c.* 700?		
Rhain	Early eighth century?		
Tewdr	Mid-eighth century?		
Maredudd	Later eighth century?	796/797	
Rhain	796/797	808	11?
Owain	808	811	3
Tryffin	811	814	3

Anarchy and Viking rule.

Hyffaid ap Bledri	c. 875?	893	c. 10/15?
Llywarch	893?	904	11?
Rhodri	?	905	

Kingdom to a cadet line of Gwynedd.

Cadell of Gwynedd	905	909	4
Hywel 'Dda' ('the Good')	905	950	45
Owain ap Hywel	950	986	36
Rhodri ap Hywel	950–3		
Edwin ap Hywel	950–4		
Einion ap Owain	c. 965–984		
Maredudd ap Owain (also Gwynedd)	986	999	13
Cynan of Gwynedd	999	1005	6
Edwin ap Einion	1005	1018	13
Cadell ap Einion	1005	1018	13
Llywelyn ap Seisyll (also Gwynedd)	1018	1023	5
Rhydderch ap Iestyn (of either Dyfed or Gwent)	1023	1033	10
Hywel ap Edwin	1033	1044	11
Gruffydd ap Llywelyn (Gwynedd) (i)	1044	1047	3
Gruffydd ap Rhydderch	1047	1055	8
Gruffydd ap Llywelyn (ii)	1055	Early 1063	7/8

Maredudd ap Owain (rival: Caradog ap Gruffydd ap Rhydderch)	Early 1063	1072	9
Rhys ap Owain	1072	1078	6
Rhys ap Tewdr	1078	April 1093	14/15

Norman Conquest.

Gruffydd ap Rhys (Cantref Mawr)	1116	1137	21
Anarawd ap Gruffydd (Ystrad Tywi)	1137	1143	6
Cadell ap Gruffydd (Ystrad Tywi)	1143	1151 (abd.)	8
Maredudd ap Gruffydd (Ystrad Tywi)	1151	1155	4
Rhys ap Gruffydd ('Y Arglywdd Rhys') ('Lord Rhys')	1155	28 April 1197	41/42

1197: Division of Deheubarth among Rhys's sons Gruffydd, Rhys, and Maelgwyn.

Maelgwyn (Ceredigion) (i)	Spring 1197	1198	1
Maelgwyn (Ceredigion) (ii)	1199	Autumn 1230	31
Gruffydd (Cantref Mawr)	Spring 1197	25 July 1201	4
Rhys 'Gryg' ('the Hoarse')(Cantref Mawr) (i)	1204	1213	9

Rhys 'Gryg' ('the Hoarse') (Cantref Mawr) (ii)	1216	1234	18
Rhys ap Gruffydd (part of CM)	1201	1222	21
Owain ap Gruffydd (part of CM)	1201	1235	34
Maredudd ap Owain (parts of CM and Ceredigion)	1235	1265	30
Maelgwyn 'Fychan' ap Maelgwyn (Ceredigion)	1230	1257	27
Rhys 'Mechyll' ap Rhys 'Gryg' (Cantref Mawr)	1234	1244	10
Maredudd ap Rhys 'Gryg' of Dryslwyn (Cantref Mawr)	1244	1271	27
Rhys 'Ieuanc' (Ceredigion)	1257	1271	14
Rhys 'Wyndod' ap R. 'Ieaunc'	1271	1283 (dep.)	12
Rhys ap Maredudd of Dryslwyn (Cantref Mawr)	1271	1288 (dep.)	17

Rulers of Ceredigion/Seisyllwg

Modern Ceredigion (Cardiganshire)

The ruling house was traditionally descended from a younger son of Cunedda of Gwynedd, the eponymous Ceredig. It became 'Seisyllwg' in the mid-eighth century in honour of its greatest ruler, Seisyll, who annexed Ystrad Tywi from Dyfed to form an expanded kingdom.

The realm passed to the dynasty of Gwynedd in 871 on the drowning of King Gwgon, whose sister was married to Rhodri 'Mawr' of Gwynedd and

Powys. It was united with Dyfed in the early 900s, under a junior line of Gwynedd princes, to form 'Deheubarth'.

Name	Date of accession	Date of death/ dep.	Years ruled
Ceredig	Mid-fifth century?		
Iusay	Later fifth century?		
Serguil	?		
Bodgu	?		
Artbodgu ap Bogdu	?		
Artglys ap Artbogbu	Seventh century?		
Clydog ap Artglys	?		
Seisyll ap Clydog	Early eighth century		
Arthgen ap Seisyll	?	807	
Dyfnwallon	807	?	
Meurig	Mid-ninth century		
Gwgon ap Meurig	?	871 (k.)	

Seisyllwg to Gwgon's brother-in-law, Rhodri of Gwynedd and Powys.

| Cadell ap Rhodri of Gwynedd 878 | 909 | 31 | |
| Clydog ap Cadell | 909 | 920 | 11 |

Union with Dyfed under Clydog's brother Hywel 'Dda'.

6

RULERS OF THE SILURES/MORGANNWG (GLAMORGAN)

Note on the Genealogy and King List

Most common version of the early genealogy, from the *De Situ Brecheniauc*, No. 10:

> Macsen Wledig – Anhun Dunawd – Tathal/Teudfal/Teithfallt   Teithrin/ Tewdr – Tewdrig (– Meurig – Arthwys).

There are two theories regarding the dating of the early rulers in this list, placing them in two different centuries. While it is accepted that Teithfallt/ Theodosius claimed descent from Emperor Magnus Maximus (d. 388) and took control after the massacre of the earlier royal family by the Saxons, his date is disputed as is that of his grandson (?) Tewdric/Theodoric. The genealogies are hazy about the line of descent from Maximus to Teithfallt, seeming to trace it through the Emperor's 'son' Anhun/Antonius who seemingly ruled in Galloway and/or Man around 400 and had no known connection to Glamorgan/Siluria. In some accounts an unknown 'Nynniaw' is intruded into the line, as father of Teithfallt; he appears elsewhere as a king of Gwent linked to the line of Pebiau. The linkage of this unusual name to the near-contemporary St Ninian, founder of the pioneering British monastery at 'Candida Casa' (Whithorn) in Galloway, is unclear – was it coincidence, or was 'Nynniaw' named after the saint?

Tewdrig appears at times as king of 'Garth Madyrn', rather than of the Silures, and his name appears bizarrely to be Visigothic – Theodoric – in origin. 'Garth Madyrn' refers to the lands of Matriona/Madyrn, legendarily daughter of Vortigern's son Vortimer, which were in Gwent. Tewdrig is given in some genealogies (e.g. Jesus College, Oxford, pedigree 9) another father, Llywarch son of Nynniaw son of Erb; was 'Erb' a ruler of Siluria or of Ergyng? Some commentators, e.g. P. Bartrum (*Early Welsh Genealogical Tracts*, 1966) think there is only one Tewdric but others believe two men have been confused. The Silurian genealogy is also extended back to suggest an unlikely connection with the rebel Roman Emperor Carausius, 'Casnar Wledig' (r. 287–93), who elsewhere appears in the family tree of Vortigern.

A connection with the earlier royal line of the Silures – that of the first-century AD Caradoc/Caratacus and Ceri – is slightly more possible, whether or not Maximus' father-in-law Eudaf 'Hen'/Octavius of Ergyng was intruded into the Silurian genealogy like Carausius because of his prestige. The long list of 'father-son' descent from Anhun to Tewdric/Theodoric also seems to suggest more generations between Maximus and Tewdric's son Mouric than would be possible from the fact that the latter had a saintly nephew born around 485 (Samson) and a royal nephew ruling around 500 (Brychan). Maximus was killed in 388, leaving one adult son and probably younger children. The explanation may be that the genealogists were wrong in suggesting a 'father-son' descent of the throne and that several rulers were of the same generation.

Nor is it altogether clear what early evidence apart from nomenclature lay behind the suppositious claim that a ruler around 400, Owain or Eugenius, was the occupant of the Late Roman villa at 'Caerworgan' near Llantwit. Owain, supposedly a younger son of Maximus and remembered as one of the 'three elders' of Britain in the Welsh Triads, is placed as the ancestor of the rulers of the sub-kingdom of Gwent in some genealogies. Logically, as he was remembered as an 'elder' rather than as a monarch he was best known to subsequent generations as some form of councillor. This was possibly to the group of 'civitates' who took over the administration in or near 410, the presumed destination of Honorius' letter authorising the Britons to look after their own defences and the organisers of the Saxon defeat around 411 recorded by Gildas. If he had achieved any sort of permanent political/military power he would have appeared in the ranks of the holders of the title of 'gwledic', with Maximus, Cunedda, and Ambrosius.

The earliest (eighteenth-century) historians to study the family placed Tewdric/Theodoric's abdication in favour of his son Mouric/Meurig and subsequent death in battle against the Saxons at Tintern around 470, as was written when a memorial was erected to him at his burial site at Mathern Church near Chepstow. More recent writers, followed by John Morris in *The Age of Arthur*, link the battle to an unsuccessful campaign of Ceawlin of the West Saxons in the area around 584. The argument is linked to the greater plausibility of a Saxon force reaching Tintern by land from the occupied Hwicce area in the 580s than in the 470s, but it is possible that a Saxon army could sail into the Bristol Channel in the fifth century and land in Gwent.

Some scholars have attributed the major divergence over dating of around 100 years here to a mistake in the main extant manuscript of the Morgannwg genealogy, claiming that two generations of kings have been missed out in the sixth/seventh centuries and that Morgan 'Mwynyfawr', 'of the Gifts', after whom Morgannwg was named, is not the 'Morgan' who died around 664 but his eponymous grandfather who lived around 600. His son Rhyhawd and a second Morgan thus bring the genealogy to around 664. This is still disputed. But it can be said that on the evidence of nomenclature Teithfallt/Theodosius is more likely to have been named in the fifth century after the Emperor Theodosius I (d. 395), or even after his father who, as a general, saved Britain from Saxon attack in 367, than someone in the sixth century when the name is unknown. His son Tewdric/Theodoric could easily have been named after the Visigothic king who ruled from 416 to 451 rather than the later Ostrogothic ruler who died in 526. The (disputed) evidence of the genealogies given for other notables linked to the royal house of the Silures who can be dated to around 500, e.g. Mouric's nephew Brychan the founder of Brycheiniog (Brecon), and saints such as Illtud, would also make it likely that Mouric reigned then rather than around 580. This all has implications for the possible identity of 'Arthur'. However, pushing Mouric back to a generation earlier than Brychan and thus his father Tewdric/Theodoric to a generation earlier than that – around 450–60? – makes nonsense of the presumed line of descent from Maximus via Anhun. Wendy Davies, who dates Mouric around 600 from the *Llandaff Charters*, prefers to place him using the genealogies as accurate 'father-son' descents to estimate the time-scale from the late fourth century to his reign.

Mouric's mother was known in the medieval period as Enhinti, sister of 'Urien'. This was taken as evidence that the later sixth century date must be the correct one, the most famous Urien being the ruler of Rheged who was murdered at Lindisfarne around 589. Accordingly, Mouric or Theodoric could be supposed to have been helped to power by their dynastic allies in Rheged. But there may be a simple confusion of names here. There was another, obscure Urien closer to hand for Siluria – Urien of 'Gore', i.e. Gower, who survived into medieval Arthurian legend as husband of one of Arthur's older sisters. It is more likely that the South Wales ruler Theodoric married the daughter of the king of Gower, a minor kingdom which later became part of Siluria/Morgannwg – and the Gower descent of the Silurian annexers may have helped their claim to it when its lords died out or were deposed. A later member of the dynasty, Yvain or Owain, is the probable origin of the Arthurian knightly hero of Chretien de Troyes' *Yvain, le Chevalier au Lion* of around 1177.

Mouric is presumably the eponymous chieftain after whom the hill-fort at 'Pentre Meurig' near Cowbridge was named; if so, this was probably his main residence. The site has not been excavated so any sixth-century settlement is unproven. His name appears frequently as a patron of the Church centred on the new see at Llandaff in the *Llandaff Charters* and he is cited as the founder of the see and buried at the cathedral, but as the charters were at least heavily edited in the later eleventh century it is uncertain how much reliance can be placed on them. They have also been variously dated, with Wendy Davies arguing in her 1979 edition of the *Charters* that the 'Mouric' named in them is more likely to have reigned around 600 (which disagrees with some genealogical evidence and Breton hagiographies). Her genealogies crucially link the line of Mouric and Tewdric to Pebiau of Ewias rather than to the longer version of Tathal, Teithrin etc. back to Maximus, and John Morris – who put Tewdric's death in battle as part of the 584 campaign against Ceawlin – muddles Tewdric up with the Cornish ruler of that name. Other claims are made for Mouric still being alive in 562, as suggested in the medieval Life of a Bishop of Llandaff, St Oudoceus (Docco?) – a saint who is alternatively linked to events in the late fifth century. Mouric is supposed by later Welsh tradition to have had an unusually long reign of around fifty years, at whatever date it occurred, and to have forged a marital link with the 'House of Coel Hen' in the north; at least one exiled prince of that line, Meirchion/Marcianus, the grandfather of Urien of Rheged, appears to have been a sub-king somewhere in Gwent in the sixth century. For what it is worth, Mouric was firmly dated at around 520 as a contemporary of Arthur by the twelfth-century Welsh *Brut Tyssilio*. The latter accurately named other rulers active at that date, e.g. Catwallaun 'Lawhir', so why should it make a mistake solely in Mouric's case?

Name	Date of accession	Date of death/ dep.	Years ruled
Nynniaw?	Late fourth century?		
Owain/ Eugenius? (Gwent?)	c. 400?		
Tathal?	c. 410?		
Teithfallt/ Theodosius?	c. 420?		
Teithrin?	c. 440?		
Tewdric/ Theodoric	450s?	c. 475? (abd.)	c. 20/5?
Mouric/ Meurig	c. 475?	c. 525?	Trad. c. 50
Arthwys	c. 525? (co-ruled c. 510?)	539/42?	

According to one interpretation of the documentary evidence, Mouric outlived Arthwys and was still alive in 562 – which would date his accession around the 520s and thus affect the earlier kings' dates too. But this is unlikely given the fixed dating of Mouric's nephew, St Paul Aurelian, at around 485–565; and Paul's (Breton) biography is near-contemporary, i.e. early seventh century, so likely to be accurate.

The alternative version:

Name	Date of accession	Death/dep.
Tewdric/Theodoric	>500	<550 (abd.)
		c. 550 (k.)
	c. 550?	c. 575 (abd.)
		584 (k.)
Mouric	c. 550	c. 600/610
Arthwys (possibly only co-ruler)	c. 600/610?	?
Morgan	c. 610?	c. 665

'King Arthur' – Was he the 'King Arthwys' of Siluria?

Arthur: the Historians, the Sceptics, and the Medieval Romances

Arthwys of the Silures is one of the current contenders for the 'original' of the figure later known as 'King Arthur' – that is, the leader of the British forces that brought a halt to the Anglo-Saxon advance around 500, resulting in the period of peace that degenerated into the misrule of which Gildas complained around 545. The name seems to be connected to the British/Welsh word for 'Bear', possibly meaning 'the Great Bear' or 'Bear Prince', and was quite possibly a nickname. But was the holder the 'Bear' referred to in the name of Dinarth in Gwynedd, or – as has been suggested recently – a nickname for a man known by a different patronymic, such as Ambrosius himself? And were the various 'Arthurs' who are recorded in the later sixth century, e.g. in Dyfed and Dalriada, named after a heroic 'original'?

The problem that has always lain at the heart of the question of the 'real King Arthur' is that he has been successively reinterpreted by each century in its own terms, building up layers of myth which cannot be regarded as applicable to the real figure of a post-Roman warlord. Indeed, we now see Arthur in the terminology of a medieval king and patron of chivalry rather than that of the fifth century, principally through the anachronistic work of the twelfth-century author Geoffrey of Monmouth who made him out as a prototypical conquering 'High King' of the British Isles, a model for his Anglo-Norman patrons to follow. To this was added a weight of equally anachronistic romance, starting with the work of the North French poet Chretien de Troyes – who seems to have modelled the feisty, adulterous Queen Guinevere on Queen Eleanor of Aquitaine. During the twentieth century, successive efforts were made to portray Arthur in realistic fifth- or sixth-century terms, and a search for the 'real' king was stepped up – aided by Leslie Alcock's archaeological finds of a fifth-century fortified military base at Cadbury Castle in Somerset, legendarily linked to Arthur. But the contemporary sixth-century Gildas does not refer to him at all in his account of the wars between Britons and Saxons that followed Ambrosius' rallying of his countrymen. Gildas' language is obscure, but it appears that the climax of the war was the great British victory at 'the siege of Mount Badon', either forty-four years before Gildas wrote, possibly in the year that Gildas was born, or forty-four years after an event referred to earlier (the start of the war? Gildas' birth?). Ambrosius is portrayed as the leader of the British, though not definitely as the victor at Badon, so why did Gildas

– the only surviving contemporary historian – not refer to the great British general 'Arthur'? Because he never existed, insist the sceptics. Similarly, the fact that the mid-tenth-century *Annales Cambriae* (Dyfed) refer to Arthur's victory at Mount Badon in 518 (?) and the fatal Battle of Camlann where he fell in 539 (?) has been written off as a late interpolation, added at a date when his legend was already established. This is debatable, but these so-called 'Welsh' annals certainly include more Irish than Welsh details for the sixth century – almost all of it religious – and seem a dubious source for allegedly genuine secular sixth-century information. Their information on the kingdoms of Wales, e.g. Gwynedd, is minimal.

The original pre-Geoffrey Welsh poems and traditions present Arthur as an 'all-Wales' figure rather than one lined to a particular dynasty – the list of Arthurian '*Mirabilia*' ('Wonders') collected by Bishop Nennius around 830 include sites in North, South, and Mid Wales. Some seem to refer to Arthwys of Dyfed, such as references to Arthur's son Nowy (the man who ruled Dyfed in the early seventh century?) or possibly the connection of Arthur with the Bishopric of Llandaff under its 'founder' Dyfrig/Dubricius. Arthur is linked to Mount Snowdon, where he is supposed to be sleeping in a cave; to Ruthin where he executed Hueil ap Caw; to Lake Bala where he was brought up at Caer Gai; to 'Carn Cafal' near Builth Wells; to Arthur's Stone in the Golden Valley, near Hay-on-Wye; and to a site near Wormelow Tump in Archenfield/Ergyng, south of Hereford. Names of places referring to him included the hill-fort of 'Arthur's Walls' near Newport and Penarth near Cardiff.

The probably eleventh- or twelfth-century tale Culhwch and Olwen placed his court at Caerleon, thus making him a king of Gwent; and gave him a band of heroes, some with mythical powers, as a forerunner of the 'Knights of the Round Table'. The Triads had courts for him at obscure sites in North and South Wales, plus the enigmatic 'Cerniw' which might be either Cornwall or a part of north-eastern Gwent – and referred to three Queen Guineveres/Gwenhwyfars, Arthur's nephew Gawain (Gwalchmai), and several prototypes for Lancelot (who only appears in twelfth-century French romance). The later eleventh-century hagiographies of Welsh saints of the sixth century – based on originals of an earlier date? – had Arthur as a contemporary of the parents of St Cadoc of Llancarfan (around 500–70), who helped them to flee from her father King Brychan of Brycheiniog (fl. 500), and a co-ruler at 'Dindraithov' in north Devon with King Cador of Dumnonia. Cadoc's 'Life' also had him coming to the River Usk in search of a fugitive and being tricked by the saint – i.e. not being the local ruler, as in Culhwch and Olwen. The – in its current state around 1100 – life of St Illtyd presented him as the saint's cousin, and thus a connection of the royal house of Morgannwg. The tale of him threatening and being punished by St Padarn, a sixth-century Dyfed holy man, seems to refer to King Arthwys of Dyfed again. The authenticity and meaning of all this literary material has been endlessly argued over by historians. But one vital element of it is that Arthur is not conceived of as a 'normal' dynastic ruler of one particular kingdom, placeable within its royal genealogy, but as an 'over-king' with a band of warriors who operates throughout Wales and has no definitive 'home area'. This has encouraged doubters to say that he was thus always conceived of as a mythical hero, a travelling 'righter of wrongs' who took on the attributes of gods and legendary warriors. If he was identifiable as the Arthwys who appears as a king of Morgannwg in either the early or the late sixth century, why all this confusion? And why do the traditions – Nennius included – not name Arthur as the son of King Mouric of the Silures if that was his parentage? Who exactly was Arthur's alleged father, usually taken as 'Uther'? As Nennius says that the British kings accepted Arthur's leadership 'though many were more noble than him', does that mean he was not royal or that he was illegitimate?

Dating the 'Silurian' Arthur

Even if it is accepted that the Morgannwg king list can be revised to date Mouric, father of the Silurian king 'Arthur'/Arthwys, to around 500, it presents problems concerning the dating of Arthwys' son and successor Morgan. He is recorded as marrying the daughter of Urien/Urbgen of Rheged (who died around 589) and fighting against Aethelfrith of Northumbria when the latter attacked Powys after the battle of Catraeth around 600. It is difficult, though not impossible, to place him as the son of a man who died around 540; he is claimed to have been the son of Arthwys' third marriage and old age and to have succeeded as an infant. In this theory Arthwys' much older elder son, Nowy 'Llacheu'('the Glittering One'?), the intended heir, had been killed in battle at Llongborth as remembered in medieval Welsh poems during his father's lifetime. Nowy is recorded as a son of Arthwys who grants land to Bishop Dyfrig/Dubricius in the *Llandaff Charters* – assuming that the 'revision' of the charters in the later eleventh century preserved accurate details from this period and that the latter is around 530, both of which Wendy Davies disputes. But he is elsewhere named as the son of a later sixth-century Arthwys, ruler of Dyfed not Glamorgan and descendant of Gildas' contemporary Vortipor. Another son of Arthur, 'Amr', is supposed to have been buried in Herefordshire according to a legend recounted in the ninth-century *Mirabilia* by Nennius – which refers to Arthur as 'amherawdr', i.e. 'emperor'. But according to the latest analyses Nennius was writing a polemical work, calling on the current kings of Gwynedd to emulate the one-time 'national 'leader Arthur and drive back the Anglo-Saxons, not a straightforward history', and gives his Arthur miraculous powers – he may have consciously modelled him on Joshua in the Old Testament. His historical accuracy is dubious.

Equally difficult for this theory is the claim that Arthwys restored Urien and his brothers Llew and Arawn to lands they had lost in Lothian. These men are named in the genealogies of the *Gwyr y Gogledd*, the northern British dynasties of Coel 'Hen's line, as the sons of Cynfarch 'Oer' – who can be presumed to be the 'St Cynfarch' recorded as a grantee of land from Arthwys in the *Llandaff Charters*. The church of Cynfarch, that is 'St Kinnemark', presumably his burial place, is near Chepstow in Gwent. The genealogies place him as fourth in descent from the early fifth-century Coel 'Hen'. Llew married Arthwys' sister Gwyar, daughter of Mouric/ Meurig of Siluria, and his sons Gwalchmai (the original of Gawain) and Medraut (possibly not 'Modred' the traitor) were adult enough to fight for their uncle before Camlann in around 539 if 'Arthwys' was 'the' king Arthur who fought this battle. This marriage must lie behind the legend of 'Lot of Lothian' as Arthur's brother-in-law, and Gwyar is thus presumably the 'original' behind Arthur's legendary sister Morgause. Medraut ap Llew married Cwyllog, daughter of Gildas (presumably the historian). Though we cannot be certain if Gildas was born around 475 or later, the inscription on the Ogmore Stone referring to a grant of lands to Gildas' close relatives by King Arthmael, i.e. 'Bear Prince' – Arthur of Siluria? – would seem to indicate the former due to Gildas' grandson Fili, a recipient, being adult before Arthwys died. Logically, if Fili was already a bishop and partner in the land-grant at Ogmore in Arthwys' lifetime he was adult by the 530s at the latest – and Gildas would be at least forty years older than him.

Llew was clearly adult around 510 to have adult sons capable of fighting around 539, whereas Urien did not succeed to his kingdom of Rheged until around 560 and was not regarded by the poets celebrating his campaigns as notably aged in the 580s. The father of these two men, Cynfarch, is recorded as marrying Nevyn, the daughter of Brychan (Arthur of the Silures' first cousin) who ruled Brycheiniog around 500–20. Brychan was the son of Mouric's sister, and Arthwys' first cousin – and was the grandfather of St Cadoc who was born around 500. Moreover, Cynfarch's uncle in the genealogies is given as Elidyr/Eleutherius, who married a daughter of Maelgwyn of Gwynedd (presumably after the latter's accession around 520) and was killed by Maelgwyn's son Rhun some time after 550 – suggesting that Cynfarch is unlikely to have been active as early as 490. There may be a simple fault in the preserved genealogies here which would explain the discrepancies. Urien might have been Llew's much younger half-brother, though it would be unusual if he was born around 530 and Llew was born around 480–90.

Archaeological Evidence for a Sixth-Century 'Arthur'

Given these problems, it is worth noting that there are two pieces of archaeological evidence that place a man with a name like 'Arthur' in Morgannwg in the early to mid-sixth century. The Ogmore Stone, a record of a land-grant now at the National Museum of Wales, gives 'Arthmael' as granting land to a group of people identifiable as contemporary relatives of St Cadoc – Glywys and Nertat, seemingly Cadoc's brother and aunt – and St Fili (of 'Caerphilly'), traditionally recorded as Gildas' grandson and the son of St Cennyd (of Llangennith in the Gower). This would imply that an 'Arthur' was ruling in the middle of the sixth century, as a contemporary of Cadoc like the eleventh-century hagiography places him. The only candidate with the right name is the father of Morgan and son of Mouric, as the Arthwys who ruled in Dyfed was a descendant (grandson?) of Gildas' contemporary King Vortipor. The 'Arthur' of the grant may be the same man as the Arthwys who is recorded in the *Life of St Cadoc* (late eleventh-century, but based on earlier sources) as granting Cadoc land at Cadoxton near Neath, though this is unclear as Cadoc's patron is sometimes given a different father. If the man who granted the Cadoxton property was not Arthwys son of Mouric, he was presumably a local king unplaced in the royal genealogies. The Arthwys who gave the Ogmore grant must however be the son of Mouric, as that estate was much closer to the centres of Silurian royal power than Cadoxton (which was on the western borders). The only recorded fifth- and sixth-century ruler of the Ogmore area apart from the Silurian royal line was Illtud's foe, Paul of 'Penychen' (the name of the local cantref east of the River Thaw).

An inscription at Llantwit places 'Artmael' (either 'the dead' or 'the ruler') as a contemporary of Abbot Samson. This may be the South Wales saint mainly active in Brittany who died around 560, but if the 'Ithael' in the inscription is the seventh-century king of Morgannwg, both the 'Artmael' and 'Samson' must be later than the 'Arthurian' period. Blackett and Wilson have also argued that the story in the *Life of St Illtud* of him receiving the body of a high-ranking personage which had arrived by sea and burying him at his cave on the banks of the River Ewenny (Chapel Hill, Merthyr Mawr) refers to the burial of Arthur after Camlann, and claim that he was reburied in an extant cave in the woods of Coed-y-Mwstwr near Pencoed and ultimately at a site by the church of St Peter on the ridge of Mynydd y Caer a few miles away (also linked by them with the monument erected to the councillors of Vortigern massacred by Hengest around 450). They claim that the 'mystery' ('anoeth') linked to the site of Arthur's burial in the literary tradition is a play on words indicating the name of the site in Coed-y-Mwstwr, or else the cave in Chapel Hill at Merthyr Mawr. But this is contentious and it is not certain that the author of the stanzas on Arthur's burial place would have known the local name of the supposed site and been able to make the connection. Moreover, the placing of the burial in the biography of Illtud puts the event as occurring when the saint was living in his cave in the lands of the hostile ruler Paul of Penychen, before he founded his school. The pupils at the school included an adolescent Maelgwyn, who was an adult king by around 520, so the incident must have taken place earlier than that date and the deceased is unlikely to have been a King 'Arthur' who died around 539.

Arthur's Father – Mouric or Uther?

It is however a major problem that any reliance on the Morgannwg genealogy comes up against the fact that none of the Arthurian legends record his father as Mouric; and his mother is stated to have been Igraine (Ygyr, daughter of Amlawdd 'Wledig') not Mouric's wife Onobrawst. The Welsh sources are in agreement in naming Ygyr, whose sisters are supposed to have been the mothers of the hero Culhwch (in *Culhwch and Olwen*) and of St Illtud. The medieval Welsh pedigrees, brought together by Rachel Bromwich (R. Bromwich, A. O. Jarman, and B. F. Roberts, eds, *Arthur of the Welsh*, 1991), name Yygyr's parents as Amlawdd 'Wledig' and Gwen, daughter of Cunedda – thus placing Arthur at three generations after Cunedda who lived around either 400 or 440. The only caveat here is that they also include Ygyr's first husband Gwrleis/Gorlois, who appears in Geoffrey's Arthurian version of the 1130s and is given 'Dindagol' as a home in twelfth- to fourteenth-century Welsh writings but has not been given an early provenance that must have evolved independently of Geoffrey.

It is notable that none of Mouric's other sons who are named in early genealogies of the Silurian dynasty seem to have survived into Arthurian legend as connections of the great king. They included Idnerth and

Comereg, Abbot of Moccas near the Golden Valley in Ewias. If Arthur was really the Silurian prince, how come the latter's brothers never appeared in the stories taken up by Geoffrey? But Mouric's daughter (Anna or Gwyar) and her marriage into the royal house of Coel 'Hen' in Lothian did survive as far as Geoffrey of Monmouth's text and the *Brut Tyssilio*. Her northern husband Llew ap Cynfarch was turned into 'Lot of Lothian' in the Anglicised stories. Geoffrey was thus using Arthwys of the Silures as an 'original' for his Arthur. Another royal marital connection of Arthur in the medieval stories, 'Urien of Gore', is another clue to the possible Silurian origin of part of the Arthurian legend; he seems to be a mix of Urien of Rheged, Llew/Lot's brother, and of a ruler of Gower ('Guyr') in South Wales around 500.

Blackett and Wilson argue that the man named as Arthur's father in all sources, Uther Pendragon, was an honorific not a personal name – it meant 'the awe-inspiring Head Dragon', i.e. chief ruler. A 'Funeral Ode' to a great commander identified as Arthur, the 'Mawrnad Uthyr Pendragon', was published in *Myrvyrnian Archaeology* in 1801, and used the word 'Uthyr' in the sense of meaning 'wonderful' not as a personal name. It also referred to Arthur as the 'kinsman of Caesar', presumably meaning the dynastic link with Magnus Maximus, and as vanquisher of the family of Caw 'of the Wall', Gildas' father, as in medieval Welsh legend. Thus a Welsh scribe writing 'Arthur mab uthr', 'Arthur the awe-inspiring', could have it misinterpreted as 'Arthur son of Uthr'. However, 'Uthyr' was a personal name – the Welsh derivation of 'Victor', a Roman name whose most famous holder was the eldest son of Emperor Maximus, Arthur's ancestor according to legend. It is not impossible that there was an Uther/Victor who succeeded Ambrosius as 'Pendragon' and that Arthur was his (illegitimate?) son, and that Geoffrey of Monmouth picked up and expanded this story that he had found in his famous 'ancient book', be it Welsh or Breton. Blackett and Wilson have gone further and claimed that early Welsh stories about Maximus' son Victor, his 'brother' Anhun/Antonius, and the general Andragaithus taking part in Maximus' successful war against the Western Roman Emperor Gratian in Gaul in 383 contributed to the stories of Arthur's Gallic campaign. Geoffrey Ashe has a different explanation (see below).

Other Candidates?

Despite southern Scottish place-names and connections with Arthur, not least Arthur's Seat, it seems likely that the eponymous prince of Dal Riada in the 570s is too late to have fought the traditional Arthurian campaigns and was rather named after the 'original' by his ambitious father, the great war-leader King Aedan mac Gabhran. The 'Arthur'/Arthwys who ruled in Dyfed in the second half of the sixth century is also probably too late to be the 'original', though he may have been called after him and/or contributed some of the Welsh place-names associated with him in later tradition. The 'Amr son of Arthur' killed and buried by his father near Wormelow in Herefordshire according to Welsh tradition could have been the son of either Arthur/ Arthwys of the Silures or Arthur/Arthwys of Dyfed. There are two 'Arthurs' in the genealogies of the 'Men of the North', one of them ruling in the Pennines within reach of the Anglian settlers of Deira, but both appear to be mid-sixth-century and neither is connected to the 'original' in Welsh tradition.

There is nothing implausible in the theory that 'Arthur' commanded a force of cavalry that used the Roman roads to campaign all over Britain, not least in Scotland, and that the widespread appearance of his name reflects his wide journeyings. Some historians prefer to argue that the Welsh connections only spread after Britons carrying stories of him were driven out of his original area and settled there, or that tales travelled along the trade-routes; one theory places him in Cornwall where there are strong topographical connections (of uncertain antiquity). The discovery of a secular settlement and a stone referring to 'Artbognu' at his legendary birthplace, Tintagel, has revived the local claims as the site now seems to be more of a secular base than the potential monastery that it was initially assumed to be. But it is not clear how old the linkage of Arthur to the area is, even if Geoffrey of Monmouth (the earliest extant source for it) used earlier Welsh or Breton books. Gorlois/Gwrleis, the 'Duke of Cornwall' and supposed husband of Ygraine/Ygyr who Arthur's father Uther seduced, is suspiciously absent from the Welsh genealogies of the rulers of Dumnonia. The identity of Arthur's court at Cylliwic/Gelliwig as the hill-fort at Killibury (Kelly Rounds) near Wadebridge is fiercely defended by protagonists of a Cornish Arthur, and opposed by the Welsh scholars who insist that 'Cerniw' is Gwent not Cornwall. Nor does the evidently fierce pride of the Cornish in Arthur as a local hero by 1113 – when a group of foreign pilgrims caused a riot by refusing to believe that he would return – mean that he was a local dynast as opposed to a British over-king and/ or 'national' general whose memory survived strongest in the areas of his activity which were still inhabited by Celts.

Geoffrey Ashe, meanwhile, concentrates on the origin of the story in Geoffrey of Monmouth that Arthur fought a campaign in Gaul in the time of the Emperor Leo (r. 457–74), and links him to a British ruler who fought there in 469. This man, 'Riothamus' ('High King') of the Britons according to Jordanes' *History of the Goths*, brought 12,000 men to a campaign in the Loire valley to assist the Roman authorities and disappeared after a battle at the significantly named Avallon in Burgundy. The 1019 *Life of St Goeznovius*, a Breton saint, portrays Arthur as campaigning in Gaul around 470, and Ashe supposes that Geoffrey used this story in constructing his account of Arthur's Gallic war. Thus Riothamus contributed at least a major part of the Arthurian legend and could have defeated the Saxons in Britain in the 460s. If an 'Arthur' fought at battles around 500 he could have been a second man with this name, or else commanded the force set up by the 'original'. Again, the theory presents major problems of dating, given the stronger Welsh traditions linking him to events and personalities of the early sixth century. This 'Arthur' is far too early to have fought at a battle at Badon around 490 to 516 – indeed, the story of the intervention in Gaul traditionally comes at the end of Arthur's career, thus putting Badon in this time-scale some years before Riothamus' ally Emperor Anthemius succeeded to the Western Roman throne in 468. This compresses the events of the seemingly long Saxon wars and the pre-Arthurian career of Ambrosius into too short a period, given that the *Gallic Chronicle*, a contemporary source unlike Gildas or Nennius, dates the main Saxon revolt at 441/2. The obscure 'Riothamus' has been more probably linked to an Armorican prince of the later fifth century, 'Iann Reath', than to a king ruling in Britain.

The Silurian ruler of the early sixth century is probably a safer (though still problematic) candidate if Arthur is to be placed in a definite kingdom instead of being a successful general who fought for assorted sovereigns. Is it possible that there were two Arthurs reigning in Morgannwg in the early sixth century, one the son of Mouric (only a local king) who was his aged father's colleague and the other the Welsh 'over-king' who was the – illegitimate? – nephew of Ambrosius? Or was there one Arthur, the son of Mouric by an extramarital relationship with the mysterious 'Ygyr', some of whose details later became confused with those of subsequent Morgannwg rulers with the same name?

It is notable that Arthur, unlike other great warrior-leaders such as Urien, was never unambiguously placed in a definite position in a royal Celtic dynasty by all subsequent writers – the early Welsh legends agreed on his location but never referred to him as the son of Mouric in a way that Geoffrey of Monmouth would have been able to utilise. Arguably this was because Mouric had become confused with 'Uther Pendragon' due to references to him in literature under his title not his name. But why then did Mouric become known as the brother of Ambrosius Aurelianus? And why did the established Arthurian stories have Uther dying before Arthur's coronation at the age of fifteen, whereas Mouric lived until his son Arthwys was an adult and the two of them ruled together? It may be that there was some mistake made by an unknown poet between the sixth century and the eleventh century about Arthur's father and/or predecessor as 'High King'. But the confusion suggests that even if he was of the Silurian dynasty and later ruled their realm he did not make his principal impact on his fellow Britons as a Silurian king, but as a 'free agent' warlord in charge of an army in the service of other rulers and subsequently as a 'national' overlord in succession to Ambrosius.

Later Silurian Kings: 'Morgannwg'

One or other of the kings called Morgan, after whom Morgannwg was named, died in 664/5 at the time of the obscure second Battle of Badon (of unknown site and participants). The dates – at times even within decades – of the later seventh-century to early ninth-century rulers are unclear. But King Ithael ap Morgan is supposed to be the founder of the church of St Nicholas, near St Fagans west of Cardiff, and so should be buried there; his son Rhys founded the church at nearby Peterston and his son Arthfael was buried at Roath. All this would suggest that their kingdom was centred around the area immediately west of Cardiff. The *Annales Cambriae* record the death of an obscure Ffernfael – from his importance, probably the ruling king – in 775; his genealogy makes him the great-grandson of Ithael ap Morgan, which confirms that the latter was probably alive in the later seventh century.

By the 880s Bishop Asser, a cleric from St David's in King Alfred's service, records that the rulers were Brochfael and Ffernfael ap Meurig ap Arthfael. Hywel ap Rhys, possibly a cousin of theirs, ruled part of Morgannwg – possibly Glywsyng, around Cardiff – and like them sought Alfred's help against Mercian attacks in the 880s. He may have been the ruler of that name who died in Rome in 884/5. The Vikings' army, which was having limited success in Wessex, arrived in the Severn valley in 895–6 and plundered across South Wales, and another major descent followed in the early 910s. That decade saw Wessex and Mercia combined into one kingdom, along with the Viking lands of eastern and northern England, and Hywel's son Owain was one of the local kings who submitted to Athelstan at Hereford in 926. Owain was buried at Ystrad Owain, near Cowbridge.

Owain was succeeded by his sons Cadwgan, Gruffydd, and Morgan around 930 after a reign of probably around forty-five years. Gruffydd, ruling Gower on the western borders, died in battle against his neighbour Hywel Dda of Deheubarth; by 950 Morgan, the only survivor, had reunified the kingdom. He also acquired Gwent on the death of Cadell ap Arthfael in 942, and acquired the sobriquet of 'Hen' ('the Old') from his long rule of over forty years. On his death in 974 a multitude of sons shared out the kingdom, with Owain (of Glywysng) as the senior. A division of Owain's lands among his own sons weakened the state's unity further; one of them, Hywel, apparently reigned for around fifty years (to around 1043). By the third and fourth decades of the eleventh century the political situation had been further muddled by the emergence of two more dynastic claims on Morgannwg – Edwin ap Gwriad of Gwent (deposed by Hywel's son Meurig in 1045) and Rhydderch ap Iestyn. The latter, whose father Iestyn ap Owain may have come from the lines of Morgannwg or Deheubarth, had secured Deheubarth on the death of Llywelyn ap Seisyll in 1023. He was the father of Gruffydd ap Rhydderch, who engaged in a long struggle for rule in South Wales with Gruffydd ap Llywelyn ap Seisyll of Gwynedd and was killed by him in 1055.

Name	Date of accession	Date of death/ dep.	Years ruled
Morgan 'the Courteous' or 'of the Gifts'	*c.* 539/542?	*c.* 600?	Over 50?
Rhyhawd ap Morgan	*c.* 600?	?	
Morgan ap Rhyhawd	?	664?	
Ithael ap Morgan	664?	?	
Rhys ap Ithael	Late seventh century?		
Arthfael ap Rhys	Early eighth century?		
Mouric ap Arthfael	Mid-eighth century?		
Brochfael ap Mouric	Mid-late eighth century?		
Ffernfael ap Ithael	?	775?	

Gweirydd ap Brochfael	*c.* 800?		
Arthfael ap Gweirydd	Early/mid-ninth century?		
Rhys ap Arthfael	Mid-ninth century?		
Brochfael ap Meurig (Gwent)	880s?		
Ffernfael ap Meurig (Gwent)	880s	?	
Hywel ap Rhys	?	Trad. 886	
Owain ap Hywel	886?	930?	44?
Morgan 'Hen' ('the Old') ap Owain	930?	974?	44?
Nowy ap Gwriad (Gwent)	<948	>955	>8?
Owain ap Morgan	974?	?	
Hywel ap Owain (Glywysng only)	990s?	1043	*c.* 50?
Rhydderch ap Iestyn (of Dyfed?) (Deheubarth from 1023)	*c.* 1015	1033	18?
Edwin ap Gwriad (Gwent)	*c.* 1015	1045	30?

Union with Dyfed 1033–47.

Gruffydd ap Rhydderch (of Dyfed?)	1047	1055	8
Meurig ap Hywel (Gwent)	1045	1055	10
Cadwgan ap Meurig (Gwent) (i)	>1045	1055	10
Gruffydd ap Llywelyn (Gwynedd and Dyfed)	1055	Mid-1063	7/8

Caradog ap Gruffydd ap Rhydderch	Mid-1063	1081	18
Cadwgan ap Meurig (ii)	Mid-1063	1074	11
Iestyn ap Gwrgan	1081	<1093	<12

It is uncertain if Rhydderch ap Iestyn, his son Gruffydd, and his grandson Caradog – the first two rulers of both Dyfed and Morgannwg – were direct male descendants of the royal houses of Dyfed or Morgannwg. Gruffydd, arch-foe of his namesake, the other Gruffydd of Gwynedd, reclaimed both Morgannwg and Deheubarth from him in a three-year war from 1047 but was killed by him in 1055. Caradog (the name derived from 'Caratacus', suggesting a claimed genealogical link to the old Silurian royal house), took control of both Morgannwg and much of Deheubarth on the killing of Gruffydd ap Llywelyn by Earl Harold in 1063. He had to share Morgannwg with Cadwgan ap Meurig, who ruled the south-east (Gwent) until losing much of it to the Norman invader William FitzOsbern, Earl of Hereford, after 1070. Some time around 1070–5 the FitzOsbern dynasty founded Chepstow Castle, thus securing control of the lower Wye valley and the lowlands west to the Usk.

Caradog killed Maredudd ap Owain of Deheubarth in 1072, lost out to the latter's brother Rhys in the succession struggle, but finally evicted his rival in 1078. He was at least defeated, and probably killed, at the Battle of Mynydd Carn by his rival Rhys ap Tewdr in 1081; Morgannwg went to Iestyn ap Gwrgan, of uncertain dynastic linkage, though Caradog's son Owain secured the lordship of Caerleon as a Norman vassal. By this stage it would appear that the Normans had at least reached the Rhymney valley, and possibly held Cardiff permanently from the Conqueror's expedition to St David's in 1081.

Norman Conquest

Glamorgan was acquired by the baron Robert Fitz Hamon, Iestyn's son-in-law, who legendarily started off as a mercenary knight called in by Iestyn to fight his rivals. Originating from Creully in Calvados, Normandy, and probably living in the Gloucester region as a tenant on King William II's lands there – he later re-founded local Tewkesbury Abbey in 1092 – and in the king's military household, he was evidently an enterprising and land-hungry adventurer fond of taking risks. He legendarily had eleven knights in his first war band as they entered Morgannwg to assist Iestyn and the twelve divided up their employer's lands into twelve fiefs. The extant literary account of their adventures was written around 1560 by the local landowner and antiquarian Sir Edward Stradling of St Donat's Castle, who had access to old records but probably invented a great deal. Setting up his own followers in castles, Fitz Hamon proceeded to evict his father-in-law from power around 1091. Having parcelled up the kingdom, he married Sybil de Montgomery, daughter of Earl Roger of Shrewsbury, and ruled to March 1107 when he was killed in a skirmish in Flanders. He was succeeded by his daughter Mabel's husband Robert, Earl of Gloucester (born around 1090), eldest illegitimate son of Henry I, who led his half-sister Empress Matilda's forces in her bid to claim the English throne from 1138 and was the linchpin of her cause. Achieving temporary victory with help from Earl Ranulf of Chester, Madoc of Powys, and Cadwaladr of Gwynedd at the Battle of Lincoln in 1141, where King Stephen was captured, he met with disaster as his bad-tempered sister entered London in triumph then quarrelled with the citizens. Rioters marched on Westminster and drove her out, and weeks later Robert was besieging Stephen's brother Bishop Henry of Winchester in that city when Stephen's wife (also called Matilda) sent an army to relieve it and Robert was captured in the retreat. He had to be exchanged for Stephen, and the war continued until 1153; he died on 31 October 1147. The 'Lordship of Glamorgan' descended to his son William (d. 23 November 1183) and thence to the latter's daughters by Hawise de Beaumont and their husbands. King John, husband of the elder Isabella from 1189 and so ruler of most of Glamorgan, divorced her on his accession in 1199; the younger daughter's De Clare descendants then succeeded to rule Glamorgan until the last earl was killed at Bannockburn in 1314.

Norman vassals also included some technically dependent principalities in the northern 'Welsh' part of Glamorgan into the thirteenth century – most notably Afan, ruled by Iestyn ap Gwrgan's descendants, and Senghenydd. Ifor 'Bach', Lord of Seneghenydd (around Machen, north of Cardiff) in the 1150s and 1160s, was most famous for kidnapping Earl William of Gloucester and his wife and children from Cardiff Castle in 1158 after the earl seized some land and refused to return it. Scaling the walls at night, he carried the earl and his family off into the remote forests inland and kept them until the lands had been restored. His son Gruffydd had succeeded to Senghenydd by June 1175, when he accompanied Rhys ap Gruffydd of Deheubarth to Gloucester to do homage to Henry II. He died in 1210 and was succeeded by his son Rhys (d. 1256); a younger son, Gruffydd 'Bychan', lived at Leckwith west of Cardiff, presumably inheriting the family's lands in the Vale of Glamorgan, and married the heiress of Roger de Sturmi, Lord of Stormy Down near Bridgend.

Iestyn's sons Caradog and Gruffydd, princes of Afan in the mid-twelfth century, were succeeded by the former's son Morgan 'Arglwydd' ('the Lord'), who died around 1208; Morgan was succeeded by his sons Lleision and Morgan 'Gam'. The latter, also lord of the borough and estate of Newcastle at Bridgend (encompassing the valley south-east of Afan), died in 1241. He passed Afan to his son Morgan 'Fychan' (d. 1288) and Newcastle to his daughter Matilda who married into the local Marcher dynasty of Turberville – originally from Dorset and so the 'original' of the literary d'Urbervilles – who were the Lords of Coity Castle (the next lordship to the east of the River Ogwr); Morgan 'Fychan's grandson John 'd'Avene' sold up the Afan estate around 1350. The dynastic descent from Iestyn continued into the modern era via the Turbervilles and via the family of John's brother Rhys of Baglan (the Mackworths and Williamses of Aberpergwm).

The rising power of the De Clare Lords of Glamorgan, controlling the earldom and the Anglicised lowlands, gradually extended northwards over the upland principalities of Morgannwg in the mid-thirteenth century. The Lords of Glynronddha were dispossessed in 1246 and Afan effectively reduced to vassalage in 1247; in 1267 Gilbert de Clare, the 'Red Earl' and grandson-in-law to Henry III, arrested Gruffydd of Senghenydd, son of Rhys (d. 1256), confiscated his lands for alleged links to Llywelyn ap Gruffydd of Gwynedd, and built the impressive Caerphilly (Caerffili) Castle in his lands to hold the locals down. The alleged 'treason' covered a naked 'land-grab'. The castle was soon sacked as the dispossessed dynasts sought the aid of Llywelyn of Gwynedd, but the annexation was made permanent as Edward I destroyed Gwynedd's power.

Gilbert, a classic 'over-mighty' subject and the greatest landowner in South Wales, had temporarily joined Simon de Montfort's rebels in 1264–5 before allying with the usurping regime's foe Prince Edward, and always had an uneasy relationship with Edward who he defied in the late 1260s; he broke a pledge to go on Crusade with him without repercussions. He died in 1295, and his son by Edward's daughter Joan 'of Acre', the 2nd Earl Gilbert, was killed at Bannockburn in 1314; this divided the huge De Clare estates in the southern Marches among Gilbert's sisters and their husbands with the Despensers soon becoming predominant. Their blatant monopoly of land and power then led to a Marcher reaction, led by the Mortimers of Wigmore Castle, and a successful revolt in 1326 which toppled their patron

Edward II. The king, accused of being the younger Despenser's homosexual lover, was to be captured fleeing from his vengeful wife and her lover Roger Mortimer near Llantrisant in Glamorgan. Mortimer, ironically, was a descendant of the aunt of Llywelyn 'the Last' of Gwynedd who Edward's father had overthrown.

The direct line of Gruffydd ap Rhydderch (Deheubarth 1047–55) continued to rule at Caerleon, held in the mid-twelfth century by Morgan (d. 1158) son of Owain son of the 1060s South Wales dynast Caradog ap Gruffydd. His brother Iorweth had killed Richard de Clare, Lord of Ceredigion, in an ambush at Grwyne Fawr near Abergavenny during the great revolt of 1136 as Morgan reconquered upper Gwent from the Anglo-Norman settlers, and succeeded Morgan as Lord of the Usk valley. In 1171 his foe Rhys ap Gruffydd persuaded Henry II, en route for Ireland, to join him in besieging Caerleon and evicting Iorweth, who had to retreat to Machen but returned in July 1173 to besiege and retake his principal fortress. He was deprived of Caerleon again by the king in 1175 after his ruthless son Hywel blinded and castrated his uncle Owain Pen-Carn in a presumed fight over the succession, but regained it later by coming to terms with Rhys – probably due to his daughter Nest's affair with that ruler. He died before 1184 and Hywel succeeded him; in that year Hywel was castellan of Newcastle, Bridgend. Hywel's son Morgan retook the confiscated Caerleon from the royal garrison during the revolt of 1216, but was driven out by the Marshal family, Lords of Pembroke; they occupied the castle but were sporadically at odds with the new King Henry III's government so Morgan was emboldened to launch a lawsuit to get Caerleon back. Cunningly using English law rather than the usual violence and benefiting from the Marshals' unpopularity at Court, he succeeded in having Caerleon taken into royal custody pending a settlement in 1223–6 and was finally awarded the castle in 1233 after assisting the Crown against Earl Richard's estates in Gwent in 1231–2. Richard's successor Earl Gilbert refused to hand it over, but had to do so in 1236. The dynasty now retained Caerleon until Morgan died childless in 1248.

Rulers of 'Glywysng' or Glevisseg

The Cardiff area; sub-kingdom of Morgannwg, the cantref of 'Penychen', named after its first ruler Glywys (grandfather of St Cadoc). The alternative name given to the area east of Cardiff was 'Gwynllwc', modern 'Wentloog', after his son Gwynllw – Cadoc's father, who is recorded as successfully abducting Gwladys, the daughter of King Brychan of Brycheiniog. The account of the early (sixth-century) dynasts thus depends heavily on the extant, late eleventh-century *Life of St Cadoc* by Lifris of Llancarfan, presumably using earlier materials then in Cadoc's monastery library though reworked for contemporary purposes (which probably means that basic genealogical and dating details are correct). Cadoc was supposed to have been the kingdom's resident bishop-cum-senior abbot, a common post-Roman practice for rural-based kingdoms most used in Ireland. He was based at the estate of Llancarfan in the Vale of Glamorgan, where he founded his monastery, but his hagiography also claimed that he travelled to Scotland and Ireland. By the later sixth century the kingdom had been absorbed into Glamorgan, and was ruled for a time by a cadet branch of its dynasty.

Nor and Filu only appear in genealogies, without any supporting evidence for dating; Paul of Penychen appears in the *Life of St Illtud* as the local ruler of the 'cantref' around Cardiff in whose territory Illtud settled around 500 (first at Merthyr Mawr and later at Llantwit).

Glywys is dateable as the grandfather of St Cadoc, born around 500; his son Gwynllw married the daughter of Brychan of Brycheiniog (fl. 500).

After Meurig, son of Gwynllw and brother of St Cadoc who nominated him as king, the original line died or was expelled; the accession of Morgan, Prince of Morgannwg, indicates that Glwysyng became the fiefdom of a cadet line of Morgannwg.

Name	Date of accession	Date of death/ dep.	Years ruled
Owain 'Finddhu'?	*c.* 400?	?	
Nor	Mid-fifth century?	?	
Filu	*c.* 470?	?	
Paul of Penychen	Late fifth century?	After 500?	
Glywys of 'Glywysng'	Late fifth century?	By 520?	
Gwynllw 'the Warrior'	By 520?	?	
Meurig	*c.* 530/540?		

Morgan of 'Morgannwg'	Mid/late sixth century?	c. 600?
Ithael	c. 600?	
Rhodri	Mid-seventh century?	
Meurig	Late seventh century?	
Rhys	c. 700?	c. 710 (abd.?)
Ffernfael	c. 710?	
Hywel	Mid-eighth century?	

United with Morgannwg.

Rulers of Gwent 'Iscoed' ('Above the Wood')

The part of the cantref of Gwent north of the Wentwood in modern Monmouthshire. Several fifth-century rulers are known: Ynyr or Honorius and his sons Caradoc and Iddron.

Honorius was presumably named after the eponymous Roman ruler who died in 423, the last to claim authority in Britain. His father is cited by the *Bonedd y Saint* pedigrees 44 and 45 as Dynfwal 'Hen', who is given in *Harleian Genealogies* nos. 4 and 5 as son of Ednyfed, son of Anhun/ Antonius and grandson of Emperor Magnus Maximus. If this is accurate it would make Ynyr, as Maximus' descendant of four generations, mid-fifth-century in dating. He is supposed (in the *Bonedd y Saint*) to have married Madyrn, daughter of Vortigern's son Vortimer, which would confirm this (Vortimer was active in the 450s). Vortimer was later known as the founder of the Gwent town of Wonastow, so this may have been the centre of his estates or sub-kingdom which his daughter duly brought to her husband and descendants.

It is presumed that this Dyfnwal was the 'Dunwallo Molmutius' annexed by Geoffrey of Monmouth as a legendary pre-Roman lawgiver. In the early sixth century: Caradoc 'Vreichvras', 'of the Strong Arm', and his son Ynyr. Ynyr's son was Iddron II. Caradoc was supposed by Welsh legend to have been a senior adviser at Arthur's court, and was claimed to have ruled as far as the 'chalk hills' which may imply a domain in the south-west Midlands or the Cotswolds stretching towards Berkshire. Is this a rare survival of a Welsh folk-memory of a ruler in pre-conquest Britain east of the Severn?

Also linked with Gwent some time in the early to mid-sixth century is Meirchion or Marcianus 'the Mad', sometimes conflated with a prince of that name from the northern dynasty of Coel Hen (see below) who was exiled from his ancestral lands and was grandfather to Urien of Rheged. He is one of St Illtud's secular foes in the latter's (around 1100) hagiography, and thus rules close to Illtud's monastery and school at Llanilltud Fawr in southern Glamorgan. If he was the northern prince, he must have reigned around 500 as his son Cynfarch was the father of Llew and Urien.

Rulers of Ergyng/Archenfield

Modern south-west Herefordshire, alternatively called 'Ewias'. The dynasty was supposedly founded by Octavius/Eudaf 'the Old', father-in-law to Emperor Magnus Maximus (d. 388), though some claim that Vortigern exercised authority here too from his ancestral lands to the north-west around Builth. Ewias has also been linked to the obscure 'Gewissae', the alternative name of the ruling family of the West Saxons, and a local connection suggested for their founder Cerdic. The similarity of the names could indicate a dynastic claim on Ewias by Cerdic's family. It is not known if there could be any truth behind the legendary linkage of Eudaf to the family of Beli 'Mawr' and other pre-Roman rulers, or if this is medieval propaganda seeking to glorify the dynasty by claiming illustrious ancestors.

Pebiau is approximately datable as the grandfather of St Dyfrig/ Dubricius, known by the time that extant Welsh tradition was written down as the first Bishop of Llandaff in the early sixth century and allegedly the man who crowned Arthur. Whether Dyfrig was more than an abbot of the kingdom's principal monastery who acted as the court's resident bishop is unclear, as is his historical link to Llandaff. His career was 'played up' and exaggerated by the ambitious first Anglo-Norman Bishop of Llandaff, Urban, in the early twelfth century. Urban even hijacked Dyfrig's remains from Bardsey Island in 1120 and installed them in the new cathedral near Cardiff as part of his long-running struggle for ecclesiastical supremacy over Wales with Bishop Bernard of St David's. Dyfrig was then claimed to have been an 'archbishop' and to have inherited the claims of the post-Roman see of Caerleon, but it is doubtful if this is historical.

Pebiau is cited by the *Llandaff Charters* and the Jesus College pedigrees as son of Erb, son of Erbin, son of Meurig; his marriage to the daughter of Custennin 'Fendigaid', who ruled Britain around 420–30, places him in the mid-fifth century at the earliest. Wendy Davies in her work on the *Llandaff Charters* in 1979, however, re-dates him to around 600 – apparently using Hector Munro Chadwick's interpretation of the reign of the first Ynyr of Gwent as being sixth-century not fifth-century. A statue of him was recorded in one of the churches of the Golden Valley in Herefordshire, within his realm, in 1536.

There are also other minor rulers of Ergyng in the fifth and sixth centuries who do not appear in the main genealogies but are referred to in documents, most notably the *Llandaff Charters*. The most prominent appears to be Gwrgant 'Mawr', the father of Onobrawst who married King Mouric of Siluria (which places him in the mid-fifth century). He was supposed by medieval Welsh tradition to have been expelled from Ergyng by Vortigern and restored by Ambrosius.

Name	Date of accession	Date of death/ dep.	Years ruled
Eudaf or Octavius 'the Old'	Late fourth century?		
Erbin	Early fifth century?		
Erb	Mid-fifth century?		
Pebiau 'the Driveller'	Late fifth century?		
Cynfyn	*c.* 500?		
Gwrgan 'Mawr' ('the Great')	Early sixth century?		
Gwrfoddw	Later sixth century		

United with Morgannwg.

It should be noted that one of the Jesus College pedigrees gives another son of Erb called 'Nynniaw', who was thus Pebiau's brother, and a 'Tewdric' as his grandson. The latter has been confused with the other Tewdric, the king of Siluria killed at Tintern, with a resulting misdating of Tewdric and Mouric of Siluria as later sixth-century.

'Nynniaw' appears in medieval documents with a tentative South Wales connection, conflated with a ruler of that name from the royal line of

Siluria and with the 'Saint Ninian' who founded the pioneering monastery of 'Candida Casa' (Whithorn) in Galloway in around 400.

Rulers of Brycheiniog

A kingdom based on modern Brecon, apparently a mixture of British and incoming fifth-century Irish settlers. Traditionally founded by the eponymous Brychan who was the son of an Irish prince, Anlach mc Cormac, and Marchell (Marcella), daughter of king Tewdric/Theodoric of the Silures. The pedigrees that crucially connect Brychan's family to Mouric's are in the *De Situ Brecheniauc* no. 10. The probability that Brychan ruled around AD 500 – his daughter was St Cadoc's mother and Cadoc was born near that year – helps to support the theory that Tewdric and his son Meurig/Mouric ruled in the fifth not sixth century (see above); Brychan was thus the cousin and contemporary of Arthwys of Siluria. Brychan's many daughters were supposed to have included a number who became proselytising saints in Cornwall, but the evidence for this is late and possibly unreliable.

The kingdom was overrun by Dyfed around 600, and independence was restored in the following century under the second King Awst and then co-rulers, his son Elwystyl and nephew Tewdwr. In the 880s or 890s Elise ap Tewdwr, the first recorded ruler of the century, sought aid from King Alfred against Anarawd of Gwynedd, but it seems to have been Morgannwg that finally annexed the kingdom when Elise's son Tewdr died some time after 934. In 1088 it was overrun by the Norman lord of the adjacent 'Golden Valley' of Herefordshire, Bernard de Neufmarche.

Name	Date of accession	Date of death/ dep.	Years ruled
Brychan	*c.* 500?	?	
Rhun 'of the Red Eyes'	Mid-sixth century?		
Awst (Augustus)	Late sixth century?		
Rhiwallon	*c.* 600?		

Rule by Dyfed through the seventh century.

Awst II	Mid-eighth century?	
Elwystyl	770s or 780s?	780s? (k.)
Tewdwr (co-ruler)	770s or 780s?	790s?
Elise ap Tewdwr	<880	890s?
Tewdwr	Early tenth century	>934

7

RULERS OF OTHER KINGDOMS

Kings of Dumnonia

The original pre-Roman tribal territory of the 'Dumnonii', modern Devon and Cornwall. The latter did not acquire its name until part of the Midlands tribe of the 'Cornovii' were moved there some time in the early to mid-fifth century to evict Irish settlers, and various rulers of Cornwall are recorded independently of contemporary Dumnonian kings. The Dumnonian dynasty was allegedly descended from Maximus, with the first king Erbin as a son of the British 'High King' of the early fifth century, Maximus' son Constantine 'the Blessed'. Its main dynastic line is recorded in the Welsh pedigrees, but this omits a number of kings who are recorded as ruling in Cornwall in the late fifth century and sixth.

Geraint (fl. around 500), son and successor of Erbin, is probably the man subsequently remembered in Welsh tradition (the Triads) as 'Llyngesog', the 'Fleet-owner', husband to Gwyar the daughter of Amlawdd 'Wledig' (and aunt of King Arthur). By the time the tales of the Mabinogi were composed he was regarded as Arthur's first cousin. According to a poem attributed to Llywarch 'Hen' he was killed the Battle of Llongborth, the 'Port of Ships'. He has been suggested as the important British prince killed at Portchester (?) around 500 by the Saxons Bieda and Maglos, but Saxon and Celtic traditions are confused about this; the *Anglo-Saxon Chronicle* refers to the said prince as 'young' but that would not fit Geraint, whose grandson Constantine was an adult ruler before 540. There is no clue as to where Llongborth was, with various English and Welsh locations being suggested – the name would indicate a harbour then in use as a port.

Cador may be the builder of the refortified military base at Cadbury Castle rather than 'Arthur' as was speculated in the enthusiasm of its discovery in the 1960s – its name implies 'Cador's burgh'. He was ruling in Dindraithov (Dunster?) with Arthur according to eleventh-century hagiography.

Constantine, one of the five kings condemned by Gildas around 545, was traditionally Arthur's successor as 'High King' according to whatever truth lay behind the stories taken up by Geoffrey of Monmouth. According to Gildas, he had already murdered two princes in a church while disguised as an abbot and later abdicated before the time that Gildas was writing; according to later Welsh legend he murdered the sons of Arthur's enemy Medraut (presumably the same boys).

Cunomorus appears to be the original of the legendary 'King Mark' in the stories of Tristram; the latter is presumably the 'Drustan son of Cunomorus' named in the memorial stone near the Cornish royal fortress at Castle Dore, but it is uncertain how authentic the tradition is. Cunomorus also ruled over part of Brittany, and was killed in battle against the Franks in around 558 after backing a rebel prince of the Merovingian dynasty, Chramn, against the senior ruler Chlotar son of Clovis (r. 511/58–61). The Frankish historian Bishop Gregory of Tours confirms the date of this, which can be used to date other contemporary foes of Cunomorus such as Bishop Paul Aurelian (a connection of the dynasty of Morgannwg). It is not certain that Cunomorus was the mysterious 'Cynfawr' from the ruling family of Rheged who appears in Welsh legend as connected to St Cynfarch and his sons Llew and Urien/Urbgen.

Tewdric is recorded in the *Life of St Gwinnear* as ruling in the Hayle estuary around 500, unusually for that period being pagan. He was also connected to the Falmouth area in Cornish tradition. He slaughtered a large group of Irish monks under Fingaras as they landed, presumably thinking they were colonists intending to seize his territory; the number of Irish inscriptions suggests strong settlement in the west of the region. His name is derived from 'Theodoric', and may or may not be connected to the Visigothic and Ostrogothic kings of that name and/or the eponymous ruler of Siluria in the mid-fifth century. He was apparently the son of Budic, suggesting a Breton connection, and commanded a strong fleet. His father may be the Budic who ruled the kingdom of Quimper in Brittany for around forty years to around 557, and who Breton tradition and the historian Gregory of Tours (590s) recorded as having been expelled as a young man (by his brother Maxentius?) and returning around 517 with naval aid from Dyfed.

There were also minor kings only remembered in local tradition, such as Clemens (around 500) who was the father of St Petroc. The latter's hagiography dates him as a contemporary of St Samson (around 486–560).

The post-Roman kingdom may originally have included the former territory of the Durotriges around Dorchester, whose rulers cannot be traced; there was certainly an important British presence in Cranborne Chase to around 600. It was gradually reduced in size and the British were driven into Cornwall by the advancing West Saxons, who seem to have conquered Dorset around 614 (depending on whether their victory at 'Beandun' was Bindon near Wareham or near Axmouth) and Somerset after their victory at Penselwood in 658. By 710 King Ine had reached the Tamar. Egbert appears to have conquered Cornwall after his victory at Galford in 825, and defeated a subsequent revolt which the Vikings assisted at Hingston Down in 838.

Genealogy from the Welsh sources (ed. Bromwich):

> Genealogy XI:
> Eudaf Hen – Cynan – Gadeon – Gorwaor –Tudwaol – Kynoar – Erbin – Gereint.

> Genealogy X:
> Erbin – Gereint – Cado – Pedur – Theudu – Peibion.

As with the Welsh sources, it is probable that several men of the same generation who ruled successively were later transcribed as a 'father-son' descent. In Genealogy XI, Eudaf Hen is in fact the ruler of Ergyng not Dumnonia; his son Cynan and the latter's successor Gadeon ruled in Brittany, though this does not rule out a domain in Britain also given that Conomorus managed this in the mid-sixth century.

Name	Date of accession	Date of death/ dep.	Years ruled
Cynan ap Eudaf	*c.* 400?		
Erbin	Early/mid-fifth century?		
Geraint ap Erbin	Late fifth century?		

Cador ap Geraint	*c.* 500?	*c.* 520?
Constantine ap Cador	*c.* 520?	*c.* 550?
Tewdric/ Theodoric (West Cornwall)	Early sixth century?	
Erbin ap Custennin (Constantine) (Co-ruler: Meirchion, cousin)	*c.* 550?	
Cunomorus/ Mark of Cornwall	?	*c.* 558
Peredur	Late sixth century?	
Tewdr	*c.* 600?	
Erbin	Seventh century?	
Geraint	Early eighth century – cited as ruling in 710 in *Anglo-Saxon Chronicle*.	

West Saxon vassals:

Doniert	?	875
Hoel	fl. 927	

Cornwall was heavily defeated by King Egbert of the West Saxons at Galford in 825, but its conquest is uncertain. The Cornish and the Vikings allied against him in 838 but were defeated at Hingston Down; final conquest was achieved by Athelstan in the 920s.

King Doniert is only known from the *Annales Cambriae* recording his drowning in 875; Hoel (a Breton name) was the ruler of the 'West Welsh' who attended Athelstan's meeting with his Celtic vassals at Eamont Bridge in Cumbria in 927.

Note on the Rulers of the Cotswolds

The former lands of the Dobunni, the prime agricultural settlements and towns of the wealthy Roman Cotswolds, had no recorded rulers apart from Aurelius Conan/Cynan, nicknamed (by Gildas or others?) 'Caninus' ('the Dog'), a contemporary of Gildas ruling at Gloucester around 540 who he denounces. He appears from Gildas' reference to have been related to Ambrosius Aurelianus. This might suggest that Ambrosius' family continued to rule the Cotswolds after him into the sixth century, but if so they left no lasting impression of stable kingdoms on Welsh or Saxon tradition. They were not conquered by the Anglo-Saxons until King Ceawlin of the West Saxons destroyed a British army at Deorham (probably Dyrham) in 577. According to the *Anglo-Saxon Chronicle* he killed three kings – Coinmail, Farinmail, and Condidan – and occupied the three cities of Bath, Gloucester, and Cirencester. These were thus still inhabited at the time and presumably had British rulers, but it is not certain that the three defeated kings were these men as opposed to neighbouring kings who had come to assist them.

The name 'Condidan' at any rate suggests a connection with the later Cyndylan of Powys, who may have been a descendant.

Kings of Northern Britain

The lands of later Anglo-Saxon Northumbria, from the Humber to the Forth. Originally in the early fifth century the kingdom of Coel 'Hen' ('the Old'), the 'original' of 'Old King Cole' (but with no known link to Colchester). It has been argued that the kingdom's military strength may have owed its origin to a cohesive body of troops – the survivors of the Roman border-forces on Hadrian's Wall left behind after the 'withdrawal' to Gaul under Constantine III in 407 and their descendants – and that Coel was their commander. Some of the forts on the Wall, e.g. the excavated Birdoswald, seem to have been occupied into the fifth century – after the end of Roman rule – and were presumably lived in by locally based bands of warriors engaged in fighting Pictish raids. It is unclear if any local sense of northern territorial unity survived from the pre-Roman kingdom of the Brigantes, whose tribal aristocracy resumed power as the Roman central government collapsed, or if the Roman province ruled from Eburacum/York was the nucleus of Coel's power.

The larger fifth-century kingdom divided into a number of smaller kingdoms – most notably Rheged (Lancashire and Cumbria), York, Elmet (south-west Yorkshire), Bryniach (Northumberland and parts of Lothian), and Lothian and Din Eidyn (Edinburgh). The genealogies make all their kings descendants of Coel, but this may be just rationalising political reality in dynastic terms. They formed the military/political leadership that defended the area against Anglo-Saxon incursions until the triumph of the new kingdom of Northumbria in the 600s, and were to be renowned in bardic poetry as the 'Men of the North ('Gwr y Gogledd') and have their traditions and genealogies preserved in Wales after their kingdoms were overrun.

Coel 'Hen' is given a long pedigree in the Welsh genealogies, stretching back to the mythical 'Afallach' in the first century. Some of it may be genuine, though his 'father', 'Guotepauc', may be a sobriquet of a man with a different personal name (or of Coel himself). His grandfather, Tecmant/Tecfan, and great-grandfather, Teuhant/Deheuwaint, may be genuine names.

Coel is supposed to have married Ystradwel, daughter of Gadeon who was one of the sons of Eudaf 'Hen' of Ergyng and a ruler in Armorica around 400. The genealogical dating would make sense, though the story may have been invented to explain a political and military alliance between the British settlers in Armorica and the post-410 kingship of northern Britain. Was there an alliance based on mutual military strength?

The date of the emergence of a number of states from Coel's unified lordship is unclear, but the second half of the fifth century would make sense. In that case, it is conceivable that the genealogies reflect the division of Coel's state into two kingdoms, led by Ceneu and Gorbiniaun (Germanianus?), in the next generation and the sub-division of those two states later.

Morcant (II) of Bryniach is datable as the murderer of his rival Urien of Rheged, the most successful British war-leader of his generation, during the siege of Anglian-held Lindisfarne around 589. The probable main royal residence of this kingdom was at the hill-fort of Yeavering Bell, reoccupied and strongly fortified in the fifth century.

Gwendolleu of Caerluel, patron of the poet Myrddin 'the Wild' alias Lailoken/Lallogen (probably one of the 'originals' behind the later legend of Merlin), was killed by his rivals, Urien and other princes of Rheged, at the Battle of Arderydd around 573. After that inter-dynastic conflict the leadership among the kingdoms passed to Rheged under Urien (patron of Taliesin) and his son Owain (patron of Llywarch 'Hen', a junior prince of the Rheged dynasty who may have briefly ruled on the Isle of Man) until the death in battle of Owain around 594. They bore the brunt of the ultimately unsuccessful struggle against Bernicia, and after the latter and Deira were united under Aethelfrith around 604 Rheged declined sharply as a military power and ended in the early seventh century as a client-state of the Angles. Its last ruler's daughter and heiress Riemmelth married King Oswy of Northumbria.

Caerleul was cited in later legend as one of the courts of 'King Arthur', and there have been attempts to link the evident military power of Rheged to Arthur's 'Knights of the Round Table' as a possible post-Roman cavalry force, inheriting the traditions and training of the Hadrian's Wall border-troops, who operated against Picts and Angles in the area from the Forth to the Tyne in the early sixth century (see in particular Alistair Moffat's *Arthur and the Lost Kingdoms*).

Accordingly, potential sites with significant etymology have been linked to the list of Arthur's battles in Nennius; Bouden Hill near Linlithgow has been cited as a possible 'Badon', Edinburgh (with 'Arthur's Seat') as a possible 'Mount Agned', the Forth estuary as 'Tribuit', and Camboglanna as 'Camlann'. But there is no potential ruler called 'Arthur' (or a near-equivalent) of around 500 in the extant genealogies, though that does not rule out that an 'Arthur' from further south could have operated as a general in the service of the local kings at some point or used the cavalry of Rheged in his army.

Peredur has been claimed as a probable 'original' for the Arthurian knight of the Round Table, 'Sir Percival', but does not appear to have been contemporary to the 'real' Arthur. He and his brother were probably evicted from York by the Anglians of Deira in or near 580.

Mynyddog of Din Eidyn was the patron of the war band who fought at Catraeth around 600 and were commemorated by Aneirin in the *Gododdin*. It is presumed that his seat was Edinburgh Rock, though this is disputed. The Irish annals date the end of this kingdom at 638.

Genealogies of the House of Coel 'Hen' from the lists in the *Laws of Hywel Dda*:

Aballac – Eudelen – Endos – Ebiud – Outigern – Titigern – Iutmetal – Grat – Urban – Tetpuil – Teuhant – Tecmant – Coel Hen – Garbiniaun – Dumnugual Moilmut – Bran Hen – Cingar Craut – Morcant Bulc.

Coyl Hen – Ceneu – Gurgust Letlum – Eleuther Cascoed Mawr – Gurci and Peredur.

Genealogies of the House of Coel 'Hen' from the Harleian Mss. 3589, reproduced in *Y Cymmrodor* No. 9 (1888), pp. 141–83:

(Rheged) Urbgen – Cinmarc – Meirchiaun – Gurgust – Coil Hen.

(Lothian) Guallauc – Laenauc – Maguic Glop – Ceneu – Coyl Hen.

(York) Gwrci and Peretur – Eleuther – Cascord Mawr – Ietlum – Ceneu – Coyl Hen.

(Pennines?) Pabo Post Prydein – Arthwys – Mar – Ceneu – Coel.

The ancestry of Coel, presumably via the tribal kingship of one of the northern Celtic realms, is traced back to the mythical 'Aballach' who was supposedly a first-century AD ruler connected to the family of Jesus Christ. This dynasty was thus the pre-Anglo-Norman 'Celtic' version of the later 'Grail Dynasty', keepers of the Holy Grail from the time of Joseph of Arimathea, which included a mysterious 'King Evelake'. As Peredur of Eburacum/York, the 'original' of Sir Perceval, was a descendant of Coel 'Hen' he was thus connected to the family of Aballach – hence the tradition of the 'Grail-finder' being of the 'Grail Dynasty' which was utilised by later medieval writers.

Over-kingship of the North

Name	Date of accession	Date of death/ dep.	Years ruled
Coel 'Hen'	*c.* 410?	Mid-fifth century?	Over 30?

Rulers of Bryniach

Gorbiniaun (Germanianus)	Mid-fifth century?
Dumnagual	Later fifth century?
Bran 'Hen'	Early sixth century?

Morcant	Early/mid-sixth century?	
Outigern	*c.* 530??	
Cynfelyn/ Cunobelinus	*c.* 550??	
Morcant	*c.* 560?	After 589

Rulers of Rheged and York

Ceneu	Mid-fifth century?
Gwrgwst 'of the Ragged Beard'	Late fifth century?

Junior line includes Ceneu's younger son Mar and his son Arthwys – the latter is probably early sixth-century and named after 'Arthur'.

Rulers of York

Elidyr/Eleutherius' title seems to indicate that he was a powerful military leader. His father may have been the elusive Arthwys, son of Mar, raising the possibility that the latter had campaigned successfully in the Yorkshire area and contributed to the legend of 'King Arthur'.

Elidyr/ Eleutherius ('of the Great Army')	Early to mid-sixth century?
Peredur and Gwrci ap Elidyr	Trad. 580

Annexation by Deira.

Rulers of Rheged

Merchiaun, according to the genealogies the son of Gwrgust 'of the ragged beard', was succeeded jointly by his sons. Elidyr/Eleutherius 'the Stout', not to be confused with his cousin Elidyr of York, was driven out by Cynfarch; his son was the poet Llywarch 'Hen', associated with the Isle of Man, who supposedly lived well into the mid-seventh century. Llywarch was remembered as a poet in exile, implying loss of his inheritance. Elidyr is supposed to have attacked Gwynedd by sea some time in the reign of Maelgwyn's son Rhun, i.e. post-550, and drawn a reprisal march into his lands on the northern princes. Logically the attack by Gwynedd can be guessed to have undermined Elidyr's power and reputation and opened the way to his dynastic rivals, Cynfarch and Urien – and to his and his son's exile?

It is not clear how Llew, 'Leodonus', presumed to be the son of Cynfarch as in later dynastic lists, achieved his apparent mid-late sixth-century rule of Lothian (supposed to have been called after him). Was this by agreement with or by defeating the local Votadini, and did he carve out a new kingdom there as an agent of his Rheged relatives? Is there any truth behind the 'Arthurian' stories about him as husband of 'Arthur's sister, originally named as Anna or Gwyar and later as 'Morgause'? Assuming Llew and the eponymous 'Loth' to be the same man, this also helps the dating via the *Life of St Kentigern*, founder of the Bishopric of Glasgow and born around 530/40, whose mother was the daughter of King Loth.

Merchiaun/ Marcianus 'the Lean'	Early sixth century?		
Elidyr/ Eleutherius and Cynfarch	Mid-sixth century?		
Llew ap Cynfarch ('Lot' of Lothian?)	Mid-sixth century?		
Urien ap Cynfarch	*c.* 560?	Trad. 589	*c.* 30?
Owain ap Urien	589?	594?	5?
Rhun ap Owain	594?	610s?	*c.* 10/20?
Rhaith	Early seventh century	*c.* 645	

Here followed annexation by Northumbria, probably by Edwin in the early 620s; Rheged seems to have been a vassal of Edwin's predecessor Aethelfrith by the early 610s and the Northumbrians would have needed to secure it before their 616 campaign to the Dee estuary. Oswy/Oswiu, Aethelfrith's youngest son and king of Northumbria in 642–70/1, had married Rhaith's daughter Riemmelth as his second wife around 640 and she was the mother of his son Alchfrith, sub-king of Deira from 655/6 to around 665.

Rhun was apparently a bishop after his abdication or deposition, possibly at the hands of Aethelfrith of Northumbria, and may have baptised the future king, Edwin of Northumbria, in this capacity while he was in exile in Gwynedd pre-617 or visited him after his restoration.

Rulers of Elmet

Centred in southern Yorkshire.

Arthwys	Early sixth century	
Pabo 'Pillar of Britain'	Mid-sixth century?	
Dunaut	Late sixth century	(d. 597 in *Annales Cambriae*)
Samuel	*c*. 600?	?
Ceredig	*c*. 610?	*c*. 625?

Annexation by Edwin of Northumbria.

Dunaut may be confused with the royally descended abbot, St Dunaut/ Donat, who contended with St Augustine's Catholic missionaries at a synod around 604.

Rulers of Caerluel/Carlisle

Ceidiaw	Mid-sixth century?	
Gwendolleu ap Ceidiaw	c.560?	Trad. 573

Gwendolleu apparently married the sister of the mysterious 'shaman' prophet and holy man Myrddin, the original 'Merlin', who was active in the border region in the 570s. Traditionally he was killed at the Battle of Arderydd (Arthuret?) by a coalition of rival princes of the Coel Hen dynasty in around 573, resulting in the eclipse of the military power of Caerluel at the hands of Rheged. Later poetry claimed the battle was a result of a quarrel over a 'lark's nest', probably a reference to the local fortress of Caerlaverock, and a poem ascribed to Myrddin had it that he went mad with guilt at the carnage there because of his own role in the dispute. The battle apparently led to the eclipse of the power of Caerluel, whose leading role in the north now passed to the kingdom of Rheged under Urien. The links of Caerleul with 'King Arthur' seem to have been due to medieval legend, but conceivably the survival of descendants of local Late Roman soldier-farmers around the western end of Hadrian's Wall provided a nucleus for a coherent and powerful military force for its kings.

Rulers of Din Eidyn

The king of this realm around 600, Mynyddog is only known as the man who collected the force of warriors from across Britain that he launched against the Anglians in the campaign commemorated in the *Gododdin*. He was renowned for his hospitality.

Mynyddog 'the Golden'	Late sixth century	After *c.* 600

Fall of kingdom to Northumbria 638.

8

THE GLYNDŴR REVOLT, 1400–16

Owain Glyndŵr, Lord of Glyndyfrdwy in eastern Powys at the time of his 'national' revolt against the preoccupied Henry IV in September 1400, was not of the direct line of Gwynedd but a descendant of the ruling house of Powys (themselves descendants of Bleddyn ap Cynfyn, d. 1075, half-brother of Gruffydd ap Llywelyn ap Seisyll) and by female descent of Gwynedd and of Dyfed/Deheubarth. His father was Gruffydd, either grandson or great-grandson of Gruffydd 'Fychan' (d. 1289) of Powys, who held lands in the ancestral 'cantref' of Edeirnion and had been steward for the Earls of Arundel in the Lordship of Chirk. His mother Elen, daughter of Owain ap Thomas of Ceredigion, brought him a half-share in the half-commote of Iscoed Llwch Hirwen and Gwynionydd; both his paternal grandmother (Elizabeth Lestrange) and wife (Elizabeth Hanmer, daughter of a King's Bench judge) were English. Born around 1354, he had succeeded his father at Sycharth in his mid-teens. His initial revolt owed much to the frustrations of the local gentry in Gwynedd and Powys, legally discriminated against and ignored by their English overlords, and immediately to grudges against the new regime of Henry IV for lack of the usual rewards in patronage. Glyndŵr himself had had an English legal training in London and probably had a residual loyalty to Richard II, overthrown by Henry in 1399, who had made much of the soldiery of his nearby County Palatine of Cheshire. Glyndŵr had served on Richard's Scottish campaign of 1385. The suspicious death of Richard in captivity at Pontefact in February 1400 had not stopped plots against the unpopular new government on behalf of its dynastic rivals the Mortimer family, who were Lords of Wigmore in the middle Marches, and at the time of his revolt Glyndŵr was being victimised by a neighbour and Henrician loyalist Reginald de Grey, Lord of Ruthin. It appears that Glyndŵr expected to be granted the chief forestership of the local 'forest' at Chirkland by the new king in 1399–1400 and was disappointed, and their pre-rebellion correspondence reveals threats by Grey to burn his lands; the latter was ordered to keep the peace by the king though his foe did not know this.

But even if Glyndŵr's decision to revolt was partly due to fear of royal punishment through Grey's connections and was linked to Ricardian plots, it quickly built up into a 'nationalist' movement as Henry's preoccupied government failed to react decisively. The small local revolt that Glyndŵr launched on the Gwynedd/Powys frontiers started with around 270 men sacking Ruthin on 18 September, followed by Denbigh, Flint, and Hawarden, only to meet a potentially disastrous reverse as local Shropshire loyalist Sir Hugh Burnell defeated his attack on Welshpool. Glyndŵr had to flee the battlefield within days of proclaiming himself 'Prince of Wales', but he survived the initial English counter-attack in 1400–1 and was aided by the counterproductive paranoia of the militant MPs in the English Parliament of early 1401 banning Welshmen from owning land or holding office in England or prosecuting Englishmen in Wales. (To be fair to Henry IV, the Commons were out of his control and used their 'power of the purse' to remove his principal ministers so he could not intervene.) Rumours spread that Parliament would ban the Welsh language next, and inflamed the revolt. Thanks to the adherence of Glyndŵr's cousin William ap Tudor and his brothers in Anglesey, a rebel attack seized control of Conwy Castle at Easter 1401 while the garrison were out at Mass – though they feared reprisal from local Royal Lieutenant Henry 'Hotspur' Percy and secured a temporary pardon and truce in return for handing over some militants for execution. Henry's local Marcher lords were unable to suppress the revolt in the north-east – Glyndŵr captured Grey in person – and in June 1401 Glyndŵr achieved victory against a larger army of loyalist Pembrokeshire settlers and their Flemish allies at 'Mynydd Hyddgen' on the western side of Mount Plynlymon. There, as later, archers were his main resource. The king's own major expedition later that year lumbered ineffectively around a countryside alive with guerrillas amid atrocious weather. A local rebel, Gruffydd Vaughan, promised to lead Henry to Glyndŵr but lured him into an ambush instead, so Henry had him hanged before looting Strata Florida Abbey and retiring to safety; once he had left Glyndŵr sacked Welshpool and tried to storm Caernarfon.

As the king had to concentrate on domestic foes and the rising threat of the Percies, Glyndŵr secured most of Wales apart from the southern coastal strip in the period from around 1403–7, making up for the English superiority in numbers, military experience, and artillery with the aid of popular support and a landscape inimical to conventional 'set-piece' warfare of battles and sieges. The Welsh won the occasional battle, e.g. Pilleth against Sir Edmund Mortimer in June 1402 (where they celebrated by cutting off the English casualties' genitals and noses), but rarely managed to take the larger English-held castles (e.g. Carreg Cennen, defended for Henry for a year in 1402–3 by Glyndŵr's later son-in-law Sir John Scudamore) or the fortified coastal boroughs. These could be supplied from the sea, and the rebels lacked the adherence of all the local lords (Dafydd Gam in Brecon, a loyalist of Henry's dynasty, being a prominent example). Later Mortimer was captured by the Welsh and (December 1401) publicly defected to their cause, bringing them the hope that he could establish a link to his interned nephew Edmund, rival claimant to Henry's throne as heir to the line of Edward III's second son Prince Lionel. The resultant attempts to rescue Edmund from Henry's hands were to lead to his unsuccessful escape from Windsor Castle in early 1405 and recapture en route to Wales. The minutiae of the campaigns are obscure, and much was magnified (or invented?) by later tradition. We cannot be certain when one allegedly major local clash, the Glamorgan rebels' victory at Stalling Down near Cowbridge, took place (1403 or 1405?).

Glyndŵr made much of contemporary prophecies about a Welsh revival, claiming to be the predicted national deliverer and using his dynastic descent to claim a bloodline back to the pre-Roman 'Trojan' dynasty. His role as an alleged 'magician' is his major legacy in British culture, thanks to Shakespeare playing this up in *Henry IV, Part One*. He formed alliances with Henry's principal international rivals, the sovereigns of Scotland and France, and even considered dividing up England with his anti-Henrician allies, Henry 'Hotspur' Percy and Edmund Mortimer. English clerics were replaced by Welshmen, including the bishops, and adherence was transferred from the Pope in Rome backed by Henry to his French-backed rival in Avignon. But Glyndŵr was crucially unable – or unwilling? – to add his forces to those of the Percy rebels in Northumbria as they marched to Shropshire to confront Prince Henry's Marcher army in 1403. The king reached his son in time, and the rebels were routed and 'Hotspur' was killed at the village of Berwick outside Shrewsbury in July – allegedly an ironic fulfilment of the prophecy that the rebel would die at 'Berwick', but not at the expected site of that name.

After the battle Henry marched across South Wales from Herefordshire to Carmarthen in September, but could do not more than secure the main castles. In spring 1405 Glyndŵr entered into a tripartite treaty with 'Hotspur's father, the exiled Earl of Northumberland, and Sir Edmund Mortimer and was promised the lands of the West Midlands up to the Severn and Mersey, but the Percy incursion into the north was defeated by the king.

A French force landed in Pembrokeshire to bring extra manpower and weaponry to the rebels' aid and had some local success, but could not decisively tip the scales against the English though it marched pointlessly as far as the outskirts of Worcester and supposedly camped on Woodbury Hill. Able to hold the only 'Welsh Parliament' at Machynlleth (1404) but outnumbered by the royal armies and with no long-term French aid, Glyndŵr was slowly forced back into Gwynedd by Prince Henry. The failure to take crucial fortresses in the south such as Coity (1404–5) showed that he could dominate the open countryside but lacked siege-engines to match the English defences, and it was only a minor comfort that the king was sporadically but increasingly incapacitated by illness from autumn 1405 (blamed by some on divine punishment for his executing rebel Archbishop Scrope of York). The king's autumn 1405 campaign fizzled out after relieving Coity and in 1406 he was unable to take the field, but Prince Henry took command and gradually wore the rebels down with the dogged ruthlessness he was to show again in Normandy in 1417–9. In 1406 English troops landed on and reconquered Anglesey. In winter 1408–9 the rebels lost control of Harlech and Aberystwyth Castles, which dominated the west coast, the former surrendering to the royal general Gilbert Talbot along with Glyndŵr's wife, daughters, and grand-daughters who had taken refuge there. Their bishops were evicted from their sees at Bangor and St Asaph, and in 1410 three of Glyndŵr's leading lieutenants were captured and executed. Glyndŵr's young son was by 1407 in custody too, in London.

Glyndŵr's effective rule was ended by English reconquest of his last domains around 1411, though he remained at large in the mountains and the revolt continued to flare up occasionally after that. His subsequent whereabouts and date of death are uncertain. On 5 July 1415 Talbot was granted a royal warrant to receive Glyndŵr into the king's obedience, so he was evidently regarded as still alive and possibly about to surrender. It was not taken up. Glyndŵr probably kept his fate a mystery to inspire people that he would return like King Arthur. A good case has been made out that he took refuge with his daughter Alys and her husband Sir John

Scudamore of Kentchurch in the Golden Valley in Herefordshire and died at Monnington Court near Vowchurch in around 1416. One theory connects him to local legends of a mysterious outlaw with magical powers, 'Jack o' Kent' of Kentchcurch.

The female line of descent from Llywelyn Fawr's daughter Gwladys survived through her Mortimer descendants; she had married Ralph de Mortimer of Wigmore Castle around 1230 and her grandson was Edmund, commander of the force that killed Llywelyn 'the Last' in 1282. His son Roger Mortimer, a baronial victim of Edward II's greedy South Wales favourites the Despensers in 1322–6, escaped from the Tower of London, fled to France, and returned as the paramour of Edward's estranged wife Queen Isabella. Effective regent of England in 1327–30, he was to be accused of having Edward II murdered at Berkeley Castle and more certainly tricked Edward's half-brother Edmund, Earl of Kent, into plotting rebellion so he could execute him. At the first opportunity Edward and Isabella's son Edward III had him arrested (in a dramatic raid on the Queen Mother's apartments at Nottingham Castle) and executed for treason in 1330. After such a disaster the Mortimers were lucky to retain their Marcher lands, based around Ludlow Castle, but staged a remarkable comeback as Roger's grandson married the daughter of Edward III's second son Lionel; their son Roger was thus the nearest heir of Richard II if female inheritance rights to the Crown were allowed. The Mortimer lands were duly transmitted by an heiress to the House of York in the early fifteenth century, Anne Mortimer marrying Henry V's cousin Richard, Earl of Cambridge (executed 1415). Accordingly, their grandson Edward IV's descent from the princes of Gwynedd was used by Welsh pro-Yorkist bards to hail him as the restorer of the family's and nation's fortunes, the 'Son of Prophecy', at the time of his seizure of the throne in 1461.

The crucial campaigns partly took place on the Welsh border, owing to Edward's father Duke Richard of York (son of Anne Mortimer) having his principal residence at the Mortimer stronghold of Ludlow Castle. In 1459 the duke and his senior lieutenants (including Edward) had to flee Ludlow after Henry VI and the royal army arrived intent on confrontation; and in February 1461 Edward destroyed the local Lancastrian army, led by Owen Tudor, at Mortimer's Cross nearby and executed Tudor at Hereford. Tudor's eldest son by Henry V's widow Catherine of Valois, Edmund (Earl of Pembroke), had been the Lancastrian lieutenant in South West Wales until his death in late 1456 and his posthumous son Henry VII was born at Pembroke Castle. Tudor's second son Jasper Tudor, his second-in-command at Mortimer's Cross, then held out against the Yorkists at Harlech Castle from 1461–8 before fleeing to France. He returned to assist Henry VI's restoration in 1470, and the king's wife Margaret of Anjou was heading for Wales to seek Jasper's aid when Edward IV caught and destroyed her army at Tewkesbury in May 1471. Jasper and his nephew Henry VII then fled to Brittany, returning in August 1485 to Milford Haven to challenge Richard III.

BIBLIOGRAPHY

1 Pre-Roman Tribal Sovereigns: Leadership in Iron Age Society

Primary Sources

Geoffrey of Monmouth, *The History of the Kings of Britain*, ed. and trans. L. Thorpe (Penguin, 1966).

The Mabinogion, ed. J. Gantz (Penguin, 1976).

The Tain, trans. T. Kinsella (Oxford: 2002).

Tacitus, *Agricola and Germania*, trans. H. Mattingley (Penguin, 1970).

Tacitus, *Annals*, ed. M. Grant (Penguin, 1969, revised 1996).

Secondary Sources

Allen, D., 'The Belgic Dynasties of Britain and their Coinage', *Archaeologia*, 90 (1964).

Arnold, C. and J. Davies, *Roman and Early Medieval Wales* (Tempus, 2000).

Atkinson, R., *Stonehenge* (3rd edn, Penguin, 1979).

Barrett, A., 'The Career of Tiberius Claudius Cogidubnus', *Britannia*, 10, pp. 227–42.

Bevan, R., *Northern Exposure: Interpretive Devolution and the Iron Age in Britain* (Leicester, 1989).

Bird, D. C., 'The Claudian Invasion of Britain Reconsidered', *Oxford Journal of Archaeology*, 19 (2000), pp. 91–104.

Blagg, T. F. and M. Millett, *The Early Roman Empire in the West* (Oxford: 1990).

Boon, G. C., 'Belgic and Roman Silchester: Excavations of 1954-8', *Archaeologia*, 102 (1976).

Boon, G. C., *The Legionary Fortress at Caerleon: Isca* (Caerphilly: 1987).

Branigan, K., 'Vespasian and the South-West', *Proceedings of the Dorset Natural History and Archaeological Society*, 95 (1974), pp. 50-7.

Branigan, K., *The Catuvellauni* (Gloucester: 1987).

Breeze, D. J., 'Agricola the Builder', *Scottish Archaeological Forum*, 12 (1980).

Breeze, D. J., *Roman Scotland* (London: 1996).

Burgess, C., *The Age of Stonehenge* (London: 1980).

Creighton, J., *Britannia: the Creation of a Roman Province* (Routledge, 2006).

Cunliffe, B., *Danebury Hill-Fort* (Tempus, 2003).

Cunliffe, B., *Fishbourne Roman Palace* (Sussex Archaeological Society, 1994).

Cunliffe, B., *Hengistbury Head* (Duckworth, 1978).

Cunliffe, B., *Iron Age Communities in Britain* (Routledge, 2005).

Cunliffe, B., *The Regni* (Duckworth, 1973).

Darvill, T. C., *Prehistoric Britain* (London: 1987).

Davies, J. and T. Williams, *Land of the Iceni* (University of East Anglia: 1999).

de la Bédoyère, G., *Defying Rome: the Rebels of Roman Britain* (Tempus, 2003).

de la Bédoyère, G., *Eagles Over Britannia: the Roman Army in Britain* (Tempus, 2001).

de la Bédoyère, G., *Hadrian's Wall* (London: 1989).

de Ligt, L. *et al.*, *Roman Rule and Civic Life; Local and Regional Perspectives* (Amsterdam: 2004).

Detsicus, A., *The Cantiaci* (Gloucester: 1983).

Dunnett, R., *The Trinovantes* (London: 1975).

Dyer, J. F., *The Hill-Forts of England and Wales* (Princes Risborough, 1981).

Elton, H., *Frontiers of the Roman Empire* (London: 1996).

Field, N. H. and N. Lock, *Badbury Rings, Dorset* (1977).

Frere, S. and M. Fulford, 'The Roman Invasion of AD 43', *Britannia*, 32 (2001), pp. 45-56.

Frere, S., *The Iron Age in Lowland Britain* (London: 1978).

Frere, S., *Britannia: A History of Roman Britain* (3rd edn, Routledge, 1987).

Fulford, M . and J. Timby, 'Late Iron Age and Roman Silchester: Excavations at the Site of the Forum-Basilica, 1977 and 1980–6', *Britannia Monographs*, 15 (London: 2000).

Gantz, J., *Early Irish Myths and Sagas* (Penguin, 1981).

Gwilt, A. and C. Haselgrove, 'Reconstructing Iron Age Societies', *Oxbow Monograph*, 71 (1997).

Hanson, W. S., *Agricola and the Conquest of the North* (London: 1987).

Hartley, B. and L. Fitts, *The Brigantes* (Sutton, 1988).

Henig, M., *The Heirs of King Verica* (Tempus, 2002).

Hingley, R., and C. Unwin, *Boudicca: Iron Age Warrior Queen* (London: 2005).

Hodson, F. R., 'Cultural Grouping within the British Pre-Roman Heritage', *Proceedings of the Prehistoric Society*, 30 (1964), p. 98ff.

Hodson, F. R., 'Some Pottery from Eastbourne, the "Marnians" and the Pre-Roman Iron Age in South-East England', *Proceedings of the Prehistoric Society*, 28 (1962), p. 140.

Hogdson, N., 'Were there two Antonine occupations of Scotland?', *Britannia*, 26 (1995).

James, S., *The Atlantic Celts: Ancient People or Modern Invention?* (British Museum Press, 1999).

Kemble, J., *Prehistoric and Roman Essex* (Tempus, 2002).

Maxfield, V. H., 'The Roman Occupation of South-West England: further light and fresh problems' in W. Hanson and L Keppie (eds), *Roman Frontier Studies 1979* (Oxford: 1980).

Nash-Williams, V. E., *The Roman Frontier in Wales* (2nd edn, Cardiff: 1969).

Niblet, R., *Verulamium: the Roman City of St Albans* (Tempus, 2001).

Pitts, M., *Hengeworld* (Century, 2000).

Pryor, F., *Britain BC: Life in Britain and Ireland Before the Romans* (Harper Collins, 2003).

Renfrew, C. (ed.), *The Explanation of Cultural Change Models in Prehistory* (Duckworth, 1973).

Renfrew, C., *Before Civilisation* (Pimlico, 1973).

Richmond, Sir I., *Hod Hill Excavations Volume 2* (Trustees of the British Museum, 1968).

Stead, I. M., 'Verulamium: the King Harry Lane Site', *English Heritage Archaeological Reports*, 12 (London: 1989).

Thom, A., *Megalithic Sites in Britain* (Oxford: 1967).

Todd, M., 'Oppida and the Roman Army: a revision of recent evidence', *Oxford Journal of Archaeology*, 4(2) (1985).

Todd, M., *The Coritani* (revised edn, Sutton, 1991).

Webster, G., *Boudicca: The British Revolt Against Rome* (Batsford, 1978).

Webster, G., *Rome Against Caratacus: the Roman Campaigns in Britain AD 43–58* (Batsford, 1981).

Webster, G., *The Cornovii* (Sutton, 1991).

Webster, G., *The Roman Invasion of Britain* (Batsford, 1980).

Wheeler, Sir M., *Maiden Castle Dorset* (HMSO, 1972).

2 The End of Roman Rule: Post-Roman Government

Primary Sources

Annales Cambriae, ed. J. Williams ab Ithel (London: Rolls Series 20, 1860).

Bede, *The Ecclesiastical History of the English People*, eds J. McClure and R. Collins (Oxford University Press, 1969).

Constantius, 'The Life of St Germanus', *The Western Fathers*, trans. F. Hoare (London: 1954).

Gildas, *De Excidio Britanniae*, trans. J. Morris (Phillimore, 1978).

Marcellinus, Ammianus, *The Later Roman Empire (AD 354–78)*, trans. W. Hamilton (Penguin, 1986).

Nennius, *British History and the Welsh Annals*, ed. J. Morris (Phillimore, 1980).

The Anglo-Saxon Chronicle, trans. M. Swanton (Phoenix, 2000).

The Chronicle of Henry of Huntingdon, trans. and ed. T. Foster (Llanerch Reprint, 1991).

The Gallic Chronicle, ed. T. Momssen (Paris: 1882).

The Mabinogion, op. cit.

William of Malmesbury, *History of the Kings of England: the Kings Before the Norman Conquest*, trans. and ed. J. Stevenson (Llanerch Reprint, 1989).

Secondary Sources

Alcock, L., *Arthur's Britain* (Penguin, 1971).

Arnold, C. and J. Davies, *Roman and Early Medieval Wales* (Sutton, 2000).

Barber, C. and D. Pykitt, *Journey to Avalon: the Final Discovery of King Arthur* (Abergavenny: Blorenge Books, 1993).

Bartholemew, P., 'Fifth Century Facts', *Britannia*, 13 (1982), pp. 262–70.

Bassett, S. (ed.), *The Origins of Anglo-Saxon Kingdoms* (Leicester University Press, 1989).

Breeze, D., *The Northern Frontiers of Roman Britain* (Batsford, 1982).

Castleden, R., *King Arthur: the Truth Behind the Legend* (Routledge, 2000).

Chadwick, H., *The Origins of the English Nation* (1907).

Cleary, E., *The Ending of Roman Britain* (London: 1989).

Collingwood, R. and F. Myres, *Roman Britain and the Anglo-Saxon Settlements* (1937).

Dark, K., *Civitas to Kingdom: British Political Continuity, AD 300–800* (Leicester: 1994).

Dark, P., *Britain and the End of the Roman Empire* (Tempus, 2000).

Davis, W., *Wales in the Early Middle Ages* (Leicester University Press, 1982).

Dixon, B., 'The Anglo-Saxon Settlement at Mucking', *Anglo-Saxon Studies in Archaeology and History*, 6 (Oxford University Committee for Archaeology, 1997), pp. 125–47.

Doble, G. K. and D. S. Evans (ed.), *Lives of the Welsh Saints* (University of Cardiff Press, 1971).

Dumville, D., 'Nennius and the Historia Brittonum', *Studia Celtica*, 10–11 (1975–6), pp. 78–95.

Dumville, D., 'Sub-Roman Britain: History and Legend', *History*, new series, LXII (1977), pp. 173–92.

Dumville, D., 'The Historical Value of the Historia Brittonum', *Arthurian Literature*, 6 (1986), pp. 1–26.

Dumville, D., 'The Welsh Latin Annals', *Studia Celtica*, 13 (1977–8), pp. 461–7.

Ellis, P., *Celt and Saxon: the Struggle For Britain AD 410–937* (Constable, 1997).

Evison, V. V., *The Fifth Century Invasions South of the Thames* (1965).

Ferguson, J., *Pelagius* (W. Heffer, 1956).

Field, P., 'Nennius and his History', *Studia Celtica*, 30 (1996), pp. 159–63.

Frere, S., *Britannia* (Routledge, 1987).

Hanning, R. W., *The Vision of History in Early Britain* (Columbia University Press, 1966).

Higham, N., *Gildas and Britain in the Fifth Century* (Manchester University Press, 1994).

Higham, N., *King Arthur: Myth-Making and History* (Routledge, 2002).

Higham, N., *Rome, Britain and the Anglo-Saxons* (Routledge, 1992).

Hoare, F. R., *The Western Fathers* (1954).

Howlett, D., *Cambro-Latin Compositions: their Competence and Craftsmanship* (Dublin: Four Courts Press, 1998).

Hughes, K., *Celtic Britain in the Early Middle Ages: Studies in Scottish and Welsh Sources* (Woodbridge: 1980).

Jones, A. H. M., *The Later Roman Empire AD 284–602* (Oxford: 1964).

Kirby, D. P., 'Vortigern', *Bulletin of the Board of Celtic Studies*, 23 (1968–70), pp. 37–51.

Lapidge M. and D. Dumville (eds), *Gildas: New Approaches* (1984).

Laycock, S., *Britannia the Failed State* (2011).

Lindsay, J., *Arthur and His Times: Britain in the Dark Ages* (Frederick Muller, 1958).

Morris, J., *Arthurian Sources Volume 2: Annals and Charters* (Phillimore, 1995).

Morris, J., *Arthurian Sources Volume 3: Persons: Ecclesiastics and Laypeople* (Phillimore, 1995).

Morris, J., *Arthurian Studies Volume 5: Genealogies and Texts* (Phillimore, 1995).

Morris, J., *The Age of Arthur: Britain AD 350–650* (1973).

O'Rahilly, T. F., *The Two Patricks* (Dublin: 1957).

Padel, O., 'The Nature of Arthur', *Cambrian Medieval Celtic Studies*, 27, pp. 1–31.

Reece, R., 'The end of Roman Britain revisited', *Scottish Archaeological Review*, 2(2) (1983).

Reece, R., 'Town and Country: the End of Roman Britain', *World Archaeology*, 12(1) (1988).

Snyder, C., *An Age of Tyrants: Britain and the Britons, AD 400–600* (University of Pennsylvania Press, 1998).

Thompson, E. A., *St Germanus of Auxerre and the End of Roman Britain* (Woodbridge: 1984).

Turville-Petre, J. E., 'Hengest and Horsa', *Saga-Book of the Viking Society*, 14 (1953–7), pp. 273–90.

Webby, D. A., 'The Roman Military Defence of the British Province in its Later Phases', *British Archaeological Reports: British Series*, 108 (Oxford: 1982).

White, N. J. D., *St Patrick* (1920).

3 Rulers of North Wales (Gwynedd)

Primary Sources

Annales Cambriae, op. cit.

Bartrum, P. C., *A Welsh Classical Dictionary* (UWC Press, 1993).

Bartrum, P. C., *Early Welsh Genealogical Tracts* (University of Cardiff Press, 1966).

Bede, *op. cit.*

British Library: Harleian Mss. 3589 genealogies.

Brut y Brenhinedd (Llanstephan Ms. 1 version), ed. B. F. Roberts (Dublin: 1971).

Brut y Tywysogion, or the Chronicle of the Princes: Red Book of Hergest Version, ed. T. Jones (University of Wales Cardiff Press, 1973).

Chronicles of the Reigns of Edward I and Edward II, ed. W. Stubbs, 2 vols (Rolls Series, 1882–3).

Chronicles of the Reigns of Stephen, Henry II and Richard I, ed. R. Howlett, 4 vols (Rolls Series, 1884–9).

Gerald of Wales/Giraldus Cambrensis, *Opera*, eds J. S. Brewer, J. Dimock, and F. Warner, 8 vols (Rolls Series, 1861–91).

Gesta Stephani, eds and trans K. Potter and R. H. C. Davis (Oxford: 1976).

Gildas, *op. cit.*

Henry of Huntingdon, op. cit.

Jesus College Oxford: Mss. 20 pedigrees.

National Library of Wales: Peniarth Mss. 183.

Nennius, *op. cit.*

Ralph of Coggeshall, *Chronicon Anglicanum*, ed. J. Stevenson (Rolls Series, 1875).

Roger of Hoveden, *Annals, Part 1*, trans. H. T. Riley (Llanerch Reprint, 1994).

William of Malmesbury, *op. cit.*

Secondary Sources

(a) Pre–800

Arnold, C. and J. Davies, *op. cit.*

Barber C. and D. Pykitt, *op. cit.*

Bartrum, P. C., 'Notes on the Welsh Genealogical Manuscripts', *Transactions of the Cymmrodorion Society* (1968, pp. 63–98 and 1976, pp. 102–8).

Casey, J. *et al.*, *Excavations at Caernarfon (Segontium) Roman Fort* (London: 1993).

Castleden, R., *op. cit.*

Dark, K., *op. cit.*

Dumville, D., 'Gildas and Maelgwyn: Problems of Dating' in M. Lapidge and D. Dumville (eds), *Gildas: New Approaches* (1984), pp. 51–9.

Dumville, D., 'Kingship, Genealogies and Regnal Lists' in P. Sawyer and N. Woods (eds), *Early Medieval Kingship* (Leeds: 1977), pp. 72–105.

Dumville, D., *op. cit.*

Ellis, P., *op. cit.*

Gruffydd, R. G., 'From Gododdin to Gwynedd; Reflections on the story of Cunedda', *Studia Celtica*, 24–25 (1989–90), pp. 1–14.

Hanning, R. W., *op. cit.*

Higham, N., *op. cit.*

Higham, N., 'Medieval Over-Kingship in Wales', *Welsh History Review*, 16 (1992–3), pp. 145–59.

Hughes, K., 'The Welsh Latin Chronicles: Annales Cambriae and related texts', *Proceedings of the British Academy*, 59 (1973), pp. 233–58.

Hughes, N., *Celtic Britain in the Early Middle Ages: Studies in Welsh and Scottish Sources* (Woodbridge: 1980).

Jarrett, M. and J. Mann, 'The tribes of Wales', *Welsh Historical Review*, 4 (1969).

Kirby, D. P., 'British Dynastic History in the Pre-Viking Period', *Bulletin of the Board of Celtic Studies*, 27 (1976–8).

Lindsay, J., *op. cit.*

Lloyd, J. E., *History of Wales from the Earliest Times to the Norman Conquest*, 2 vols, (3rd edn, 1939).

Miller, M., 'The Foundation Legend of Gwynedd', *Bulletin of the Board of Celtic Studies*, 27 (1976–8), p. 515–30.

Morris, J., *op. cit.*

Nash-Williams, V. E., *The Roman Frontier in Wales* (2nd edn, Cardiff: 1969).

Nicholson, E. and B. Williams, 'The Dynasty of Cunedag and the Harleian Genealogy', *Y Cymmrodor*, 21 (1908), pp. 63–105.

Padel, O., *op. cit.*

Phillips, G. and M. Keatman, *King Arthur: the True Story* (Random House, 1995).

Snyder, C., *op. cit.*

(b) 800–1200

Bartrum, P. C., *op. cit.*

Carr, A. D., 'Anglo-Welsh Relations, 1066–1282' in M. Jones and M. Vale (eds), *England and Her Neighbours 1066–1453: Essays in Honour of Pierre Chaplais* (London: 1989).

Charles-Edwards, T. L., 'The Heir Apparent in Welsh and Irish Law', *Studia Celtica*, 9 (1971), pp. 180–90.

Charles-Edwards, T. L., M. Owen, and P. Russell (eds), *The Welsh King and His Court* (University of Wales Press, 2000).

Crouch, D., 'The March and the Welsh' in E. King (ed.), *The Anarchy of Stephen's Reign* (Oxford: 1994), pp. 255–89.

Davies, R. R., 'Henry I and Wales' in H. Mayr-Harting and R. I. Marre (eds), *Studies in Medieval History Presented to R. H. C. Davis* (London: 1981), pp. 133–47.

Davies, R. R., *Conquest, Co-Existence and Change: Wales 1063–1415* (Clarendon Press/University of Wales Press, 1987).

Davies, W., *Patterns of Power in Medieval Wales* (Oxford: 1990).

Davies, W., *Wales in the Early Middle Ages* (Leicester University Press, 1982).

Higham, N. (2), *op. cit.*

Hughes, K., *op. cit.*

Hughes, N., *op. cit.*

Insley, C., 'The Wilderness Years of Llywelyn the Great' in M. Prestwich, R. Britnell and R. Frame (eds), *Thirteenth-Century England Volume 9* (Woodbrdge: 2003), pp. 163–73.

Jack, R. I., *Medieval Wales* (London: 1972).

King, D. J., 'Henry II and the Fight at Coleshill', *Welsh Historical Review*, 2 (1964–5), pp. 367–75.

Kirby, D. P., *op. cit.*

Latimer, P., 'Henry II's Campaign against the Welsh in 1165', *Welsh Historical Review*, 14 (1988–9), pp. 523–52.

Lloyd, J. E., *op. cit.*

Loyn, H. R., *The Vikings in Wales* (1976).

Maund, K. L. (ed.), *Gruffydd ap Cynan: a Collaborative Biography* (Woodbridge: 1996).

Maund, K. L. (ed.), *Handlist of the Acts of Native Welsh Rulers, 1132–1283* (University of Wales Press, 1996).

Maund, K. L., *Ireland, Wales and England in the Eleventh Century* (Woodbridge: 1991).

Pryce, H. and C. Insley (eds), *The Acts of Welsh Rulers, 1120–1283* (University of Wales Press, 2005).

Sims-Williams, P., 'Historical Need and Literary Narrative: a Caveat from Ninth Century Wales', *Welsh Historical Review*, 7 (1994–5), pp. 1–40.

Smith, J. B., 'Dynastic Succession in Medieval Wales', *Bulletin of the Board of Celtic Studies*, 33 (1986), pp. 199–232.

Smith, J. B., 'Owain Gwynedd', *Transactions of the Carnarvonshire Historical Society*, 32 (1971), pp. 8–17.

Stephenson, D., *The Governance of Gwynedd* (1984).

Walker, D., *Medieval Wales* (Oxford: 1990).

Warren, W. L., *Henry II* (1973).

(c) 1200–1283

Carr, A. D., *op. cit.*

Carr, A. D., 'The Last and Weakest of his Line: Dafydd ap Gruffydd, the Last Prince of Wales', *Welsh Historical Review*, 19 (1989–90), pp. 375–99.

Carr, A. D., 'The Last Days of Gwynedd', *Transactions of the Carnarvonshire Historical Society*, 43 (1982), pp. 7–22.

Carr, A. D., *Owen of Wales: The End of the House of Gwynedd* (Cardiff: 1991).

Charles-Edwards, T. L. *et al.*, *op. cit.*

Jack, R. I., *op. cit.*

Jones, G. R., 'The Defences of Gwynedd in the Thirteenth Century', *Transactions of the Carnarvonshire Historical Society*, 30 (1969), pp. 29–43.

Lloyd, J. E., *op. cit.*

Lloyd, J. E., 'Llywelyn ap Gruffydd and the Lordship of Glamorgan', *Archaeologia Cambria*, sixth series, 13 (1913), pp. 56–66.

Maund, K. L. (3), *op. cit.*

Powicke, F. M., *Henry III and the Lord Edward: the Community of the Realm in the Thirteenth Century*, 2 vols (1947).

Pryce, H. and C. Insley, *op. cit.*

Pryce, H., 'Negotiating Anglo-Welsh Relations: Llywelyn the Great and Henry III' in B. Weiler and I. Rowlands (eds), *England and Europe in the Reign of Henry III (1216–72)* (Ashgate Press, 2002).

Richter, M., 'Daffyd ap Llywelyn, the first Prince of Wales', *Welsh Historical Review*, 5 (1970–1), pp. 205–19.

Roderick, A. J., 'The Feudal Relations between the English Crown and the Welsh Princes' in *History*, 37 (1952), pp. 201–12.

Sims-Willams, P., 'The Death of Llywelyn ap Gruffydd: the Narratives Reconsidered', *Welsh Historical Review*, 11 (1982–3), pp. 200–13.

Smith, J. B. (2), *op. cit.*

Smith, J. B., 'Llywelyn ap Gruffydd, Prince of Wales and Lord of Snowdon', *Transactions of the Carnarvonshire Historical Society*, 45 (1984), pp. 7–36.

Smith, J. B., 'Llywelyn the Great and the March of Wales', *Brycheiniog*, 20 (1982–3), pp. 9–22.

Smith, J. B., *Llywelyn ap Gruffydd, Prince of Wales* (University of Cardiff Press, 1998).

Smith, L., 'Llywelyn ap Gruffydd and the Welsh Historical Consciousness', *Welsh Historical Review*, 12 (1984–5), pp. 1–28.

Smith, L., 'The Gravimina of the Community of Gwynedd Against Llywelyn ap Gruffydd', *Bulletin of the Board of Celtic Studies*, 30 (1984), pp. 158–96.

Stephenson, D., *op. cit.*

Stephenson, D., 'Llywelyn ap Gruffydd and the Struggle for the Principality of Wales 1258–83', *Transactions of the Historical Society Cymru* (1983), pp. 36–49.

Studd, J. R., 'The Lord Edward's Lordship of Chester 1354–72', *Transactions of the Historical Society of Lancashire and Cheshire*, 128 (1979), pp. 1–25.

Taylor, A. J., 'The Death of Llywelyn ap Gruffydd', *Bulletin of the Board of Celtic Studies*, 15 (1982–3), pp. 200–14.

Tout, T. F., 'Wales and the March during the Barons' War, 1258–67' in his *Collected Papers*, vol. 2 (Manchester: 1933), pp. 47–100.

Walker, D., 'A Note on Gruffydd ap Llywelyn', *Welsh Historical Review*, 1 (1960–3), pp. 83–98.

Walker, R. F., 'Hubert de Burgh and Wales 1218–32', *English Historical Review*, 87 (1972), pp. 465–92.

Williams, G., 'The Succession to Gwynedd, 1238–47', *Bulletin of the Board of Celtic Studies*, 20 (1962–4), pp. 393–417.

4 Rulers of Mid Wales (Powys)

Primary Sources
As for Chapter 3.

Secondary Sources
(a) Pre-800
as Chapter 3 and:

Brooks, D. A., 'A Review of the Evidence for Continuity in British Towns in the Fifth and Sixth Centuries', *Oxford Journal of Archaeology*, 5(1) (1986), pp. 77–102.

Eyton, R. W., *Antiquities of Shropshire*, 12 vols (1854–60).

Kirby, D. P., 'Vortigern', *Bulletin of the Board of Celtic Studies*, 23 (1968–70), pp. 37–59.

Nash-Williams, V. E., *The Roman Frontier in Wales* (Cardiff: 1969).

Webster, G., *The Cornovii* (Sutton, 1991).

White, R., *Britannia Prima* (Tempus, 2005), pp. 180–5 on Viroconium.

(b) 800–1287

Bartrum, P., *op. cit.*

Bridgeman, G. T., 'The Princes of Upper Powys', *Montgomeryshire Collections*, 1 (1868), pp. 5–194.

Carr, A. D., *op. cit.*

Cathcart King, D. J., 'Two Castles in Northern Powys; Dinas Bran and Caergwrle', *Archaeologia Cambria*, 123 (1974), pp. 113–39.

Charles-Edwards, T. L., *op. cit.*

Crouch, D., *op. cit.*

Davies, R. R., *op. cit.*

Davies, W., *op. cit.*

Higham, N., *op. cit.*

Hughes, N., *op. cit.*

Jack, R., *op. cit.*

Kirby, D. P., *op. cit.*

Latimer, P., *op. cit.*

Lloyd, J. E., *op. cit.*

Lloyd, J. Y., *The History of the Princes of Powys Fadog*, 6 vols, 1881–7.

Mason, J. F., 'Roger de Montgomery and his Sons, 1067–1102', *Transactions of the Royal Historical Society*, fifth series, 13 (1963), pp. 1–28.

Maund, K. L., *op. cit.*

Powicke, F., *op. cit.*

Pryce. H. and C. Insley, *op. cit.*

Roderick, A. S., *op. cit.*

Smith, J. B., 'The Middle March in the Thirteenth Century', *Bulletin of the Board of Celtic Studies*, 24 (1970–2), pp. 77–93.

Stephenson, D., 'The Politics of Powys Wenwynwyn in the Thirteenth Century', *Cambridge Medieval Celtic Studies*, 7 (1984), pp. 39–61.

Tout, T., *op. cit.*

Walker, D., *op. cit.*

Walker, D., 'The Lordship of Builth', *Brycheiniog*, 20 (1982–3), pp. 23–33.

Walker, D., *The Norman Conquerors* (Swansea: 1977).

Warren, W. L., *op. cit.*

5 Rulers of Dyfed and (Tenth-Century) Deheubarth

Primary Sources

As Chapters 3 and 4 and:

James, J. W., 'The Harleian Mss. 3859 Genealogy, II. The Kings of Dyfed down to Arthur map Petr, died *c.* 586', *Bulletin of the Board of Celtic Studies*, 23(2) (1969), pp. 147–96.

Secondary Sources
(a) Pre-900
As Chapters 3 and 4 and:

Doble, G. H., *Lives of the Welsh Saints*, ed. D. S. Evans (University of Wales Press, 1971).
Kirby, D. P., 'A Note on Rhigyfarch's Life of St David', *Welsh Historical Review*, 4 (1968–9), pp. 292–9.
Miller, M., 'Date-Guessing and Dyfed', *Studia Celtica*, 12–13 (1977–8), pp. 33–61.
The Black Book of St David's, ed. J. W. Willis-Bund (London: Cymmrodorion Society Record Series, 1902).
The Welsh Life of St David, ed. D. S. Evans (University of Wales Press, 1988).

(b) 900–1287
Bartrum, P., *op. cit.*
Bartrum, P., 'Plant y Arglwydd Rhys', *National Library of Wales Journal*, 14 (1965–6), pp. 97–114.
Brooke, C. N., 'The Archbishops of St David's, Llandaff and Caerleon-on-Usk', in N. K. Chadwick (ed.), *Studies in the Early British Church* (Cambridge: 1958), pp. 201–42.
Carr, A. L., *op. cit.*
Charles-Edwards, T. L., *op. cit.*
Crouch, D., *op. cit.*
Crouch, D., 'Oddities in the Early History of the Lordship of Gower 1107–1166', *Bulletin of the Board of Celtic Studies*, 31 (1984), pp. 133–42.
Crouch, D., *William Marshal: Court, Career and Chivalry in the Angevin Empire 1147–1219* (London and New York: Longman, 1990).
Davies, R. R., *op. cit.*
Davies, W., *op. cit.*
Higham, N., *op. cit.*
Hughes, N., *op. cit.*
Jones, N. and A. Pryce (eds), *Y Arglwydd Rhys* (University of Cardiff Press, 1996).
Kirby, D. P., *op. cit.*

Kirby, D. P., 'Hywel Dda: Anglophile?', *Welsh Historical Review*, 8 (1976–7), pp. 1–13.

Latimer, P., *op. cit.*

Lewis, F. R., 'A History of the Lordship of Gower from the Missing Cartulary of Neath Abbey', *Bulletin of the Board of Celtic Studies*, 9 (1939), pp. 149–54.

Lloyd, J. E., *op. cit.*

Lloyd, J. E., 'Carmarthen in Early Norman Times', *Archaeoloiga Cambria*, sixth series, 7 (1907), pp. 281–92.

Maund, K. L., *op. cit.*

Miller, M., *op; cit.*

Nelson, L., *The Normans in South Wales 1070–1171* (Austin, Texas: 1966).

Powicke, F., *op. cit.*

Pryce, H., *op. cit.*

Pryce, H., 'The Dynasty of Deheubarth and the Church of St David's' in J. S. Evans and J. M. Wooding (eds), *St David of Wales: Cult, Church, and Nation* (Woodbridge: 2007).

Roderick, A. S., *op. cit.*

Rowlands, I. W., 'The Making of the March: Aspects of the Norman Settlement of Dyfed', in R. Allen Brown (ed.), *Proceedings of the Battle Conference*, 3 (Woodbridge: 1981) pp. 142–57.

Rowlands, I. W., 'William de Braose and the Lordship of Brecon', *Bulletin of the Board of Celtic Studies*, 30 (1982–3), pp. 123–33.

Smith, J. B., 'The Cronica de Wallia and the Dynasty of Dinewr: A Textual and Historical Study', *Bulletin of the Board of Celtic Studies*, 20 (1962–4), pp. 262–82.

Tout, T., *op. cit.*

Turvey, R., *The Lord Rhys* (Llandysul, 1997).

Walker, D. G., 'Miles of Gloucester, Earl of Hereford', *Transactions of the Bristol and Gloucester Archaeological Society*, 77 (1958–9), pp. 66–84.

Walker, R., *op. cit.*

Warren, W. L., *op. cit.*

Wightman, W., 'The Palatine Earldom of William FitzOsbern in Gloucestershire and Herefordshire', *English Historical Review*, 77 (1962), pp. 6–17.

6 Rulers of the Silures/Morgannwg (Glamorgan)

Primary Sources
As Chapters 3–5.

Secondary Sources
(a) 400–900
As Chapters 3–5 and:

Alcock, L., *Arthur's Britain* (Harmondsworth: 1971).

Ashe, G., 'A Certain Very Ancient Book: Traces of An Arthurian Source in Geoffrey of Monmouth's History', *Speculum*, 56 (1981), pp. 301–23.

Ashe, G., 'The Origins of the Arthurian Legend' in *Arthuriana*, 5(3) (1995), pp. 1–24.

Ashe, G., *King Arthur's Avalon* (London: 1982).

Ashe, G., *The Discovery of King Arthur* (London: 1985).

Blackett, B. and A. Wilson, *Artorius Rex Discovered* (Pontypridd: 1985).

Blake, S. and S. Lloyd, *The Keys to Avalon* (Random House, 2003).

Bromwich, R., 'Concepts of Arthur', *Studia Celtica*, 10–11 (1975–6), pp. 163–81.

Bromwich, R., A. O. Jarman and B. Roberts, *The Arthur of the Welsh* (University of Wales Press, 1991).

Dark, K., 'A Famous Arthur in the Sixth Century? Reconsidering the Origins of the Arthurian legend', *Reading Medieval Studies*, 26 (2000), pp. 7–95.

Green, T., *Concepts of Arthur* (Tempus, 2007).

Jackson, K., 'The Arthur of History' in R Loomis (ed.), *Arthurian Literature in the Middle Ages* (Oxford: 1959).

Jackson, K., 'The Site of Mount Badon', *Bulletin of the Board of Celtic Studies*, 2 (1953–8), pp. 152–5.

Lacey, N. (ed.), *Arthurian Studies: Volume 15* (Woodbridge: 2005).

Liber Landavensis, ed. Revd W. S. Rees (Llandovery: 1840).

Littleton, C. S. and L. Malcor, *From Scythia to Camelot* (New York and London: 1994).

Moffat, A., *Arthur and the Lost Kingdoms* (Weidenfeld and Nicolson, 1999).

Phillips, G. and M. Keatman, *King Arthur: the True Story* (Random House, 1992).

Reno, F., *The Historical King Arthur* (Jefferson, North Carolina: 1996).

The Book of Llan Dav, ed. J. Gwenogwyn Evans and J. Rhys (Oxford: 1893).

The Llandaff Charters, ed. W. Davies (Aberystwyth: 1979).

Thomas, N., 'Arthurian Evidences: the Historicity and Historicising of King Arthur', *Durham University Journal*, 87(2) (July 1995), pp. 385–92.

Williams, *History of Monmouthshire* (1984).

(b) 900–1295

Bartrum, P., *op. cit.*

Carr, A. L., *op. cit.*

Charles-Edwards, T. L., *op. cit.*

Crouch, D., *op. cit.*

Crouch, D., 'The Slow Death of Kingship in Glamorgan', *Morgannwg*, 29 (1985), pp. 20–41.

Davies, R. R., *op. cit.*

Davies, W., *op. cit.*

Griffiths, R. A., 'The Norman Conquest and the Twelve Knights of Glamorgan', *Glamorgan Historian*, 3 (1966), pp. 153–69.

Higham, N., *op. cit.*

Hughes, N., *op. cit.*

Jack, R., *op. cit.*

Kirby, D. L., *op. cit.*

Maund, K. L., *op. cit.*

Nelson, L., *op. cit.*

Powicke, F., *op. cit.*

Pryce, H., *op. cit.*

Pugh, T. B. (ed.), *Glamorgan County History*, vols 2 and 3 (1971).

Rees, W., 'The Lordship of Cardiff', *Transactions of the Cardiff Naturalists Society*, 63 (1932), pp. 18–35.

Smith, J. B., 'The Lordship of Glamorgan' in Morgannwg, 9 (1965), pp. 9–38.

Tout, T., *op. cit.*

Walker, D., *op. cit.*

Warren, W. L., *op. cit.*

7 Rulers of Other Kingdoms

Primary Sources

Genealogies, as Chapters 3–6, and:

J. Gwenogfryn Evans, *The Book of Aneirin Volume 2* (Llanbedrog: 1922).

J. Gwenogfryn Evans, *The Book of Taliesin: Facsimile and Text* (Llanbedrog: 1910).

Dumnonia/Cor

Alcock, L., *By South Cadbury is that Camelot …* (Thames and Hudson, 1972).

Anon, 'Tintagel', *Current Archaeology*, 159 (1998), pp. 84–8.

Ashe, G., *op. cit.*

Baring-Gould, S. and J. Fisher, *The Lives of The British Saints* (Cymmrodorion Society, 1913).

Batey, C., A. Sharp and C. Thorpe, 'Tintagel Castle: Archaeological Investigation of the Steps Area, 1989 and 1990', *Cornish Archaeology*, 32 (1993), pp. 47–66.

Bidwell, P. T., *Roman Exeter: Fortress and Town* (Exeter: 1980).

Blackett, B. and A. Wilson, *op. cit.*

Branigan, K. and P. J. Fowler (eds), *The Roman West Country: Classical Culture and Celtic Society* (Newton Abbot: 1976).

Breeze, D., *op. cit.*

Broadhurst, P., *Tintagel and the Arthurian Myths* (Launceston: 1992).

Castleden, R., *op. cit.*

Doble, G. H., *Saint Carantoc: A Cornish Saint* (Long Compton: 1932).

Doble, G. H., *Saint Petroc* (Long Compton: 1938).

Harry, R. and C. Morris, *Tintagel: Excavations 1994* (English Heritage, 1994).

Hoskins, W. G., *The Westwards Expansion of Wessex* (Leicester University Press, 1960).

Kirby, D. P., *The Earliest English Kingdoms* (Routledge, 1992), pp. 40–60 on Wessex.

Major, A. and E. Burrow, *The Mystery of Wansdyke* (Cheltenham: 1926).

Morris, J., *op. cit.*

Padel, O., 'The Cornish Background of the Tristan Stories', *Cambridge Medieval Celtic Studies*, 1 (1981), pp. 53–81.

Pearce, S. M., *The Kingdom of Dumnonia: Studies in History and Tradition in South-West Britain* (Padstow: 1978).

Radford, R., *Tintagel Castle* (Cornwall, London: 1939).

Thomas, C., 'Cornwall in the Dark Ages', *Proceedings of the West Cornwall Field Club*, new series, 2(2) (1957), pp. 59–72.

Thomas, C., 'The Context of Tintagel: a New Model for the Diffusion of Post-Roman Mediterranean Imports', *Cornish Archaeology*, 27 (1988), pp. 7–25.

Thomas, C., *Tintagel: Arthur and Archaeology* (Batsford, 1993).

van der Geest, A., 'Tintagel', *Pendragon*, 26(3) (1997), pp. 5–9.

The North

Arnold, T. J., *Roman Britain to Saxon England* (Tempus, 2000).

Breeze, A., *Medieval Welsh Literature* (Dublin: Four Courts Press, 1997).

Breeze, D. J., *Roman Scotland* (London: 1996).

Canu Llywarch Hen, ed. I. Williams (1935).

Cessford, C., 'Northern England and the Gododdin Poem', *Northern History*, 37 (1997), pp. 218–22.

Dark, P., *op. cit.*

de la Bédoyère, G., *Hadrian's Wall* (Tempus, 1998).

Dornier, A., 'The Province of Valentia', *Britannia*, 13 (1982).

Elton, H., *Frontiers of the Roman Empire* (London: 1996).

Esmonde Cleary, S., *The Ending of Roman Britain* (London: 1989).

Koch, J. T., *The Gododdin of Aneirin* (University of Wales Press, 1997).

Morris, J., *op. cit.*

8 The Glyndŵr Revolt, 1400–16

Allemand, C., *Henry V* (Yale University Press, 1997).

Bradley, A. E., *Owen Glendower and the Struggle for Welsh Independence* (1901).

Davies, R. R., *op. cit.*

Davies, R. R., 'Owain Glyndŵr and the Welsh Squirearchy', *Transactions of the Cymmrodorion Society* (1968), pp. 150–69.

Gibbon, A., *The Mystery of Jack of Kent and the Fate of Owain Glyndŵr* (2009).

Goodman, A. E., 'Owain Glyndŵr before 1400', *Welsh Historical Review*, 5 (1970–1), pp. 67–70.

Jack, R. I., 'New Light on the Early Days of Owain Glyndŵr', *Bulletin of the Board of Celtic Studies*, 21 (1964–6), pp. 163–6.

Jack, R. I., 'Owain Glyndŵr and the Lordship of Ruthin', *Welsh Historical Review*, 2 (1964–5), pp. 303–22.

Lloyd, J. E., *Owen Glendower* (Oxford: 1931).

Mortimer, I., *The Fears of Henry IV: the Life of England's Self-Made King* (Vintage, 2008).

Phillips, J. R. S., 'When did Owain Glyndŵr Die?', *Bulletin of the Board of Celtic Studies*, 24 (1970–2), pp. 69–77.

Smith, J. B., 'The Last Phase of the Glyndŵr Rebellion', *Bulletin of the Board of Celtic Studies*, 22 (1966–8), pp. 250–60.

Williams, G., *Owen Glendower* (1966).

INDEX

Also available from Amberley Publishing

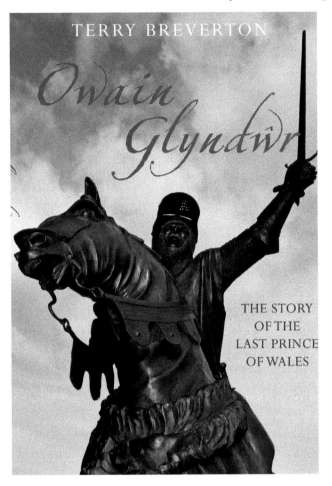

The first ever full-scale biography of the last native Prince of Wales who fought to maintain an independent Wales

If it had not been for Owain Glyndŵr's 15-year struggle against overwhelming odds, the Welsh would not have survived as Europe's oldest nation. His war for Welsh independence (1400-1415) is the defining era in the history of Wales. Yet Glyndŵr is hardly known – a cultured, literate warrior who was never betrayed or captured and vanished into history. This book tells us how Glyndŵr came to stir Wales into war, and why his name still resonates today as one of the greatest warriors the world has seen.

£15.99/$29.95
32 colour illustrations
208 pages
978-1-84868-328-0

Available from all good bookshops or to order direct
Please call **01453-847-800**
www.amberleybooks.com